Double trouble

DOUBLE TROUBLE

DOUBLE TROUBLE

IRAN AND NORTH KOREA AS CHALLENGES TO INTERNATIONAL SECURITY

Edited by Patrick M. Cronin

PRAEGER SECURITY INTERNATIONAL
Westport, Connecticut • London

Library of Congress Cataloging-in-Publication Data

Double trouble: Iran and North Korea as challenges to international security /
edited by Patrick M. Cronin.
    p.   cm.
  Includes bibliographical references and index.
  ISBN 978–0–275–99960–5 (alk. paper)
  1. Nuclear nonproliferation.   2. Nuclear weapons–Iran.   3. Nuclear
weapons–Korea (North)   4. United States–Foreign relations–2001-   5. Security,
International.   I. Cronin, Patrick M., 1958-   II. Title: Iran and North Korea as
challenges to international security.
  JZ5675.D68   2008
  327.1′747095195–dc22   2007035888

British Library Cataloguing in Publication Data is available.

Library of Congress Catalog Card Number: 2007035888
ISBN-13: 978–0–275–99960–5

First published in 2008

Praeger Security International, 88 Post Road West, Westport, CT 06881
An imprint of Greenwood Publishing Group, Inc.
www.praeger.com

Printed in the United States of America

The paper used in this book complies with the
Permanent Paper Standard issued by the National
Information Standards Organization (Z39.48–1984).

10 9 8 7 6 5 4 3 2 1

Copyright Acknowledgments

Earlier versions of chapters two and seven appeared in the Institute for
International Strategic Studies journal, *Survival*, and are reprinted in part here with
permission of the IISS.

Every reasonable effort has been made to trace the owners of copyright materials in
this book, but in some instances this has proven impossible. The author and
publisher will be glad to receive information leading to more complete
acknowledgments in subsequent printings of the book and in the meantime extend
their apologies for any omissions.

Better never trouble Trouble
Until Trouble troubles you;
For you only make your trouble
Double-trouble when you do.

Attributed to poet David Keppel

Contents

Preface

This volume emanates from the intellectually rich research program of the International Institute for Strategic Studies (IISS). For half a century, the IISS has provided comprehensive, international, fact-based analyses of salient global security issues, at once defining the field of strategic studies and describing the major contours of international security.

In the first decade of the Institute's prestigious series of monograph studies, the Adelphi Papers, some of the intellectual giants of Western strategic thinking set out their thoughts about problems related to nuclear weapons and proliferation, including Michael Howard, Bernard Brodie, Sir Solly Zuckerman, Raymond Aron, Lester B. Pearson, Curt Gasteyger, Sir John Slessor, Thomas Schelling, Morton Halperin, Albert and Robert Wohlstetter, Alastair Buchan, Philip Winsor, Coral Bell, Hedley Bull, and Pierre Hassner. In the past decade the Adelphi Papers have sought to delve into the domestic political variables driving proliferating state and nonstate actors in order to provide a more complete account of the challenges posed by them and the potential levers on which outside nations might pull to help contain these challenges. For instance, Robert L. Carlin and Joel S. Wit, both seasoned American nonproliferation specialists, wrote Adelphi Paper No. 382 in 2006 on *North Korean Reform: Politics, Economics and Security* and Shahram Chubin, a contributor to this volume, wrote Adelphi Paper No. 242 in 2002 on *Whither Iran? Reform, Domestic Politics and National Security.*[1] Significantly, in recent years, the Institute has also published in-depth net assessments or dossiers on Iran and North Korea.[2] Numerous other analyses have appeared in the IISS journal *Survival*, the Institute's annual publications *Strategic Survey* and *The Military Balance*, and in the Institute's series of short analyses known as *Strategic Comments*.

Each year the Institute's staff and members come together with other leading strategic thinkers from around the world for an annual Global Strategic Review. In September 2006, I wove into the agenda detailed assessments of Iran and North Korea from different international points of view. Many of those initial papers and presentations have been updated through April 2007 and incorporated into this volume. Some have been significantly rewritten and only two have been printed before in earlier versions. All of the sections that I have written are new and represent the understanding of the problem as of the spring of 2007. I have put together appendices providing selected chronologies of events and key documents and statements to make this volume a useful reference source.

There are many people to thank for this volume, not least the complete cast of contributing authors whose perspicacity has certainly broadened and deepened my own understanding of the twin challenges posed by Iran and North Korea. I also want to thank two of the bright young intellectual forces of the Institute, Raffaello Pantucci and John Wooding, for their assistance in enabling the completion of this report. I am grateful to Robert Silano for making this volume possible. Last, but by no means least, I thank Caitlin Brannan for making the Global Strategic Review conference possible at all. All mistakes in this volume, however, are solely my own responsibility.

NOTES

1. Also see Wyn Q. Bowen, *Libya and Nuclear Proliferation: Stepping Back from the Brink*, Adelphi Paper No. 380 (2006); Robin M. Frost, *Nuclear Terrorism After 9/11*, Adelphi Paper No. 278 (2005); William Walker, *Weapons of Mass Destruction and International Order*, Adelphi Paper No. 370 (2004); and David Reese, *The Prospects for North Korea's Survival*, Adelphi Paper No. 323 (1998).

2. See *Iran's Strategic Weapons Programmes–A Net Assessment* (IISS, September 2005) and *North Korea's Weapons Programmes: A Net Assessment* (January 2004). Published in London by the International Institute for Strategic Studies.

Introduction: The Dual Challenge of Iran and North Korea

Patrick M. Cronin

How do Iran and North Korea pose trouble to regional stability and world order? Why have attempts to curb their nuclear programs and broader political ambitions failed? How have Iran and North Korea, each in their own way, managed to defy the world's preponderant power, the United States, as well as other major powers and the United Nations? Where are the fractured and oscillating relations with these two nettlesome actors heading? What are the long-term implications of their current trajectories for nuclear proliferation, deterrence, alliance management, regional security, and world order? These timely and pressing questions about two of the world's most dangerous powers are the focus of this volume.

DOUBLE TROUBLE TIMES FIVE

Iran and North Korea pose serious challenges to international order. For all the differences between the Islamic Republic of Iran and the contentedly isolated Democratic People's Republic of Korea (the DPRK or North Korea), these two states create similar strategic challenges to the United States, the Middle East and the Northeast Asian regions, respectively, and to relations among major states. It is not simply that this duo represents the remaining charter members of what President George W. Bush famously dubbed: "the axis of evil." The trouble posed by this pair of powers runs far and wide, as potential catalysts for future war, as proliferators threatening the tenuous global nuclear nonproliferation regime, as agents frustrating America's alliance management and regional diplomacy, as potential spoilers of regional peace, and even short of war exerting influence on future regional security architectures, and ultimately, as maverick wild cards in the global order.

First, Iran and North Korea remain amongst the most likely potential triggers for interstate war in an era when most wars are intrastate or civil wars or, as in the case of terrorism, perhaps transnational conflicts. When security planners in Washington—and in other capitals around the globe—contemplate the myriad ways in which future interstate wars could break out, the precarious relations between the United States and Iran and North Korea are at the apex. Indeed, some commentators contend that conflict with Iran and North Korea has been held off this long in part because of America's exhaustion after launching a global offensive, a "war on terrorism" that left it broadly committed in terms of potential foes and deeply mired in specific insurgencies, especially in Iraq. As the epigraph of this volume admonishes, preempting trouble before one even knows for sure that it is trouble, is a swift way for a major power to experience overstretch. Toppling Saddam Hussein, who held together his Sunni-minority government through brute force, pervasive intelligence, and corruption, was a modest security objective aside the more ambitious but poorly planned strategy of establishing a model democracy in the Middle East. The high cost of intervening in Iraq—whether counted by a metric of human lives, state treasure, regional instability, or political capital—has tempered Washington's enthusiasm about any other headlong rush into Tehran or Pyongyang. But a weakened, hesitant United States is also a hindrance to keeping the peace, as an emboldened Iran and North Korea each march forward with their nuclear programs and political aims. In fact, the perception that the United States is timorous or a "paper tiger" may well create the perception and misperception that may trigger future war. When Iranian Revolutionary Guard Corps troops took fifteen British sailors and marines hostage in March 2007, the world witnessed precisely the kind of local incident that could have been the spark to ignite a larger war. Hence, by the criterion of being a potential trigger of conflict, Iran and North Korea are clearly troublesome.

Iran and North Korea are also clearly trouble in the sense that their nuclear programs pose challenges to security in general and to the nonproliferation regime in particular. The spectre of war with Iran or North Korea is sufficiently grim even before one recalls that, unlike Iraq, these countries either have, or are clearly erecting the capabilities to have, nuclear weapons. Furthermore, even if those prospective weapons are never to be fired in anger or by accident, the sheer scope of their nuclear programs are, everyday, posing a challenge to the viability of the regime of treaties and agreements—especially the Nuclear Non-Proliferation Treaty (NPT)—that have helped in past decades to contain the threat posed by the rampant spread of nuclear weapons and their supporting technologies. Even while the last five-year review of the NPT in 2005 concluded in such a manner as to cast doubt on its future relevance, Iran has accelerated its full nuclear fuel cycle program and North Korea has conducted a nuclear test. Moreover, North Korea has been granted a diplomatic process, despite the fact that it has left the NPT, while Iran remains a constant threat to also walk away from the international agreement. The expanding nuclear and missile capabilities of Iran and North Korea are changing facts on the ground. Iran abandoned a go-slow approach to uranium enrichment and North Korea also accelerated its own program before acceding—again—to multilateral diplomacy in February 2007. Both countries have cooperated with the nuclear black market, and Pakistani scientist A.Q. Khan has admitted to providing each of these countries with gas centrifuge technology needed to help create a nuclear bomb. If these two countries are allowed to succeed, some analysts predict that further nuclear proliferation—even a second nuclear era—will be nearly inevitable in the Middle East and East Asia. As Henry Kissinger wrote, "The world is faced with the nightmarish prospect that nuclear weapons will become a standard part of national armament and wind up in terrorist hands. The negotiations on Korean and Iranian nuclear proliferation mark a watershed."[1]

War may well be prevented, and the international agreements aimed at curbing wider nuclear proliferation may continue to stagger forward like a drunken sailor (i.e., teetering but still standing). But Iran and North Korea will also threaten double trouble to existing regional security mechanisms, which in the absence of agreed upon and effective multilateral forums in the Persian Gulf and Northeast Asia, are based on a rough balance of power underpinned by America's bilateral alliances and security partnerships. These alliances are increasingly strained by the continuing challenges of managing a rising Iran and a potentially failing North Korea. In the Gulf and Middle East, long-standing U.S. partners (and predominantly Sunni Arab states), like oil giant Saudi Arabia and peace supporter Egypt, have become increasingly assertive in their foreign policies and vigilant in their domestic policies because of Iranian power. Not only has the United States failed to reverse the Iranian threat, its intervention in Iraq has now limited the potential financial, human, and political capital that the United States could dedicate toward stifling Iranian regional hegemonic ambitions. The largely Sunni Arab world in particular feels the tug of power moving in Iran's direction, especially with Iran freed from its two most proximate past foes in Afghanistan and Iraq. At the same time, an American tendency to equate good governance with democracy, particularly in the Middle East, has done little to challenge the autocratic theocracy of those running Iran, but it has certainly accentuated concerns about future stability in Saudi Arabia and Egypt. The concern that Saudi Arabia may intervene in Iraq to defend the Sunni minorities left behind after the fall of Saddam Hussein, or that Israel could take it upon itself to strike Iran's nuclear facilities rather than wait for the seemingly inevitable arrival of a nuclear weapon, are demonstrative of the new tensions Iran is creating in America's alliance management. Meanwhile, America's regional ally Israel is isolated and feeling more threatened by the potential emergence of an Iranian nuclear weapons program and support for surrogate insurgents in the region.

North Korean diplomacy and strategy has seriously troubled the U.S.-South Korean alliance since the late 1990s and especially since 2001. Since then the divergence in perception between the American and the South Korean sense of the North Korean threat has become starker. At the same time, the North Korean issue is strengthening the U.S. alliance with Japan—which is now eager to behave like a normal power and is on the verge of rewriting its constitution to allow it to assume the same military posture as other powers—though this is having a corrosive effect on the U.S.-South Korean alliance. Meanwhile, China's influence is growing with South Korea, while Chinese-Japanese relations remain locked in a historic time warp of distrust. Consequently, it is no surprise that China and South Korea have forged incredibly thick and deep ties in the past several years. Whether the diplomatic process designed to channel diplomatic efforts for dealing with North Korea—namely, the Six-Party Talks comprising North and South Korea, the United States, China, Japan, and Russia—can succeed in keeping the nuclear issue in check and transform it into a useful multilateral security mechanism in Northeast Asia, remains an open question. What is not in question is that North Korea, as well as Iran, produce a sober challenge for America's alliance system—a collection of security obligations and arrangements that undergird security in the absence of effective multilateral institutions.

Iran and North Korea pose a fourth kind of trouble as regional spoilers. In the greater Middle East, Iran has the capability to spoil stability in Iraq and Afghanistan, as well as with countries surrounding Israel; at the same time, Iran's nuclear power and flexing of political muscle might well confound future attempts at erecting a more peaceful regional order. In Northeast Asia, the largest strategic challenge may well be reconciling the three-sided balance of power among a reemerging China, a more normal Japan, and a relatively declining United States. The power discrepancies in both regions make it difficult for major powers to agree to constraints on their powers; those powers, believing that time is on their side, hope to accrete more power, and those fearing a loss of at least relative power are reluctant to agree to a further diminution of their clout. As suggested above with the complication to America's alliances, Iran and North Korea each have the ability to significantly alter the future course of regional peace and security and the sets of relations that emerge in the event of a watershed event, such as war or a significant arms agreement.

Iran and North Korea generate a fifth type of trouble, namely to world or international order, by which we mean especially relations among the major powers. World order came to mean something specific after the Second World War, and the permanent members of the United Nations Security Council have since held considerable sway in global security affairs. In

America, many have seen world order—like globalization—as one and the same phenomenon as American order. But the distribution of global power is today much more diffuse than it was more than three score years ago. How the United States will reconcile its role in the world in the coming decade is a crucial question for international security. To answer that question, one will have to consider America's relations with its traditional allies, including those in Europe, the Middle East, and East Asia. Also, one must understand the potential for harmony and conflict between the United States and a rising China. Finally, there is the issue of newly formed relations among regional powers in the Middle East and East Asia. Taken together, Iran and North Korea suddenly can be seen as posing much larger challenges than they should do, given their limited contributions to that same order. This fifth type of trouble, times two, rounds out a full complement of ten challenges to security.

IRAN AND NORTH KOREA

The first four chapters of this volume delve into the trouble with Iran.

Chapter 1 describes some of the specific military and political challenges posed by Iran. The failure to find a diplomatic means of taming Iran's nuclear ambitions suggests that Iran and the United States may well be on a collision course in the coming decade. Limited trust and a difficulty in fashioning a framework for political resolution means that future regional peace and security could well be at the mercy of individual events, whether intentional or accidental. At the same time, the various challenges of the region—including instability, terrorism, and political violence in Iraq—seem unlikely to be advanced by a continuing standoff on the nuclear issue. Whether the nuclear issue can be resolved peacefully or not may determine the future of regional security in the Persian Gulf and the Middle East.

In Chapter 2, nonproliferation expert and former Deputy Assistant Secretary of State Mark Fitzpatrick describes the technical progress and impediments facing Iran's recent developments. However likely it may seem, Fitzpatrick does not judge an Iranian nuclear weapon as an inevitability. At the same time, Iran's pursuit of uranium enrichment, despite international pressure to desist, and the country's other nuclear facilities, including its plutonium reactor at Arak, suggests that Iran is seeking more than a peaceful nuclear program as it claims. He makes clear the complex issues of Iran's nuclear developments and the policies arrayed against those developments. He crystallizes the technical issues and outlines how diplomatic overtures have been designed to slow down or stop progress toward Iran's capacity to build nuclear weapons. Although the record is punctuated with a less than spectacular success rate, he notes that diplomacy has slowed Iran's nuclear program and he remains hopeful that diplomacy may yet find a resolution to the fundamental problem of dealing with Iran.

In Chapter 3, Shahram Chubin explains how Iran's ever-shifting motivations behind its proliferation program relate to security, prestige, and domestic politics. The security aims center on the suspicion that Iran's nuclear program only makes sense if it has a military goal of building a nuclear weapon; otherwise, a full fuel cycle makes little sense for a uranium-poor Iran. Exploiting every opportunity within the existing NPT is seen as a less confrontational way of achieving progress toward that capability. With respect to prestige, Chubin notes that the program is in a real sense an end in itself rather than a means to some larger security objective. Internally, the nuclear issue is first and foremost a political tussle for power and legitimacy, and only secondarily about ideology. Despite the regime's insistence on its benign intentions, it has also studiously prevented any public debate over the nuclear program. For instance, a true debate in Iran might raise the risks that the regime is exposing its people to by its headlong pursuit of nuclear energy. Even so, Chubin believes a final decision about converting Iran's nuclear capabilities into a nuclear weapon has not been fashioned.

In Chapter 4 leading Russian strategic thinker Alexei Arbatov describes the profound dangers posed by the continuing tensions between Iran and the United States. He is starkly dire in his predictions of what could happen in the coming decade when Iran is faced with making a final decision as to whether to proceed with forging nuclear weapons. He also explains why Russian officials put their policy of practical cooperation with Iran over a single-minded pursuit of nonproliferation. After all, Arbatov notes, Iran's transgressions in not complying with international demands from the International Atomic Energy Agency and the United Nations Security Council must be compared with North Korea's quitting the NPT altogether and yet still being rewarded with concessions and negotiation. Arbatov is constructive in portraying the steps that Iran, the United States, and other international actors might take to convert the challenge of dealing with Iran into an enduring milestone in regional security.

The next five chapters deal with North Korea.

In Chapter 5, I have sketched out some of the ways in which North Korea poses trouble to security. Nuclear proliferation is only the most obvious concern created by North Korea's nuclear program. The fact that North Korea has twice resisted coercive diplomacy, and American and international demands, suggests that the regime has more determination and resiliency than it is credited with possessing. At the same time, the potential for sudden regime collapse and possible Korean unification remain real concerns for all neighbouring countries in the region. The changes in the U.S.-South Korean alliance in recent years have, for the most part, weakened this partnership even in the absence of multilateral security mechanisms. North Korea magnifies these other troubles as well.

In Chapter 6, former South Korean Foreign Minister Sung-Joo Han focuses on the tenuous peace on the Korean Peninsula, which is buffeted by both North Korea's nuclear and missile proliferation but equally by a shifting American-South Korean alliance. He also portrays some of the futility of American attempts to rely more on pressure on North Korea to abandon its nuclear weapons than on diplomacy, and the indirect strain this placed on a changing U.S.-South Korean alliance. Ambassador Han describes the dangers of a shifting balance of power on the Korean Peninsula as North Korea builds and retains nuclear weapons and long-range missiles, the lingering potential for an outbreak of regional war, and the growing arms buildup if not arms race in Northeast Asia. In detailing some of the potential calculus behind North Korea and China's endgame, he further shows the complexity of resolving the dilemmas posed by North Korea. Meanwhile, the South Korean-U.S. security alliance and deterrent system has been weakened in recent years, despite the absence of a clear mechanism for replacing it. The chief implication for South Korea, however, is that it will increasingly have to take responsibility for deterrence on the Peninsula.

In Chapter 7, former U.S. State Department Policy Planning Director Mitchell Reiss analyzes why attempts to use coercive diplomacy against North Korea backfired and North Korean escalation of tensions in 2006 through missile and nuclear tests ended up producing a return to diplomacy. At the same time, Dr. Reiss describes many of the reasons for pessimism about securing from North Korea any quick and lasting agreement over nuclear disarmament. Looking at the crisis-like tensions of the latter half of 2006 as a low point in U.S. diplomacy, Reiss writes that, "The real failure has been Washington's inability, after several years of on-again, off-again negotiations in Beijing, to learn whether North Korea is actually willing to surrender its nuclear weapons program, and if so, at what price." He adds that, after years of negotiations with North Korea, we still know very little about the scale, dimensions, and scope of its nuclear program. Even while finding much fault in the procedure and substantive of negotiations with North Korea, particularly surrounding the Six-Party Talks, Reiss notes that critics of the Bush administration would have been hard pressed to show that North Korea would have seized bilateral negotiations with the United States in good faith. Alas, Reiss observes that North Korean recalcitrance has not brought significant, if any, penalty. Only with a basic reappraisal of the priorities and approaches to curbing North Korea's nuclear program by China and South Korea can we expect real progress in disabling the North Korean problem.

In Chapter 8, Dr. Liru Cui, who heads a prestigious think tank in Beijing—the China Institute for Contemporary International Relations which provides classified reports to Chinese Communist Party officials—explains how a combination of China's domestic priorities and politics and its foreign policy interests have combined to push China to the forefront of diplomacy with North Korea. China's emphasis on stability over nonproliferation and the importance attached to improving relations with South Korea have been notable features of recent Chinese diplomacy. Chinese diplomacy is driven by the view that the problem is cold war between North Korea and the United States and requires Chinese mediation as an honest broker to prevent open conflict. Dr. Cui also accentuates the critical role played by the United States in whether peace or insecurity prevails in the region. He portrays a benign version of China's interests in the region. He also observes how China is encroaching on America's role as a regional provider of the public good of peace and security.

In Chapter 9, one of the best of Japan's next generation of strategic analysts, Narushige Michishita, portrays why the combination of missile and nuclear programs threatens Japan above all others. *Scud* and *No-dong* missiles can reach Japan, which remains a primary target of North Korea. Even so, Michishita recognizes that North Korea's primary goal in escalating tensions in 2006 was to coerce the United States and Japan back to the bargaining table from a more advantageous position to North Korea. Ultimately, he believes North Korea wants to win acceptance of the status quo, receiving benefits for cooperation but never fully disarming its unconventional programs. From this perspective, a further defensive military buildup by Japan, with the United States, is an inevitable consequence of living with a nuclear North Korea. The impact that China's enlarged regional role has had on Japan should not be underestimated; for Japan, China, and not the United States, has shown that it can play a decisive role in shaping the course of regional relations. China's rise continues to be an assumption on which the surrounding powers, including Japan, determine their strategy and defense posture. Meanwhile, North Korea has two choices: it can make a real strategic decision to forsake its nuclear weapons and begin doing so; or it can bandwagon further with a growing China. That choice will be a bellwether of future regional security and it highlights why the careful management of the North Korean problem is so important for international security.

Finally, in the conclusion to this volume, I return to troubles posed by Iran and North Korea, especially related to their nuclear programs. I have highlighted how Iran and North Korea have succeeded in preserving and countering American-led coercive diplomacy to disable their nuclear facilities and verifiably abandon a nuclear weapons program. Alliance management and regional institution building remain vital long-term endeavours to be tackled by future leaders. Hopefully the creative juxtaposition will help augment the sizable corpus of literature on these countries and issues, and ease the way for prudent but strategic approaches to grappling with Iran and North Korea.

NOTE

1. Henry A. Kissinger, "A Nuclear Test for Diplomacy," *The Washington Post*, May 16, 2006, p. 17.

PART I

Iran

1

The Trouble with Iran

Patrick M. Cronin

Iran invites violently opposing viewpoints. Optimists see Iran's historic civilization, potent trading power, mounting oil wealth, teeming collection of youth, a country more pluralistic than any other in the Middle East but Turkey, a victimized state richly deserving of more equality with other states, and a middle power desiring an expansive set of regional responsibilities. Pessimists tend to see Iran through the glass darkly: a government dead set on a full nuclear fuel cycle with a weapon in mind; an emboldened, risk-taking nation waging indirect and proxy warfare against the United States and Britain, for instance, by providing Iraqi insurgents with explosively formed projectiles and apprehending British sailors in Iraqi waters; an Iran that uses the discourse of rights and justice but fails to support any internal debate on its nuclear program; a country whose officials seem to have a deeply warped view of the West; and a nation that has rebuffed liberal political reforms in favor of the zealotry of President Mahmoud Ahmadinejad, whose scorching rhetoric frequently raises regional tensions. The reality is that both of these clashing perspectives on Iran inform the intricate mosaic that is the whole picture of modern Iran.[1]

The trouble with Iran is that, in the midst of starkly different realities and trends, it is unambiguously augmenting its power and challenging the status quo in the Persian Gulf and greater Middle East. Whether right or wrong, Iran is shifting the regional balance of power and the resulting tensions with local and outside powers may well fuel a more intense and larger conflagration. In the past several years, Iran's prominence has been boosted by the profoundly weak states of neighboring Afghanistan and Iraq, a United States that is overencumbered fighting to stand up fledgling governments in those two countries, and Tehran's relentless pursuit of a nuclear option. Iran's self-assurance has swollen concomitant with the rising costs imposed on the United States since it led an intervention into Iraq, deposed Saddam Hussein, and then found itself in the midst of a counterinsurgency from which both success and exit appeared to be distant options at best. Indeed, the misconceived "war on terrorism" of which Iraq was part of only by conflating the heinous but separate behavior of Saddam Hussein and the egregious acts of terrorism on the United States on September 11, 2001, highlighted the heavy yoke of providing global security, regardless of whether that role was a self-appointed American one, or more collegially shared.

Unfortunately, Iran appears to have decided that a nuclear program, backed by other military means, is the best means of demonstrating its rising prominence, despite the risks attendant to such an exhibition. Tehran's nuclear program, which had been dialled back during seesawing negotiations with the European states of Britain, France, and the Germany, accelerated in 2006 and 2007, hastening the time when Iran would have to make a final decision—assuming it had not already done so—about whether to acquire a nuclear weapon. Thus, at a time when the United Nations Security Council had demanded that Iran halt its limited uranium enrichment work, Iran signalled defiance by opting to announce that it had started industrial production of nuclear fuel.[2] Although the veracity of the announcement was met with skepticism, Iran undoubtedly remained headed in a dangerous direction. President Ahmadinejad cast the issue as one of rights, glossing over legitimate violations documented by the International Atomic Energy Agency (IAEA) and obvious security concerns about Iran's nuclear posture. "The great Iranian nation," Ahmadinejad said in a speech at its Natanz nuclear facility in April 2007, "...will not allow some bullying powers to put obstacles in its path of progress. ... We will go on to reach the summits." The president admonished others against applying pressure on Iran lest Iran "reconsider its behavior," a reference to unspecified Iranian countermeasures.[3] Does Iran want to fabricate and amass an inventory of nuclear weapons, or does it merely want the wherewithal to build one, should it feel the need to do so in the future? No one appears to know the answer to that question. Meanwhile, Iran's missile ranges continue to grow; the limited accuracy of its longest-range missile, the extended range *Shahab-3*, makes it a more logical candidate for a nuclear rather than a conventional warhead. But even the short-range missiles of Iran, such as the *Zezal*, is dangerous, as the reported use of it by Hezbollah during its five-week war with Israel in the summer of 2006 made clear. Far less visible is Iran's network of forces and nonstate actors which can sow trouble throughout the region.

Iran is no small power. It has 65 million people, which makes it more populous than the United Kingdom with some 60 million people. Demographically, Iran is less a homogenous Persian empire than a collection of many frontier minorities. Iran is only half Persian, with the other half divided among Azeris, the most numerous minority having migrated from the Caucasus; Kurds near northern Iraq and Turkey; Gilani and Mazandarani of northwest Iran; Lurs in western Iran; Arabs from across the Shatt al-Arab waterway, the Persian Gulf, and Gulf of Oman; the Baloch adjacent to Pakistan and Afghanistan; and Turkmen astride the border with Turkmenistan. Four-fifths of the population are under thirty years of age, and thus 80 percent of the population have only ever known Iran as the Islamic Republic of Iran, and only one in five may remember that Iran and the United States were once close allies. Indeed, along with Turkey and Pakistan, Iran formed a critical front line of states to thwart Soviet power. With the Soviet Union a relic of history, however, youthful Iranians see the United States as the leading country trying to deny it a larger regional role, even while a majority appear to want a modern, not a medieval Iran to emerge. Thus, Iran's youth will ultimately determine whether Iran continues to harbor an ethos of a revolutionary Islamic state or transforms into a modern regional power.

Neither is Iran a trivial military power. Iranian forces include some 350,000 soldiers in the army, 125,000 members of the Islamic Revolutionary Guard Corps (IRGC), a small navy with about 18,000 forces, and about 52,000 air forces. The IRGC, although seen as having primarily an internal security role, also controls some 40,000 paramilitary forces. It was IRGC forces that apprehended fifteen British sailors and marines in March 2007, and it was IRGC commanders who were detained by U.S.-led coalition forces in Irbil, Iraq, two months prior to that. The IRGC Air Force controls Iran's strategic missile force, including one brigade of *Shahab-1/2* intermediate-range ballistic missiles with twelve to eighteen launchers; and one battalion with six single launchers each with four *Shahab-3* intermediate-range ballistic missiles. Iran also supports a number of nonstate groups associated with insurgency and terrorism, including most notably Hezbollah in Lebanon.[4]

THE EVOLUTION OF THE IRANIAN NUCLEAR PROBLEM

The Iranian nuclear problem has been long in evolution. During the course of four decades, Iran's nuclear ambitions and the readiness of foreign suppliers to assist, have followed a circuitous route with four distinct phases. In the first phase, during Iran's embryonic nuclear program in the late 1960s and early 1970s, peaceful nuclear cooperation was but one aspect of a burgeoning allied relationship. The United States provided Iran with basic nuclear research facilities, and in 1968 Iran signed the Nuclear Non-Proliferation Treaty (NPT). The United States deemed it necessary to promote Iranian power to help police the Persian Gulf region at a time when the United States was fully committed in Vietnam and the British withdrew from East of Suez in 1971. Iran was eager to fill the vacuum of power, not least because of competition with its main neighbor and rival, Iraq. However, in the mid-1970s the United States successfully persuaded its European allies not to sell Iran dual-use nuclear technology, which in this case meant fuel cycle facilities with both civilian and potential military applications. For the Shah (Muhammad Reza Shah Pahlavi), as for Iran's leaders today, the prestige associated with being a nuclear power was at least as important as objective security concerns.[5]

Cooperation, nuclear and otherwise with Iran, took a very different turn with the Iranian Revolution in 1979. In this second phase, Washington led the global opposition to nuclear assistance for the Islamic Republic of Iran. The development of nuclear power was a low priority for Iran's Supreme Leader Ayatollah Ruhollah Khomeini. However, even during this time of turmoil, Iran undertook at least a small-scale clandestine program with the help of centrifuge technology acquired from Pakistan.

After the death of Ayatollah Khomeini in 1989 and the end of the Cold War shortly thereafter, Iran embarked on a concerted effort to expand its nuclear activities. From Russia and China rather than Europe, Iran gained help with uranium conversion and heavy-water production. Once again, however, the United States prevailed upon foreign suppliers to limit exports to Iran to something less than full fuel cycle facilities. What was not well understood at the time, was Iran's growing covert nuclear program, which included research into nuclear conversion, enrichment, and plutonium separation. With the help of the now-exposed network of A.Q. Khan, Iran was able to begin the construction of pilot-scale and industrial-scale enrichment facilities as Natanz around 2000.[6]

The fourth and current phase of relations over Iran's nuclear program can be dated to 2002, when President George W. Bush included Iran, along with Iraq and North Korea, as part of an "axis of evil" during his 2002 State of the Union address. Public explanation of this escalating rhetoric shortly followed, with the revelation in August 2002 of the previously secret Natanz research and enrichment facilities by an Iranian opposition group. The United States tried to ratchet up the pressure on Iran, indirectly by justifying the overthrow of Saddam Hussein largely on the basis of proliferation concerns, and directly by threatening to refer the matter to the UN Security Council. Meanwhile, European countries took the lead in brokering a deal. In October 2003, Iran reached an agreement with the United Kingdom, France, and Germany (the so-called European Union-3 or EU-3) to acknowledge its previously undeclared nuclear activities, allow more intrusive IAEA inspections under the Additional Protocol and "temporarily" suspend all uranium enrichment and reprocessing activities as defined by the IAEA. The accord soon faltered over the scope of suspension, as Iran resumed production of centrifuge components and began trial operations at its conversion facility in Esfahan. A new confrontational round of diplomacy ensued that once again produced a deal with the EU 3 in November 2004 and thereby averted referral of the matter from the IAEA to the UN Security Council. The accord restored full suspension of Iran's enrichment activities, including uranium conversion, manufacture of centrifuge components, and the installation, testing, and operation of centrifuges at the Natanz facility. This cyclical crisis diplomacy repeated itself in late 2005. As Iran resumed limited preenrichment steps, the EU-3 sought to strike a new bargain, and the IAEA agreed in principle but not in practice to refer the matter to New York and the UN Security Council.[7]

THE COLLISION COURSE OVER NUCLEAR ENERGY

Especially since 2006, Iran has appeared on a collision course with the international community in general and the United States in particular. In the spring of 2006, the IAEA reported to the United Nations Security Council that Iran has not heeded calls to suspend a uranium enrichment program that could be diverted for making nuclear weapons. UN Security Council members have since deliberated over a series of sanctions, each one fraught with peril.

Despite international overtures to Iran, it has failed to grasp the olive branch of diplomacy. Although the George W. Bush administration began to adopt a more pragmatic approach to nonproliferation issues during the final two years of its tenure, it simultaneously held onto all of its options, including the use of force; meanwhile, other members of the Security Council supported either mandatory or voluntary sanctions but not the threat of force to coerce Iran to comply with its demands. Tehran's policy approach was to eschew offering proposals of its own, while lambasting the major powers, and seeking to shift the debate to issues other than sanctions.

It is worth considering the author's first-hand experience while participating in the first two conferences on security and nuclear power allowed after Ahmadinejad's ascent to power. In fact, President Ahmadinejad reportedly tried to thwart the meetings; when he failed to prevent them from taking place, he then sought to upstage them by holding a press conference of his own and impeding an international inspection of Iran's nuclear facility at Esfahan. The conferences were hosted by the Centre for Strategic Research, which is under the jurisdiction of Iran's Expediency Council, whose Chairman—the Ayatollah Akbar Hashemi Rafsanjani—Ahmadinejad had defeated in the presidential contest.

The conference boasted far more passionate rhetoric than is typical of a conference in Washington or at an American or European university campus. The fiery rhetoric emanating from Iran appeared to be fuelled by a perception that Iran was negotiating from a position of strength vis-à-vis the permanent members of the UN Security Council. The conference's histrionics also appeared to disclose a fierce jockeying for power among Iran's political elite. Speaking at the conference he helped to arrange, Chairman Rafsanjani was most content with garnering praise for having laid the cornerstones of Iran's longstanding nuclear program. Although Rafsanjani is considered the moderate beside a president who uses the spectre of an external threat to solidify his domestic power base, his words were more caustic than measured. He noted that Iran's nuclear enrichment program was peaceful "for the moment," and that it was "irreversible, like a bullet fired from a gun, and it can't be taken back." Rafsanjani glossed over Iran's violations as a voluntary signatory to the NPT, dismissing them as "minor transgressions" by forgetful bureaucrats who were doing nothing that the IAEA wasn't aware of; however, he then contradicted that reasoning by arguing that in some cases Iran could not report purchasing critical materials from "immoral sources" (such as the A.Q. Khan network) because "if we had told you, you wouldn't have let us do it."[8]

Although the Secretary of the Supreme National Security Council, Dr. Ali Larijani, has distinguished himself as an able interlocutor with the outside world, his words at this largely domestic-oriented conference were far from temperate. Indeed, Larijani delivered an equally blustery diatribe, denouncing the United States for its "lies" and for serving as "the center for the demolition of international law." Iran speaks "with one voice on this national issue," Larijani said in regard to its civilian nuclear program, a nuclear program that was started under the Shah with the backing of the United States. But even while Larijani repeated the chorus of Iranian rights, he also left the door ajar for a diplomatic resolution—the only question being whether Iran would be willing to meet the world partway to defuse the escalating crisis. On that front, most evidence pointed in the opposite direction. For instance, Larijani declared a tit-for-tat policy of suspending cooperation with the IAEA should the UN adopt sanctions and he said military strikes would force Iran's nuclear program underground.

Meanwhile, President Ahmadinejad and Ayatollah Seyyed Ali Khamenei declared on consecutive days Iran's unswerving commitment to a full nuclear fuel cycle. The Iranians would, said Khamenei, "respond to any strike with double the force." These statements seemed part of a comprehensive, well-calibrated campaign of public diplomacy. I and other international visitors participating under the auspices of the Nobel Prize-winning Pugwash organization were party to the charade. For the second year in a row, a trip was planned for the visitors to fly to Esfahan, 400 kilometres away, to underscore the transparency of Iran's nuclear program—after all, Iran unlike North Korea remained a signatory to the NPT and still allowed restricted IAEA inspections. Unfortunately, the April 2006 excursion took place in a less hospitable climate and forced the group to travel day and night by slow bus, leaving barely enough time for Iranians to snap pictures of foreign experts garbed from head to toe in protective gear freely viewing a rudimentary element of the uranium conversion facility. Iran revealed, as it would again in March 2007 with the capture of fifteen British sailors shown on television "confessing" their transgressions, that it understands effective public relations.

Even without help from the regime in Tehran, experts concluded from the facility visit that Iran could be three to five years away from a nuclear weapon, should it choose to build one. Iran had recently declared its successful enrichment experiment with 164 centrifuges, as part of a plan to build 3,000 centrifuges; this is separate from the industrial scale that Iran also seeks to complete within a decade. Either way, Iran would be able to acquire sufficient fissile material for a nuclear weapon, should it choose to do so; the only difference was whether it would take months or weeks. But no one could be certain of Iran's real capabilities or intentions, not least because even under the NPT, Iran had no obligation to disclose weapon designs and verification was impossible in any event.

Despite the brinkmanship, propaganda, and lab escapade, the door for diplomacy remained open with Iran for two reasons. First, sanctions and military force would entail unknown but huge risks, and Iran has made it very clear it will not sit by idly should the UN adopt draconian sanctions. Second, Iran has kept open all options, including a deal to freeze in place its enrichment program now that it has shown the world that it can do it and has every right to do it. Unfortunately, as more time has passed, a freeze on Iran's enrichment capacity diminishes in value.

Nevertheless, the options for members of the UN Security Council have been limited. On the one hand, they retained the desire for diplomacy and on the other, a negotiated settlement of the issue. Such a fresh starting point might resemble the bargain reached in February 2007 with North Korea, which entailed a step-by-step approach based on the facts on the ground as they existed, rather than as the United States and other powers wished for them to exist. The second option entails a constant turning of the screw, an array of ever-tightening sanctions, with the risk that Iran's reaction could trigger a wider conflict rather than a cessation to its nuclear program.

The moment for a potential freeze in 2006 and even 2007 appeared to come and go. The advantage of a freeze was that it might have bought time, critical time that could allow a modicum of trust to be built with Iran, while perhaps eventually ushering in an Iranian president more interested in realistic dialogue than Ahmadinejad. Already Iran had cooperated to some extent on the stabilization of Afghanistan. In contrast, there was a missed opportunity for diplomacy over Iraq in 2006, and as the insurgency deteriorated in Iraq, accusations between the United States and Iran over Shia militias in Iraq escalated. Equally problematic was the question of whether the United States and Iran could narrow their perceptions over how to deal with terrorism. From Iran's perspective, there was a desire to make a distinction between the Al-Qaeda network and those groups using political violence to pursue their nationalist aspirations in Palestine and Lebanon. From the U.S. perspective, Iran was sponsoring terrorism through Hezbollah, Hamas, and other groups, and was unlikely to relinquish their ability to exert indirect regional influence by stopping that support. Privately, thoughtful Iranian spokesmen could sketch out a scenario that would end with Iran's de facto acceptance of the state of Israel (in contrast to President Ahmadinejad's Holocaust-denying oratory); but the absence of a serious process for building a better common understanding and step-by-step cooperation meant such a vision could not even attempt to get started. Instead, the "moderate" rhetoric was easily dismissed as stalling tactics while Iran acquired its nuclear deterrent, and Iranian hardliners could portray the United States as not taking Iran's claims seriously.

A second advantage of a freeze is that it might avert a repeat of the Iraq intervention, which has made Iraq a catalyst for radicalism, both inside Iraq and in Islamic communities more broadly. An initial diplomatic decision to freeze would also unite rather than further divide the international community—or at least the permanent five members of the UN Security Council plus Germany. A beneficial agreement would cede the moral and legal high ground to the UN, should harsher steps be needed. Although Iran likes to portray the United States as isolated, any observer of the Iranian press discerns the company that Iran is able to celebrate, including such notable partners as Sudan, Zimbabwe, and Cuba.

The downside to the freeze option, however, is that it would seemingly reward an obstreperous Iran, which appeared to be using salami tactics—slicing away at its ambitions in a way that makes each slice look unlike the whole salami—to pursue a clandestine nuclear option. Delay only abets this process, and it also gives Iran the know-how that will make effective military action, should it be necessary, that much more problematic. Decision makers are often said to have to choose between options that are bad and worse. Clearly in this case, there appears to be no good option; but some options seem worse than others.

As Alexei Arbatov argues in this volume, wars can be ignited by specific events, whether intended or accidental. What is disturbing is that the Iranian leadership appears to condone considerable risk-taking that could well erupt into a larger conflict. At least, it is difficult to interpret Iran's seizure of fifteen British sailors and marines in Iraqi territorial waters in March 2007 as anything but a callous gambit designed to substitute the fate of the sailors for the fate of Iran's nuclear program.

The diversion away from the nuclear issue was only short-lived, but the incident spoke volumes about how Tehran pursues room for diplomatic maneuver when it feels hemmed in by international action, such as UN Security Council sanctions. The Persian Gulf seizure appears to have been premeditated, not inadvertent. Officials in Tehran clung to a narrative of rights, but far from appearing like a law-abiding country fighting alleged

American double standards, they seemed interested in only the thinnest veneer of justice—just enough to justify its headlong pursuit of nuclear power and feed Iran's growing appetite for regional influence. At a tactical level, according to Arab media reports, the operation was a carefully calculated retaliation for the arrest and detention of the Commander of the *Al-Quds* Bridgade, Brigadier Tayshizri, and four other Iranian Revolutionary Guard Corps officers from the Iranian consulate in Irbil by U.S. forces on January 11, 2007, as well as the recent disappearance and possible defection of a key *Al-Quds* intelligence officer, Colonel Amir Muhammad Hussein Shirazi, in Turkey.[9]

At a strategic level, it is hard not to see the hostage-taking operation as part of a broader plan to promote Iranian regional and nuclear power. Iran's nuclear progress is held back only by technology: Iranian scientists were closing in on assembling 3,000 centrifuges in a pilot enrichment program. To be sure, in the spring of 2007, Iran still faced technical problems that were likely to make it difficult for the machines to operate at a high speed over a sustained period of time, which was essential for creating enough fissile material for a nuclear weapon. Without policy or regime change in Tehran, however, nuclear success looked like just a matter of time.

Perhaps most disturbing of all was that the main pressure point employed by the United States and Europe, together with more lukewarm support from Russia and China, focused on sanctions. And yet each time the UN Security Council announced sanctions—in particular, in December 2006 and March 2007—Iran responded with a rhetorical broadside, accompanied by steps to accelerate its uranium enrichment program. The fact that North Korea was allowed to return to Six-Party Talks without promising more than sealing its old plutonium reactor at Yongbyon—and not yet touching its nuclear stockpile, other fissile material, or a suspected highly enriched uranium reactor—was surely not lost on officials in Tehran trying to calculate how far they could push back without crossing a "red line" that might trigger open war.

THE TURBULENT PERSIAN GULF REGION

Iran's sundry motivations for coveting nuclear power include fundamental security concerns. In the past four decades, the region has been jolted by an Iranian revolution, an Iran–Iraq war, an Iraqi invasion of Kuwait, a small war in Yemen, conflict between Israel and its neighbors, and the ongoing conflict in Iraq. Today, security challenges include not just Iran's nuclear ambitions but also stability in Iraq and the general problem of religious extremism and terrorism (both state-sponsored and that conducted by nonstate actors). These challenges have produced strategies focused on basic objectives of national interest: preserving national and territorial sovereignty, preserving prosperity, hedging against uncertain neighbors outside the Gulf, and seeking ways to tamp down terrorism. A large Gulf country, such as Saudi Arabia, sees a singular role for itself in the region and the wider Islamic world, whereas smaller Gulf countries, such as Kuwait, are keen to advance collective security. As Iran has seemed to emerge the "winner" of the Iraq war, however, large Arab powers like Saudi Arabia and Egypt have openly sought to challenge Iran for regional leadership. Just because Washington may be more sympathetic to Saudi or Egyptian foreign policy goals, it does not obviate the fact that Iran, too, is surrounded by a turbulent and competitive region.

The security challenges to the region have altered considerably over the past decade. State weakness rather than state strength and transnational terrorism are at the apex of security concerns. Instability in Iraq poses the most immediate security challenge to the region. Clashing forces challenge a fledgling government whose future remains uncertain. Foreign forces are at once part of a solution and a problem in the eyes of Gulf States, which agree on the objectives but not necessarily the means of stabilizing Iraq. No one expects an early end to Iraq's insurgency or to sectarian political violence, whether because of a U.S. "surge" or a potential U.S. disengagement. The United States was in a good position in 2007 to help "clear and hold" certain contested areas of Iraq; but no foreign or domestic entity possessed the power to quickly erect the institutions of state required for rudimentary security, a civil policy, and shared economic weal. While Gulf States hope to play a larger role in supporting the emerging Iraqi government, they also generally want the United States to continue to play a leading security role—and to listen and learn from others in and outside the region. Iran, in contrast, called on the United States to leave Iraq; however, it also seemed rather content with watching the United States pay a heavy price for its intervention.

Terrorism poses another critical challenge. Whereas most in the region see this as a vital common threat, there is no consensus on specific threats or remedies, other than the need for multifaceted national and regional policies, in which military intervention is only one policy instrument. Among the remedies offered, there could be wider cooperation among Muslims on confronting the false narratives of those using a distorted version of Islam to justify indiscriminate killing. Although terrorism is a common threat, it is paradoxically difficult to forge effective international cooperation against it. The definition of terrorism itself is value-laden, with some in the region insisting that Al-Qaeda's acts differ little from "state-sponsored" terrorist acts such as humiliating if not torturing prisoners, bombing civilian populations, or the practice of targeted assassination. Terrorism is also viewed as a personal issue for each nation. Despite the obstacles to cooperation, including the fundamental issue of trust, many support deeper and wider intelligence sharing. Speed, precision, calibration of power, expertise, justice, leadership, and deep interdependence all are seen as needed if terrorism is to be countered. More Muslims die from international terrorism than any other group.

There is also the challenge revolving around the domestic institutions of regional states. Some in the region see the need for more democracy and popular legitimacy, while others hope to integrate the region into the global marketplace of ideas and commerce, and still others want to shore up state security in the face of unfettered communications, porous borders, and political violence. The effort of the United States to promote democratic reform in the greater Middle East and beyond has drawn mostly ire from the region and at best has created urgency to the pace of political reform throughout the region.

These perceptions relate to a final issue of the challenge by external actors: some want a responsible role for the United States in the Gulf, but few are happy with the status quo. Many welcome Europe's participation, but are skeptical about how vibrant that role can be; others are interested in linkages between the region and the rising Asian powers of China, India, as well as Japan. The region has depended heavily on "imported security" to deal with volatility in the past two decades. It lacks an indigenous balance of power, which causes instability and tensions.

The solutions to handling these diverse—and diversely viewed—challenges center on either new security structures and institutions or specific actions. The idea of pursuing a broader Gulf regional forum that ties together the six Gulf Cooperation Council states (Saudi Arabia, Kuwait, Bahrain, Oman, the United Arab Emirates, and Qatar) as well as Iraq, Iran, Yemen, and perhaps Jordan, remains an unfulfilled notion—with the important exception of the annual Manama Dialogue facilitated by the International Institute for Strategic Studies. Others worry that attempts at all-encompassing inclusivity are premature, and that for the time being like-minded nations ought to coalesce in order to deal with at least the scourge of terrorism and Iraq. Still others prefer dealing with specific issues and put a premium on bilateral cooperation, whether intelligence sharing or combined military exercises. Iran will be operating from its region, not just a piece of territory surrounded by many other states, and thus in the final analysis a regional approach will be essential to coping with security challenges and troubles that transcend Iran's nuclear program. Even so, the trouble posed by Iran's nuclear ambition appears to be a principal barrier—and yet could become the key medium—for fashioning greater regional security cooperation in the years to come.

NOTES

1. See, inter alia, the optimistic review of Dilip Hiro, *Iran Today* (London: Politicos Publishing, 2006); the pessimistic account of Alireza Jafarzadeh, *The Iran Threat: President Ahmadinejad and the Coming Nuclear Crisis* (New York: Palgrave

Macmillan, 2007); and the more balanced accounts of Ray Takeyh, *Hidden Iran: Paradox and Power in the Islamic Republic* (New York: Times Books, 2006) and Ali Ansari, *Confronting Iran: The Failure of American Foreign Policy and the Next Great Crisis in the Middle East* (London: Perseus Books, 2006).

2. Dafna Linzer, "Iran Asserts Expansion of Nuclear Operation," *The Washington Post*, April 10, 2007, p. A9.

3. "Powers Won't Thwart Iran Nuclear Drive," AFP, April 9, 2007.

4. See *The Military Balance 2007* (London: IISS, 2007), pp. 224–226.

5. For instance, see, Gordon Corera, *Shopping for Bombs: Nuclear Proliferation, Global Insecurity and the Rise and Fall of the A.Q. Khan Network* (London: C. Hurst & Co., 2006), pp. 59–61.

6. Ibid.; *Iran's Strategic Weapons Programmes: A Net Assessment* (London: IISS, 2005), pp. 11–15.

7. *Iran's Strategic Weapons Programmes*, pp. 16–28.

8. Author's notes from the conference, April 24–25, 2006.

9. Ali Nourizadeh, "Tehran Wants to Swap British Sailors for Iranian Officers Detained in Iraq–Iranian Military Source," *Asharq Al-Awsat*, March 25, 2007.http://www.aawsat.com/english/news.asp?section=1&=8425

2

Is Iran's Nuclear Capability Inevitable?*

Mark Fitzpatrick

Likely though it now seems, the prospect that Iran will soon come to possess nuclear arms is not inevitable. Greater dexterity will be needed, however, if Iran is to be persuaded to keep the capability latent. The odds are low that a combination of sanctions and incentives will induce Iran to give up uranium enrichment or to dismantle any part of its nuclear program. If the Bush administration concludes that diplomacy and financial pressure is not working, it may be drawn to military options to try to push back the date by which Iran could have a nuclear weapon. Low confidence that air strikes could delay Iran's weapons program and the high costs and possible consequences of military action, however, should lead policymakers to consider whether the nuclear timeline might be prolonged through negotiation. Bowing to reality and accepting small-scale, intermittent enrichment activity in exchange for far greater access to international inspectors holds some appeal, and the asking price will rise over time. But legitimizing Iran's program has significant disadvantages, especially without an assurance of swift and severe penalties in the event the deal is broken.

ASSESSING IRAN'S PROGRESS

Nobody on the outside knows if Iran has made a decision to produce nuclear weapons. Although there should be no doubt that, at the very least, Iran

---

* A version of this essay was published in *Survival* 49(1) (Spring 2007).

seeks a latent nuclear weapon capability, actually producing the weapon can be a later decision than the decision to obtain the capability. For now, Iran may still be "playing it by ear."[1] Although the Central Intelligence Agency (CIA) reportedly has found no conclusive evidence of a parallel military nuclear program,[2] Western intelligence agencies continue to give priority to the task. The International Atomic Energy Agency (IAEA) is also continuing its investigation of unanswered questions, without any help from Iran. The questions include at least ten indicators of Iranian military involvement in the nuclear program and of weapons intentions. Together these indicators strongly suggest that, until 2003 at least, there was a coordinated military connection for purposes of exploring a nuclear weapons program.[3]

Evidence Trail of Military Indicators

For now, the trail stops in 2003, the date of the last documents about explosives testing and missile reentry vehicles and other damning evidence, found on a computer hard drive turned over by an Iranian walk-in at an American embassy. It is possible that the apparent weapons development and testing plans found on the hard drive were only feasibility studies that never left the drawing table. Not coincidentally, 2003 is when the Iran program was formally exposed and when Iran felt at its most vulnerable, watching the ease with which American troops rolled up Iraqi forces during Operation Iraqi Freedom. Steered by an exposé of the exiled National Council of Resistance of Iran, which made public what Western intelligence agencies already knew, IAEA inspections that year were able to visit the uranium enrichment plant being built at Natanz and the heavy-water reactor building site at Arak; together they documented an eighteen-year history of systematic safeguards violations.

It may be that, facing intense inspection scrutiny and relieved of a presumed nuclear, chemical, or biological threat from Iraq, Tehran's leaders decided in 2003 to lay low and put their military program, or at least those parts of it that might become visible to inspectors or informants, on ice for the time being. In May 2003, Iran offered comprehensive talks with the United States on all outstanding issues. In October, in negotiations with France, Germany, and the United Kingdom (the European Union-3 or EU-3) Iran agreed for the first time to suspend its uranium enrichment program, partially and temporarily, and to sign and provisionally implement the Additional Protocol to its Nuclear Non-Proliferation Treaty (NPT) safeguards agreement. Hassan Ruhani, Iran's chief negotiator at the time, said the suspension was a negotiation tactic.[4] It is unknown whether a similar tactical calculation led to a suspension of the military program. Iran may simply have found a way to tighten information security over the weapons program. Even if a decision were taken in 2003 to go no further with the weapons feasibility plans, Iran's improved geostrategic position since then may have produced a different calculation. Indeed, Iran's insistence, in the face of strong international opprobrium, on going ahead with uranium enrichment as well as the research reactor at Arak, ideal for plutonium production, suggests that it is moving ahead to put in place the wherewithal for a weapons capability.

The intensity of inspections and sharp international attention in the past three years probably did help to postpone the date by which Tehran could produce a nuclear weapon if it chose to do so. By October 2003, Iran had assembled a 164-machine cascade at the Natanz uranium enrichment pilot plant. The Iranians could have begun testing that cascade at any time by introducing uranium hexafluoride (UF6). One reason they waited is that they were experiencing problems with that step in single centrifuges. The Iranians could also have kept single centrifuges and smaller cascades running continuously in a vacuum to gain crucial data about their durability and ways in which they can fail, and also to improve quality in the centrifuge manufacturing process. As far as is known, and bearing in mind the possibility of clandestine work, they did not do so until early 2006. The Iranians had other reasons for delaying, most importantly so that they could run several batches of natural uranium concentrate through the uranium conversion facility at Esfahan, producing, by January 2007 (according to Gholamreza Aghazadeh, the head of Iran's Atomic Energy Organization), 250 metric tons of UF6. This is enough, when enriched, for thirty to fifty implosion-type nuclear weapons. Production of sufficient feed material may have enabled Iran to overcome one key bottleneck, although it is unclear whether Iran has been using domestically produced UF6 to test the cascades or is still relying on purer quality feed material imported from China in 1991. One day of suspension of the enrichment activity thus did not equal one day's postponement of the date by which Iran could produce a nuclear weapon. Nevertheless, it is fair to say the on-again, off-again suspension of enrichment activity, resulting from the EU-3 engagement strategy, did have a beneficial impact in slowing down the program.

It is more difficult to assess the current speed of Iran's program because of the restrictions Iran has placed on IAEA inspector access. Up until February 2006, under the terms of the EU-3 suspension deal, the IAEA was able to inventory all the spinning parts of the centrifuges as well as key raw material, including high-strength maraging steel. Although access was imperfect and could not guarantee that Iran was not producing centrifuge components in unreported workshops elsewhere in the country, the IAEA's verification measures exceeded the terms of the Additional Protocol, which Iran had been following as if it were in force. If Western analysts are correct that Iran cannot itself manufacture maraging steel, which is necessary for bellows for Iran's P-1 centrifuges (and for the rotors of the more advanced P-2 machines Iran has been pursuing), monitoring the imported material was a critical verification tool.

The status of the P-2 development program remains one of the outstanding questions about Iran's nuclear activities. The IAEA continues to seek clarification of the P-2 work Iran carried out in 2003 and previous years and what President Mahmoud Ahmadinejad meant, when he spoke in April 2006 of research on new types of centrifuges that were four times more powerful. Iran's only response, on June 16, was that this was "an ongoing and progressing R&D activity without using nuclear materials."[5] Unreported progress in the P-2 program could give Iran the ability to produce highly enriched uranium more quickly than Western analysts predicted.

The IAEA's ability to monitor Iran's program was reduced in January 2006 when Iran asked the Agency to remove seals from centrifuge-related raw materials and components. Iran continued provisionally to implement the Additional Protocol until February 6, 2006, when it suspended all provisions of the protocol and other nonlegally binding safeguards measures in response to the IAEA Board's February 4 decision to report the Iran case to the UN Security Council. The IAEA can no longer monitor production of centrifuge components and warehousing of imported material. Iran continues to provide the bare minimum access required by its full-scope safeguards agreement, allowing verification of enrichment activity at Natanz. However, Iran gradually has put obstacles on this as well, for example by restricting the frequency of inspections at the underground fuel-enrichment plant and not granting inspectors visas until the last moment. Because its access is so restricted, the IAEA is unable to confirm the status of Iran's program.

The IAEA does know the number of centrifuges installed at Natanz and the level of enriched uranium being produced. The aboveground pilot plant has about 360 centrifuges: two 164-machine cascades, a 10- and a 20-centrifuge cascade, and a handful of individual centrifuges. As of the end of February 2007, Iran also had two 164-machines cascades installed in the underground enrichment facility at Natanz and was nearing completion on another two cascades. Iran announced that by May 2007 it would have 3,000 centrifuges installed in the underground facility. As of the end of February 2007, only the cascades in the pilot plant were operating with UF6. Between June 6 and August 23, 2006, the first cascade in the pilot plant operated with UF6 for nineteen days, or less, then 25 percent of the time, using 6 kilograms UF6. Between August 23 and November 2, 2006, Iran reported having fed 34 kilograms of UF6 into the two cascades, nearly a six-fold increase over the summer campaign, enriching it to levels below 5 percent.[6]

Technical Difficulties

More important than the enrichment level or number of installed centrifuges is the intermittent operation of the cascades, as reported by IAEA Director General Mohamed ElBaradei to the Board in November 2006.[7] As of that date, an inability to run the cascades continuously was the largest hurdle remaining in Iran's path to fissile-material production. Moreover, the enriched product was not being collected. Instead it was being remixed with the depleted uranium tails into the same collection cylinder from where it could be refed through the cascade as natural uranium feed. The two cascades were not serially linked, with the output from one being fed into the second for further enrichment, an operation that requires a high degree of competence.[8] Running the two cascades as two separate testing lines was an indication of continuing technical trouble. The essence of a cascade, after all, is that the machines are linked, not that 164 of them are standing together. Remixing and reusing the product may indicate that Iran is still testing the cascade with its limited Chinese-origin UF6, rather than its domestically produced feed material.

Iran would like the world to believe that its mastery of the fuel cycle is already a fait accompli. Ahmadinejad boasted on November 14, 2006, that the United States and its allies had "finally agreed to live with ... an Iran possessing the nuclear fuel cycle."[9] Iran has proven that it can produce centrifuges, balance and spin them for months at a time, and enrich uranium in small amounts to reactor fuel-grade levels (3.5–5 percent) in a cascade of 164 centrifuges. Iran has been enriching uranium intermittently since April 2006. But if Iran cannot yet run the centrifuge cascades for a sustained period, it cannot produce enriched uranium beyond a research and development level. In September 2006, IAEA analysts reportedly told U.S. and European officials that Iran was unable to control an overheating problem when UF6 was injected into the centrifuges; after a short period they had to be stopped because the high temperatures had been causing some centrifuges to crash.[10] The breaking of centrifuges alone is not necessarily an indication of problems, because the testing program would in any case seek to find the breaking point of the machines. Problems were also reported, however, with the integrity of the complicated piping linking the centrifuges. These technical troubles gave the transatlantic allies reason to believe they had more time than previously feared to find a diplomatic solution, which partly explains Washington's willingness to go along with the slow diplomatic dance, beginning in the autumn of 2006 over a UN sanctions resolution. According to Western enrichment experts, any new start-up facility should run test cascades continuously for a year before it could be certain the machines worked properly. The CIA's worst-case scenario for when Iran could produce a nuclear weapon therefore is still the end of the decade at the earliest.

Technical difficulties were one reason that Iran did not follow through with plans to install five to six cascades (nearly 1,000 centrifuges) in the pilot plant by the end of summer 2006.[11] Full installation of all six cascades at the pilot plant was also postponed out of concern that they would be susceptible to air strikes and to keep some centrifuges in reserve for use elsewhere. By mid-October 2006, however, IAEA officials concluded that the summer slowdown was also politically driven. Iran could have completed more cascades in late summer, but chose not to in order not to appear to be overly provocative. In short, Iran would not bow to the Security Council demand for full suspension by August 31, 2006, but it did try to temper international reactions by not racing ahead with more cascades. When the Europeans resumed Security Council consultations on a sanctions resolution in October, Iran responded by beginning operation of the second cascade—a clear political signal that it would not bend under pressure. Installation of additional cascades was kept in reserve for the next tit-for-tat response, the announcement of which came after the Security Council imposed sanctions on December 23, 2006.

Centrifuge Numbers

Since January 2006, the IAEA has had no ability to monitor how many centrifuges Iran has been producing, nor how many centrifuges were breaking during test operations. Before the October 2004 suspension, Iran was producing 70–100 centrifuges a month in a single work shift. Assuming Iran could have doubled the production tempo by adding another shift, IAEA officials estimated in late 2006 that Iran was on track to meet its announced goal of having 3,000 centrifuges, albeit uninstalled, by the end of the Iranian calendar year in March 2007, or shortly thereafter. Although 500 of them are second-hand imports from Pakistan and others are of still unproven domestic production, IAEA officials believe they are at least serviceable.[12]

Although Iran announced in April 2007 that it had made further progress toward installing 3,000 centrifuges in the underground enrichment plant at Natanz, connecting them together and getting them to run smoothly will take until 2008 or 2009 at the earliest. Unless Iran follows the North Korean path by pulling out of the NPT, thereby annulling its safeguards agreement completely, the IAEA will be able to monitor progress at Natanz. Once a 3,000-centrifuge enrichment plant is operational, Iran could produce a weapon worth of highly enriched uranium (enriched over 90 percent) in nine to eleven months.[13] That time would be cut to as little as thirty-six to forty-eight days if Iran first built up a stock of low-enriched uranium, then went for breakout by enriching it to weapons grade. As soon as the plant began enriching beyond the 3.5–5 percent level needed for reactor fuel, however, the IAEA would know—and blow the whistle. Another breakout scenario would involve Iran building a hidden enrichment facility unreported to the IAEA. A hidden facility of 1,500 centrifuges could produce a weapon worth of highly enriched uranium (or HEU) in one and a half years.

EXPORT CONTROLS

Strict export controls on any materials and technology that can aid Iran's enrichment program must continue to be an essential part of transatlantic strategy. Iran has a more advanced industrial sector than Pakistan. Western officials believe Iran is largely self-sufficient in enrichment-related materials and technology, with the exception of maraging steel, of which it has imported a certain quantity. Iran already may have on hand what it needs to produce a few nuclear weapons. To make the 54,000 centrifuges planned for the underground commercial facility at Natanz, Iran would need to rely on additional material from black market sources. In any case, to enhance its breakout capability, Iran will continue to try to procure better equipment and parts through its extensive black-market procurement operations. Iran's missile program is also dependent on foreign procurement.

ENGAGEMENT

Although policymakers must consider the worst-case scenario, the earliest possible date—2009—is not the most likely. In seeking a suspension in enrichment activity, Western governments hope to push the date further back. Delaying the nuclear program until such time as Iran had a more representational government has long been the unstated transatlantic policy. Washington has also sought to speed up another timeline—the "democracy clock," by which Iran's youthful demographics and anticlerical mood will bring about a less threatening government in Tehran. If present trends continue, there is little chance that the democracy timeline will advance fast enough to overtake the ticking nuclear clock. Most objective experts on Iran doubt that Washington's unsubtle reform-promotion efforts will have much impact, other than to stigmatize any Iranian reformers who take American money. Although outside help has assisted democratic successions in Georgia, Ukraine, and elsewhere, there is little by way of a comparable civil society to support in Iran.

The real issue is not the race between the democracy clock and the ticking nuclear bomb, but whether those who advocate a less confrontational foreign policy will prevail over Ahmadinejad's revolutionary radicals. Those who might be called pragmatists, characterized by Akbar Hashemi Rafsanjani and Ali Larijani, are fully part of the leadership consensus on acquiring a nuclear weapon capability. Nevertheless, they are willing to negotiate over the timing and they realize the benefits of normal international intercourse, both for Iran's commercial interests and for its relations with its Sunni neighbors. Unless national pride in Ahmadinejad's nuclear pronouncements overshadows popular dissatisfaction with his disastrous economic stewardship, he stands a good chance of losing to the pragmatists in the next presidential election in 2009. In a hopeful sign of things to come, pro-Ahmadinejad hard-liners lost badly in the December 15, 2006, elections for city and village councils and the eighty-six-member Assembly of Experts (which elects and oversees the Supreme Leader), taking less than 20 percent of the vote in each, outpaced by both pragmatic conservatives and reformists. Although Iran will not see reformist government soon, real changes in the political environment are very possible before Iran can acquire a nuclear weapon.

MISSED OPPORTUNITIES

The strength of hard-line views in the leadership camp is evident in the failed talks in early autumn 2006 between Larijani, chief Iranian negotiator and Secretary of the Supreme National Security Council, and EU foreign policy chief Javier Solana, acting loosely on behalf of the permanent five members of the UN Security Council and Germany (the so-called P5+1 including China, France, Russia, United States, UK, and Germany). The talks—actually talks about talks—were to explore ways Iran and the P5+1 could begin negotiations on the basis of the package proposal Solana transmitted on June 6, 2006. The extraordinary incentives in the package included direct U.S. engagement in the negotiations and state-of-the-art Western nuclear technology with explicit U.S. backing (in effect, the promise of a lifting of U.S. sanctions, although the Congress would still have to agree). The Europeans anticipated that the prospect for direct U.S. engagement would be the most alluring element of the package for Iran. Indeed, offering direct engagement (in a multilateral context, as with North Korea) was a major policy shift for the Bush administration, which up until Condoleezza Rice moved to the State Department in 2005 refused to have anything to do with the EU engagement strategy with Iran.

Since late 2005, U.S. Ambassador to Iraq, Zalmay Khalilzad, had also been authorized to meet with his Iranian counterpart and appropriate Iraqi authorities over Iran's role in the worsening security situation there. In March 2006, when Iraqi Shia leader Abdul Aziz al-Hakim called on Iran to respond positively, it gave Larijani, backed by Supreme Leader Khamenei, an excuse to say "yes." This was a significant change on the part of Iran, where not long ago, dealing with the Great Satan was a formidable taboo. The talks never materialized, however, as they became freighted with too much baggage as each side sought to structure the talks on its own terms. On one hand, the United States backed off when Iran upped the ante on Khalilzad's request for talks between ambassadors, and decided to send Larijani and the commander of the Revolutionary Guard to Baghdad. The Iranian leadership backed off as well, when Ahmadinejad said in April 2006 that talks on Iraq were not necessary now that the Iraqis had established a permanent government. The Iranians said they wanted to discuss issues with the

United States comprehensively, not just the individual issue of Iraq security. American advocates of engagement hoped that, in Khalilzad's able hands, talks about security in Iraq could become a vehicle for broaching broader issues between the United States and Iran. However faint a hope that might have been, the moment passed, and, like previous attempts at engagement by President Clinton in 1999 and President Mohammad Khatami in 2003, the Khalilzad gambit can be chalked up as another missed opportunity.[14]

Prospects for U.S.-Iran talks on Iraq appeared to grow in late 2006, when the Iraq Study Group advised opening talks with Iran and Syria about ways to end the violence in Iraq. On November 5, 2006, Iranian Foreign Ministry spokesman Mohammad Ali Hosseini said Iran would consider talks with the United States over regional issues, including Iraq, if Washington requested. President Bush ruled that out, however, unless Iran first suspended its enrichment program, although there is no reason Iran would make trade-offs on its nuclear program in order to help the United States repair its position in Iraq.[15] American and Iranian representatives did meet at a one-day international conference in Baghdad on March 10, 2007, to discuss Iraqi security; but the broad regional participation and nature of the session provided for little real interaction between the two main protagonists beyond an exchange of accusations.

The possibility of U.S.-Iran engagement through multilateral negotiations over the June 2006 package fared no better. The incentives came with the precondition that Iran first suspend enrichment activity before negotiations could commence. The Iranians were unwilling to make that concession up front, seeing it as a trap. They feared that Washington would pocket the suspension then make additional demands on missiles, terrorism, human rights, recognition of Israel, and whatever else, without ever lifting sanctions. Moreover, the P5+1 proposal omitted the prospect for security guarantees that the previous EU-3 offer had contained. However, some in Iran thought there was room to maneuver, so Larijani engaged Solana in September 2006 to explore a diplomatic solution on how to begin negotiations without Iran capitulating on the suspension precondition. In the second week of September, Larijani signaled that, once negotiations began, Iran could suspend for a short, defined period, perhaps two or three months. Whether it was a serious attempt or not, Larijani soon found his negotiating room constricted by the uncompromising mood in Tehran, where Supreme Leader Khamenei sided with hard-liners who believed it was not the time for Iran to make any concessions. With the United States bogged down in Iraq, oil prices high, and Iran's protégé Hezbollah having fought Israel to a standstill, Iran was in a strong position. It imposed conditions Solana could not accept, and when the transatlantic allies held firm, Ahmadinejad announced on September 28, 2006, that Iran would not suspend enrichment for even one day. Larijani had to pull his suspension offer off the table, and Solana finally had to overcome his natural optimism and report to EU foreign ministers that the pre-talks had run aground. The Europeans then moved their consultations on a Security Council resolution to the foreground.

CLINGING TO ENRICHMENT

Notwithstanding Secretary Rice's artful diplomacy in joining the EU engagement strategy, and putting the onus on Iran, the West has not moved a step closer to meeting its objective of denying Iran a fissile material production capability. By joining the EU in offering carrots, Washington persuaded the Europeans to join in on threatening sticks. Moving the issue to the Security Council and imposing sanctions, however, was only a tactic, not the goal. Meanwhile Iran has moved closer to its goal of mastering the enrichment process.

To date, at least as of the summer of 2007 when this book went to press, negotiations have failed over the fundamental incompatibility between these two goals. The Western allies continue to hope that Iran will be willing to forego enrichment if only the right inducements and incentives package can be found. As anyone who visits Iran knows, however, there is no visible prospect that Iran will give up this technology. The issue has taken on too much political weight. Every man on the street in Tehran now knows—or thinks he knows—what enrichment is, and believes it to be indispensable to Iran's energy future and technological standing in the world. The more emphasis that the West places on stopping enrichment, the more Iranians come to believe that it is a valuable technology they cannot do without. A few Iranian reformist leaders realize the price the country could pay for its confrontational stance, but even the reformers only advocate a temporary suspension.[16]

European negotiators understand that Iran will not totally give up enrichment, which is why the incentives packages offered to Iran in August 2005 and June 2006 included a review process mechanism under which enrichment would be possible after Iran has restored international confidence. In both offers, Iran was asked to forego enrichment for a period, not give it up forever. The difference is that in the August 2005 offer, Iran was asked to make a "binding commitment" not to pursue fuel cycle activities, although this commitment could be reviewed every ten years, whereas in June 2006 Iran was asked to suspend its fuel cycle activities during the negotiations. The June 2006 offer said that a moratorium would be reviewed when "international confidence in the exclusively peaceful nature of Iran's civil nuclear program has been restored." The rub in this for Iran is a disbelief that Washington would ever agree that Iran has restored confidence, whatever conclusions the IAEA reaches.

At some point, the hope that Iran can be persuaded to forego enrichment before it acquires the necessary knowledge will be overtaken by events. While Iran may agree to pause in its march along the technology learning curve, it is unlikely to settle for less than the evolving status quo, short of a seismic shift in its security situation. A compromise by Iran cannot be ruled out altogether. It has suddenly shifted ground before on other intractable positions, such as agreeing to a cease-fire with Iraq in 1988. Hopes for a similar shift on the nuclear question, however, rest on the thin chance of a major change in Iran's security calculus. Examples of other nations that have given up weapons programs are not relevant. South Africa gave up its nuclear weapons only when its apartheid system was about to change. Libya gave up its nuclear weapons only when it realized that it would not be able to complete importing necessary parts and that more was to be gained by trading the weapons program for Western investment and trade. North Korea agreed in 1994 to freeze its plutonium-based nuclear program but never dismantled a single part, and resumed the program in 2003. Whether Iran would be willing to agree to a freeze of its nuclear program at the current level or operating tempo is unknown unless negotiators are able to ply their craft. It is a good bet, however, that Iran will not agree to dismantle what it has now. It is also a good bet, in light of the recent record, that Iran would not stick to a freeze.

SANCTIONS

On July 31, 2006, the Security Council mandated, in Resolution 1646 (passed 14-1 with only Qatar voting no), that Iran suspend all enrichment-related and reprocessing activities. If Iran failed to do so by August 31, the resolution expressed the Council's intention "to adopt appropriate measures" under Article 41 of Chapter VII of the UN Charter—economic sanctions. On December 23, nearly four months after Iran ignored the deadline, the Council finally adopted sanctions, in Resolution 1737, this time unanimously. The resolution banned technical and financial assistance to Iran's enrichment, reprocessing, heavy water and ballistic missile programs, and froze the foreign-held assets of twelve Iranian individuals and ten organizations involved in those programs. The resolution also put some restrictions on IAEA's technical cooperation with Iran (although most current assistance programs were exempted) and called on states to "exercise vigilance" in allowing travel by Iranians involved in these activities or training of Iranians in disciplines that would contribute to these programs. The resolution did not touch Russian support for the Bushehr reactor, including delivery of fuel. If Iran did not comply within sixty days, the resolution affirmed that the Council would adopt further measures under Article 41.

The technology ban was less extensive than what members of the Nuclear Suppliers Group and the Missile Technology Control Regime already embargoed, and was significantly weaker than what the EU-3 authors originally proposed. The significance of the resolution was its unanimous adoption and global application. To win Russian approval, the Europeans repeatedly had to revise the draft, never knowing until the end what Russia's bottom line was. One key compromise was to change what had been an over-all ban on "proliferation sensitive" nuclear technology and missile delivery systems to a specific listing of embargoed items. Another was to make the proposed travel and training bans voluntary.

When Iran defied that deadline, the Security Council responded with surprising speed on March 24, 2007, with a second sanctions resolution, again with unanimity. Although new Council members South Africa and Indonesia sought to drop new punitive measures, they reluctantly agreed to support the text largely as agreed to by China and Russia. Resolution 1747 doubled the list of Iranian entities subject to an asset freeze because of their involvement in Iran's nuclear and missile work, including seven more Iranian Revolutionary Guard Corps officers. Also included in the list was Bank Sepah. The only new mandatory sanction barred Iranian arms exports. To maintain Security Council unanimity, the EU-3 sponsors dropped several penalties. UN member states were only asked to "exercise vigilance and restraint" in transferring arms to Iran, and were called upon, but not required, to cut off financial assistance and concessionary loans to Iran. In addition, member states must report whether an individual sanctioned by the Council has entered through their territory, but these persons are not subject to a travel ban.

Iran's response to these resolutions was calibrated. President Ahmadinejad had warned that any move toward sanctions would prompt a "decisive and appropriate answer" from Iran. Hard-line Majlis members and newspapers demanded that Iran pull out of the NPT. That threat remained a bluff, however, because it would destroy Iran's claims to the legitimacy of its nuclear program. Giving up its NPT claim to legality would play into the hands of American hard-liners, who believe that Iran is only using the NPT anyway as a cover for its nuclear weapons intentions. Rather than the provocative step of pulling out of the NPT, the Majlis passed a law obliging the government to revise its cooperation with the IAEA. In line with this law, the government banned thirty-eight IAEA inspectors from Canada, France, Germany, the UK, and the United States, refused to accept newly designated inspectors, and demanded that the IAEA remove Belgian citizen Christian Charlier as section head for Iran. Iran also refused to allow the IAEA to install remote monitoring cameras and declared that it no longer would provide advance notification to the IAEA of nuclear facility construction or modification. Iran argued that all of these steps were within its legal right, but in exploiting the gray area in its NPT-required full-scope safeguards agreement, Iran came close to impeding the Agency's ability to conduct inspections, and thereby providing another basis for Iran being found in safeguards noncompliance.

Sanctions are an essential element of the Western negotiating position, and they caution against pessimism about the efficacy of sanctions, lest this becomes a self-fulfilling prophecy. The sanctions resolutions were an important test of Security Council resolve in acting in unison to bring enforcement action. Any further Security Council injunctions to Iran would be meaningless if the Council had not carried through with sanctions as forecast in Resolution 1646. Disrespect of a Security Council Chapter VII mandate should not be without consequences. Sanctions are a way to protect the credibility of the international system, to provide an objective lesson to other potential proliferators, and to globalize export controls. It nevertheless seems very unlikely that sanctions alone will change Iran's calculus in time. The historical record of sanctions is largely dismal; when they have worked, as in South Africa and Libya, it was only after a prolonged period of time and in conjunction with incentives.

The unanimity of Resolution 1737 appeared to take Iranians by surprise, and contributed to a groundswell of criticism of Ahmadinejad's rhetoric on the nuclear issue. Ahmadinejad came under fierce criticism over his handling of the nuclear issue, including from a newspaper connected with Supreme Leader Khamenei. The parliament held a public debate on whether the defiant attitude of the government was providing the basis for additional sanctions and a major reformist party called for public discussion to inform the people of the depth and scope of the costs and benefits of the nuclear program. In the debate that followed Resolution 1737, however, few Iranian voices called for suspension of enrichment or opposed the government's announced plans to install 3,000 centrifuges in the underground facility at Natanz.

The Europeans emphasized that sanctions should be progressive, proportionate, and reversible, although they realized that Iran would only be induced to change its policy if it faced a serious economic cost that might threaten regime stability. Washington realized the psychological value of consensus resolutions, but wanted to move more quickly toward sanctions with real teeth. Embargoing the sale of refined petroleum products to Iran, for example, would severely crimp an otherwise oil-rich economy that can only refine 60 percent of the petroleum needed to fuel its own trucks and cars. Iranians who now choke the nation's city streets and highways in cars run on highly subsidized gasoline (paying as little as $.09 per liter) may react in anger if the government is forced to reduce those subsidies to cope with an embargo-caused shortage. Forcing a reduction in gasoline consumption, however, would actually help the Iranian economy.[17] And persuading all of Iran's suppliers to join an embargo on refined petroleum exports would be very difficult. Iran's neighbors and diversified trading partners are unlikely to enforce sanctions any better than they enforced the embargo the United Nations imposed on Iraq. Any trade sanctions on Iran would be undercut by unofficial deals and smuggling. Even leaky sanctions would drive up the cost of gasoline in Iran and put pressure on the government, but the Iranians do not believe the Security Council will impose any sanctions that would hurt. So far, they are right. Russia and China refuse to accept any measures that leave open the possibility of UN-sanctioned military action. Resolutions 1737 and 1747 thus did not state that the situation constituted "a threat to international peace and security."

De Facto Sanctions

Washington is urging other nations to interpret the resolution aggressively, by cutting ties with any businesses involved with the sensitive nuclear and missile programs and the Iranian Revolutionary Guard Corps, two commanders of which are named in an annex to the resolution. This effort builds on the U.S. Treasury's strategy to apply pressure on Iran by seeking to deny international financial services. Well before the Security Council action, Iran already was paying the price of de facto sanctions. It could not get letters of credit for trade and had to forego work on most oil and gas development projects. In September 2006, Oil Minister Kazem Vaziri-Hamaneh suggested that, with no new investment, output from Iran's fields would fall by about 13 percent a year. Switzerland's two largest banks, UBS AG and Credit Suisse and Germany's second-largest bank Deutsche Bank have ceased operations in Iran, based on internal risk assessments. Several other European financial institutions and industrial groups, reportedly including British Petroleum, ABN Amro in the Netherlands, HSBC and Standard Chartered, have stopped new investments and dollar transactions with Iran. Japan pulled out of the Azadegan oil field development deal because profit margins were not worth the risk and the Japan Bank for International Cooperation has halted all new financing of projects in Iran until it meets the Security Council mandate for suspension.

The U.S. Treasury on January 9, 2007, barred Bank Sepah, Iran's fifth-largest bank, from any business with U.S. financial institutions on grounds of its transactions with Iranian entities named in UN Security Council Resolution 1737. The Treasury action prevents Bank Sepah from doing business in U.S. dollars. In mid-September 2006, the U.S. Treasury took similar action against another of Iran's major banks, Bank Saderat, because it was Iran's channel for funneling money to Hezbollah. Several other countries joined the action against Bank Saderat (although only Japan did so publicly), which has had a serious impact in Iran. The United States asked the EU to impose similar official sanctions on Bank Sepah and U.S. Treasury officials have been trying to persuade European financial conglomerates unofficially to stop doing business with any Iranian banks involved in illicit activities. Iran must increasingly stop selling oil for dollars and turn to investments from Russia, China, South Korea, India, and other non-Western countries. The

United States is putting pressure on these sources of investment as well, facing them with a choice of either stopping business with Iran or losing the American market. Private companies will respond accordingly.

MILITARY OPTIONS

If the combination of diplomacy and financial pressure does not show evidence of slowing Iran's drive toward a nuclear weapons capability, many American political observers believe President Bush will feel a responsibility (or a recklessness) to seek other ways to reduce the threat, rather than to hand it off unresolved to his successor in 2009. The coincidence of the American presidential cycle and the timeline for the worst-case scenario for Iran producing a nuclear weapon may argue for consideration of a military option in the final months of the administration, notwithstanding all the counterarguments. Israel may feel the need to take action against the "existential threat" even earlier than that, if it judges that the United States will not do so and that waiting will make it harder.

At best, air strikes will only delay the program by a few years, and probably not at all, unless the United States or Israel are prepared to extensively widen the bombing campaign and to repeat it in a few short years—in effect, to launch an interminable war against a Middle East foe stronger, larger, and more cohesive than Saddam's Iraq. America's disastrous experience in Iraq post-Saddam should make such a scenario unacceptable.

Iran's nuclear facilities are more dispersed than were Iraq's in 1981, the time of Israel's preemptive air strike popularly credited with having significantly set back an Iraqi nuclear weapons program. In any case, as Richard Betts convincingly argues, the Israeli 1981 example is a fallacy: destroying the nuclear reactor at Osirak did not delay Iraq's nuclear program and probably accelerated it.[18] After the bombing, Saddam increased the budget and number of scientists dedicated to the nuclear weapons program twenty-fold.[19] Without accurate intelligence about Iran's dispersed nuclear facilities and hidden equipment, air strikes that only target the known facilities would not cripple the nuclear program. An unnamed senior U.S. official said November 7, 2006: "We do not have enough information about the Iranian nuclear program to be confident that you could destroy it in a single attack. The worst thing you could do is try and not succeed."[20]

The uranium conversion plant at Esfahan is vulnerable, but Iran may no longer need it for a small weapons program, having already produced enough uranium hexafluoride for at least thirty bombs, as noted above. According to a knowledgeable Western official, the UF6 produced to date is of sufficient purity for Iran's initial purposes and is stored in dispersed locations safe from air strikes.[21] Iran could also build smaller uranium conversion facilities elsewhere, if it has not already done so. The aboveground pilot enrichment plant at Natanz, with its 360 installed centrifuges, is also vulnerable. The additional centrifuges in the underground facility at Natanz are a harder target but still vulnerable. Bombing Natanz, however, would not destroy Iran's other centrifuges and centrifuge components. Iran may already have up to 2,000 centrifuges stockpiled in unknown locations.[22] By accelerating to round-the-clock production, Iran could conceivably triple the 70–100 a month centrifuge production rate at which it was known to have operated two years ago, and replace the 360 centrifuges at the Natanz pilot plant within two months. Iran would also have to build a new facility and equip it with replacements for the autoclaves, piping, and other equipment in the Natanz pilot plant, but it is prudent to assume that Iran already has a replacement facility being readied. Above all, short of commando operations to target scientists and engineers, bombing would not destroy the knowledge in nuclear and related sciences and engineering skills that Iran has amassed to date.

Consequences of Air Strikes

Assuming that air strikes could set back Iran's program for a few years, those years would be bought at a high cost in lives, property, alliance relationships, oil prices, and regional stability. Buoyed by an inflamed nationalism that can be expected to close the nation's ranks around an otherwise increasingly unpopular government, Iran's response would be predictably lethal and asymmetrical. Retaliation options would include the following:

- Attacking American and European cities with radioactive "dirty bombs" and suicide bombers by proxy groups with plausible Iranian deniability or by self-styled terrorist groups acting on their own
- Targeting of Western citizens, embassies, and business concerns throughout the Middle East by Hezbollah, Hamas, and other proxies
- Overt retaliation against shipping in the Persian Gulf, at least temporarily shutting off the flow of oil through the Straits of Hormuz[23]
- Sabotaging oil production in Iraq and elsewhere in the Gulf
- Chemical or biological warhead missile attacks against U.S. forces and allies in the region
- Employing Iran's intelligence services and Revolutionary Guard forces to lead Iraq's Shia majority in waging full-scale guerilla war on coalition forces
- Inciting Shia minorities in the Gulf to destabilize U.S. allies.[24]

None of these responses are inevitable—Iran is concerned, for example, not to exacerbate the Sunni-Shiite divide—but all are possible. Washington could soon have no allies in the Gulf and no friends in Europe. The resulting alienation in much of the Muslim world would make it even harder for the United States fight a "global war on terror" against an additional set of enemies.

TAILORED ACQUIESCENCE

Given the uncertain effectiveness and high costs of military action, if diplomacy and sanctions do not work, the Western allies should consider whether negotiations could have at least the same probability of delaying Iran's nuclear weapons status without the attendant negative consequences. IAEA Director General ElBaradei and his senior staff have no doubt that this is so. American officials would agree only if negotiations were to produce a halt to Iran's program. The ideal outcome is zero enrichment (and zero plutonium reprocessing) in Iran, because only that will provide the confidence that Iran cannot produce a nuclear weapon. Unfortunately, zero enrichment is an increasingly elusive dream. The question for the United States and its allies is whether it makes sense to try to negotiate an outcome that would limit Iran's program to a small pilot plant, coupled with intrusive IAEA monitoring to provide the highest possible level of confidence that Iran was not cheating, realizing that no verification system will provide 100 percent confidence. This strategy has been called "tailored acquiescence"[25] —accepting the reality of Iran's enrichment capability but seeking to constrain it as much as is possible from the breakout weapons scenario.

It is impossible to assign real numbers to most of the variables: how long air strikes would postpone the program, if at all, and the delaying impact of intrusive inspections. One part of the equation can be calculated, however: how long it would take a set number of centrifuges of known quality to produce weapons-grade enriched uranium. Taking into account the efficiency gains that operators would achieve as they became more proficient, 500 P-1 centrifuges, for example, would take about four to five years to produce a weapon worth of highly enriched uranium.

Throughout 2006, various Iranian would-be intermediaries who claimed insider status suggested that Iran would be willing to settle, for now, for several hundred centrifuges in the pilot plant, postponing an industrial level capability for several years. The exact size of the research program and the number of years the industrial-level program would be postponed can be a matter of negotiation, the intermediaries say. One unnamed "insider" told the *Financial Times* in June 2006 that Iran might settle for a limit of three cascades of 164 centrifuges for six or seven years. Another said: "Around 70 percent of senior people may be prepared, under pressure, to accept an eventual limit ... [of] hundreds or thousands."[26] In November 2006, a well-placed Iranian academic said Tehran would aim in negotiations for acceptance of 1,000 to 3,000 centrifuges. Iran has also strongly hinted that it would agree to forego plutonium reprocessing technology, although it has shown no sign of willingness to stop work on the Arak heavy-water plant and heavy-water-moderated research reactor.

Now that Iran has installed additional centrifuges at the underground facility at Natanz, it will be difficult to induce it to stop at the number of centrifuges operating at the pilot plant. Even if Iran were willing to stop at a certain number, the United States would suspect that it was a temporary, tactical delay in order to gain more experience at this level and iron out technical problems before expanding. Nevertheless, on the assumption that Iran will not agree to walk back the program, but may agree to freeze it, any deal that could be struck today is probably better than the deal that might be possible next year and worse than a deal that could have been possible a year ago. The same could have been said last year and the year before. Of course, the assumption that Iran would accept any limitations for more than a limited period of time is itself unsupported by the historical record.

In November 2004, Iran was holding out for exempting 20 centrifuges from the suspension agreement. IAEA officials believe that if this had been accepted, Iran may also have been willing to put off UF6 production—a former U.S. red line. In spring 2005, Iranian negotiators let it be known that if a 64-centrifuge pilot cascade was accepted, they would be willing to put off industrial-scale enrichment for ten years.[27] In spring 2006, Iran still might have accepted freezing the program at 164 centrifuges, but for a period less than ten years. If Iran assembles 3,000 functioning centrifuges, that number will be its new benchmark.

ElBaradei has advocated striking a deal with Iran to cap the program before it gets to an industrial scale and Iran has a breakout capability with which it could produce HEU for a nuclear weapon in a matter of weeks or months. IAEA officials expect Iran would not agree to cap the program for more than a few, perhaps five years, and they acknowledge that Iran may well break the deal before then. They argue that such a deal would buy some amount of time, probably at least as much as would be gained through a bombing campaign. During that time, meanwhile, the situation could improve in various ways. Without the nuclear issue with which to drum up popular support, Ahmadinejad's mismanagement of the economy would likely see him gone from power and replaced by leadership that, while not "moderate" and certainly not antinuclear, would be less hostile and uncompromising. If an agreement on the nuclear deal allowed Iran access to Western investment and other technology, enrichment would become less of a political flashpoint. Buying time also allows more time for Iran's youthful demographics to change the political landscape in other ways.

Judging that the preferable "zero option" is likely unachievable, the International Crisis Group in February 2006 proposed a "delayed limited enrichment" plan under which the international community would explicitly accept Iran's right to domestic enrichment, in return for Iran agreeing to delay commencement of the program (perhaps for two to three years), limit its initial size to several hundred centrifuges for three to four years, and accept highly intrusive inspections.[28] In March 2006, Russia reportedly floated a similar proposal, under which Iran would temporarily suspend all uranium enrichment activities, but then be allowed to undertake "limited research activities" to supplement a joint venture to produce enriched uranium on Russian soil, while putting off Iran's own industrial-scale enrichment for seven to nine years, and granting the IAEA intrusive inspections.[29] These proposals found favor in many European circles and the IAEA, as well as among some Iranians. According to one report, Rafsanjani was himself promoting a ten-year suspension of enrichment.[30] Washington absolutely would not accept any uranium enrichment in Iran, however, and the EU-3 agreed.

If a deal that allows Iran to keep the enrichment activity it now has were to be struck, it is better to focus on the operating tempo than on the number of centrifuges. The number of centrifuges installed at Natanz matters far less than what Iran can learn by running the centrifuges continuously with UF6, because once the knowledge is acquired it can be applied to any number of centrifuge cascades. One compromise that the P5+1 may wish to consider is keeping enrichment at the Natanz enrichment pilot plant intermittent. Stopping the cascades from enriching uranium continuously would keep Iran from passing this crucial step in the learning curve. Freezing the centrifuge- and component-production capacity should also be part of any deal.

TIGHT INSPECTIONS

More important than the level at which the program is frozen is the level of confidence that Iran is not enriching uranium in unreported facilities. No matter how intrusive the IAEA inspections are and how many inspectors are assigned to the task, they could not guarantee that a country the size of Iran was not operating secret cascades using UF6 produced secretly or diverted from IAEA monitoring.[31] Given the necessary access and inspection rights, going beyond the Additional Protocol, however, and with sound baseline knowledge, IAEA inspectors believe that they could, with a reasonable level of confidence, impede Iran's ability to cheat.

To have any confidence that it can detect and monitor changes in Iran's nuclear program, the inspectors must have confirmed knowledge of Iran's program as it exists today and how it reached that point. They need to know how Iran's program got started and how much material and technology was obtained through the A.Q. Khan network and other foreign procurement activity and how much has been produced domestically. The IAEA needs complete answers to its outstanding questions about the 1985–2003 period of documented safeguards violations and the additional questions that have arisen since, including questions about military involvement and weapons connections. IAEA inspectors believe it is possible to reach an understanding with Iran on the baseline measurements they need, even though by now Iran has had plenty of time to conceal and destroy all incriminating evidence.

In an April 27, 2006, letter to ElBaradei, Iran said it was prepared to resolve the remaining questions, provided that the issue remained with the IAEA and not with the UN Security Council. The letter was a negotiating ploy by Iran, but also an important acknowledgment that they had the answers. Iran does not want to give the answers away without something in return, and to be held to account for further admissions of safeguards failings and previous misrepresentations. Before it is ready to admit to the skeletons in its closet, Iran would want some kind of grandfathering waiver. From Tehran's point of view, this means the IAEA closing the Iran nuclear file and treating Iran on par with other countries the IAEA inspects in accordance with standard safeguards agreements. A lack of confidence that Iran's program is for peaceful purposes makes it very difficult for the United States and its allies to allow the IAEA to close its file on Iran any time soon. It will be possible, however, when the IAEA is able to conclude that Iran's declarations are correct and complete and that there is no undeclared nuclear material or activity.

Former IAEA Safeguards Department head Pierre Goldschmidt advocates strengthening the IAEA verification and investigation authority and rights in a legally binding and well-defined way, until the Agency can make this conclusion. This can be done impartially, by Security Council adoption of a binding resolution applicable to any state found to be in noncompliance with its safeguards obligations.[32] ElBaradei has called for transparency measures that "extend beyond the formal requirements of the Safeguards Agreement and Additional Protocol and include access to individuals, documentation related to procurement, dual use equipment, certain military owned workshops and research and development locations."[33] The IAEA Board of Governors in September 2005 urged Iran to implement the transparency measures requested by ElBaradei. Such requests by the IAEA Board have no legal force, however, unless backed by a Security Council resolution.

The transatlantic allies have not sought a Security Council resolution along the lines Goldschmidt recommends, out of concern that doing so could dilute attention from the main emphasis on calling for Iran to suspend enrichment and because adopting generic resolutions would turn the Council into a legislative body and set embarrassing precedents. They also may believe that focusing on inspections would signal a willingness to accept some level of enrichment activity. Regardless of whether or not a deal is struck that accepts some level of enrichment activity, a tighter inspection regime is necessary to keep tabs on Iran's program and restrict its ability to conduct clandestine operations. It is highly unlikely that Iran would provide the requisite inspector access, regardless of what the Security Council mandates, other than as part of a deal. Resolutions requiring Iran to grant access are useful if the purpose is to undercut Iran's legal position, but for the inspectors' purposes, it is more important to have the actual access. The IAEA cannot do much with legal access rights if it does not have Iranian cooperation on the ground. If Iran is going to try to replicate clandestine cascades, it is better to have as many inspectors having access to as many places as possible, to try to detect and impede the effort.

DANGERS OF A DEAL

Striking a deal with Iran that accepts some level of domestic enrichment activity has its own costs and dangers. From a legal and political standpoint, it would confer legitimacy on a program the Security Council officially delegitimized as recently as July 2006. Backing down from the Security Council mandate for full suspension would likely encourage further defiant behavior by Ahmadinejad. A deal would not "give" Iran enrichment, because whether or not the United States and its allies strike a deal, Iran will continue its enrichment program. However, a deal would confer a right to enrichment that once granted, is not reversible. Security Council pressure on Iran would come to a halt and financial institutions would resume loans, insurance, and investment activity with Iran. Resuming this pressure if Iran broke the deal would be neither quick nor certain. Even though Iran repeatedly broke the October 2003 suspension deal with the EU-3, it took two and a half years and a total abrogation of the agreement on Iran's part, before the IAEA Board belatedly agreed to report Iran's safeguards noncompliance to the Security Council. Legitimizing the program also would obviate the Western allies' ability to block Iran's foreign procurement effort. A tight, international export control system is the best tool for impeding progress in Iran's enrichment program. If the enrichment program is legitimized, controls would inevitably weaken, and Iran would be able to hide all purchases behind the mask of the acknowledged program.

From a technical standpoint, an ongoing authorized enrichment facility would mask signals from a clandestine program, which Western policymakers have to assume Iran would try to pursue. The risk of even a small acknowledged enrichment program is not so much that Iran would put it to weapons use (although it would allow Iran to build up a store of low-enriched uranium that, in a breakout scenario, would reduce four-fold the time needed for enriching the uranium to weapons grade). Rather, the risk is that once Iran masters the technology of running a cascade, it can replicate the capability at clandestine facilities unreported to the IAEA. Environmental sampling is the IAEA's best tool for detecting clandestine enrichment activity, but it is an imperfect method in the best of circumstances, useful only if inspectors have access to suspect sites. Wide-area environmental sampling and other advanced monitoring techniques are being developed, but their utility in detecting the presence of undeclared enrichment activity will be severely hampered if Iran is allowed to enrich uranium legitimately.

A legitimized enrichment program would also make it impossible for inspectors to prove that any evidence they found of centrifuge component production was for clandestine purposes and not part of the replacement cycle for the acknowledged program. On the other hand, Iran may already be operating centrifuges in clandestine facilities. Suspending its aboveground operations at Natanz would not necessarily have any effect on such a clandestine operation, other than to make it somewhat less difficult for IAEA inspectors to detect the hidden facility, assuming they had the necessary access rights (which, as noted, they now lack).

Finally, there is the risk that legitimizing the existing program would not buy the Western allies any time at all. If Iran cannot do much more for the time being anyway, because of technical problems encountered in the enrichment process and/or because of resource constraints in their ability to manufacture more components and install more centrifuges, then freezing the program at its current level would be a dubious diplomatic achievement. Granting the Iranians the right to continue working on a small cascade is all they need right now to perfect the process. A natural progression of this "what you see is what you get" scenario is easy to imagine: once the Iranians are able to surmount the technical problems with a legitimized small-scale program, they would break the deal, first in small ways and by exploiting loopholes, and gradually by moving on to larger-scale production. Inspector access would again be restricted if the Security Council took any enforcement action. Unfortunately, Iran's recent history provides no basis for believing that it would abide by a deal unless it reached a strategic decision to stop.

On the other hand, if the "what you see is what you get" scenario unfolded and Iran did not have a hidden program and therefore a deal bought no time, at least the United States and its partners would not have gone to war again over another misjudgment.

NOTES

1. Shahram Chubin, *Iran's Nuclear Ambitions* (Washington DC: Carnegie Endowment for International Peace, 2006), p. 13

2. Seymour Hersh, "The Next Act: Is a Damaged Administration Less Likely to Attack Iran, or More?" *The New Yorker*, November 27, 2006. See http://www.newyorker.com/archive/2006/11/27/061127fa_fact

3. Mark Fitzpatrick, "Assessing Iran's Nuclear Programme," *Survival* 48(3) (Autumn 2006), 5–26.

4. Hassan Rohani, "Beyond the Challenges Facing Iran and the IAEA Concerning the Nuclear Dossier," *Rahbord*, September 30, 2005, 7–38 (in Persian). Translated by FBIS in 2006 (FBIS-IAP20060113336001) and available at www.armscontrolwonk.com/file_download/30.

5. IAEA, "Implementation of the NPT Safeguards Agreement in the Islamic Republic of Iran," GOV/2006/53, para 13, August 31, 2006.

6. IAEA, "Implementation of the NPT Safeguards Agreement in the Islamic Republic of Iran," GOV/2006/64, para 2, November 14, 2006.

7. Ibid.

8. David Albright and Jacqueline Shire, "Latest IAEA Report on Iran: Continued Progress on Cascade Operations, No New Cooperation with the IAEA," Institute for Science and International Security (ISIS), November 14, 2006, http://www.isis-online.org/publications/iran/continuedprogress.pdf

9. Gareth Smyth, "Iran Says It Will Be 'Fully Nuclear' Soon," *Financial Times*, November 15, 2006.

10. David Ignatius, "Iran's Uranium Glitch; Technical Troubles Offer Time for Diplomacy," *Washington Post*, September 29, 2006, A21.

11. Council on Foreign Relations, "Albright: 'Room for Optimism' in Confrontation with Iran," interview with David Albright, September 12, 2006, http://www.cfr.org/publication/11435/albright.html.

12. Interviews with IAEA officials, October 2006.

13. International Institute for Strategic Studies, *Iran's Strategic Weapons Programs: A Net Assessment* (Abingdon: Routledge for the IISS, 2005), p. 54. Other reputable analysts estimate a 3,000-centrifuge facility could produce a bomb's worth of HEU in 4–6 months. See David Albright and Corey Hinderstein, "The Clock Is Ticking But How Fast?" Institute for Science and International Security, March 27, 2006, http://www.isis-online.org/publications/iran/clockticking.pdf.

14. Talks between Khalilzad's successor, Ambassador Ryan Crocker, and Iran's ambassador to Baghdad, Hassan Kazemi Qomi, were finally held in late May 2007.

15. Flynt Everett, among others, argues that engagement with Iran will not work unless the major issues of concern to each side are included. See Flynt Everett, "Dealing with Tehran: Assessing U.S. Diplomatic Options Toward Iran," New York and Washington, D.C. The Century Foundation, December 4, 2006, http://www.tcf.org/publications/internationalaffairs/leverett_diplomatic.pdf.

16. Patrick Clawson and Michael Eisenstadt, "Forcing Hard Choices on Tehran; Raising the Costs of Iran's Nuclear Program," The Washington Institute for Near East Policy, Policy Focus no. 62, November 2006, http://www.washingtoninstitute.org/pubPDFs/PolicyFocus62.pdf.

17. Ibid., p 16.

18. Richard K. Betts, "The Osirak Fallacy," *The National Interest* (Spring 2006), 2225. As Betts explains, Iraq did not have a reprocessing facility to separate out the plutonium that would have been produced once the Osirak reactor went on line. When it was destroyed, Iraq embarked on a fast-paced effort to produce weapons through the alternate route of enriching uranium.

19. Dan Reiter, "Preventive Attacks against Nuclear Programs and the 'Success' at Osiraq," *Nonproliferation Review* 2(2) (Summer 2005), 263. Before the bombing, Iraq had committed 400 scientists and $400 million to the program; afterwards the numbers grew to 7,000 personnel and a budget of $10 billion.

20. Tovah Lazaroff, "US official: Israel won't bomb Iran," *The Jerusalem Post*, December 8, 2006, http://www.jpost.com/servlet/Satellite?cid=1162378347825&pagename=JPost%2FJPArticle%2FShowFull.

21. Interview, October 2006.

22. Ibid.

23. Closing the Straits would also stop Iran's oil exports and, more importantly, its import of 40 percent of its consumption of gasoline (refined petroleum), the consumer price of which is heavily state-subsidized. Iran would therefore not want to close the straits entirely or for long.

24. Among the many published analyses of the likely consequences of air strikes, one of the best is in Anthony H. Cordesman and Khalid R. Al-Rodha, "Iranian Nuclear Weapons? Options for Sanctions and Military Strikes," Center for Strategic and International Studies, August 30, 2006.

25. Steven Miller, Director of the International Security Program at the Harvard Kennedy School of Government's Belfer Center for Science and International Affairs, coined this phrase at a June 23, 2006, workshop on Iran hosted by the International Institute for Strategic Studies in London.

26. Gareth Smyth, "Iran 'ready to limit nuclear program,' " *Financial Times*, June 18, 2006.

27. Interviews with IAEA officials, October and December 2006.

28. International Crisis Group, "Iran: Is There a Way out of the Nuclear Impasse?" Middle East Report no. 51, February 23, 2006, http://www.crisisgroup.org/home/index.cfm?id=3976&CFID=14546738&CFTOKEN=26322303.

29. Elaine Sciolino, "Russia Plan for Iran Upsets U.S. and Europe," *New York Times*, March 7, 2006.

30. Volker Perthes and Eva Wegner, "Enriching the Options: Europe, the United States, and Iran," discussion paper for the 4th Annual GMF Think Tank Symposium in Vienna, May 2006, p. 9, http://www.swp-berlin.org/en/common/get_document.php?id=1688. The authors source this report to personal communications with an Iranian journalist. Another European source with close dealings with Iranian officials discounts the Rafsanjani story but says an Iranian negotiator claimed Khamenei himself agreed to a ten-year moratorium (interview, December 2006).

31. In April 2006, the IAEA lost continuity of knowledge over one cylinder of UF_6 at Esfahan when Iran moved it in the absence of inspectors. The amount involved was not enough for a weapon but it would be enough for a clandestine research program if, in fact, the UF_6 was diverted. Loss of continuity of knowledge is not proof of diversion.

32. Pierre Goldschmidt, "The Urgent Need to Strengthen the Nuclear Non-Proliferation Regime," January 2006, http://www.carnegieendowment.org/files/PO25.Goldschmidt.FINAL2.pdf. Goldschmidt expanded on this suggestion at a presentation at Wilton Park on December 19, 2006.

33. IAEA, "Implementation of the NPT Safeguards Agreement in the Islamic Republic of Iran," GOV/2005/67, para 50, September 2, 2005.

3

Understanding Iran's Nuclear Ambitions

Shahram Chubin

Iran has had no pressing security rationale for nuclear weapons and its rationale for a nuclear program has varied over time. The program itself has not been characterized by urgency, but by persistence. Iran's motivations are vague and fluctuate, with no indication that a definitive decision has been made to continue irrespective of cost. The nuclear program is a popular national cause, as it relates to access to advanced technology and scientific potential. Most Iranians want the country to play a more important role internationally. This does not necessarily translate into support for a nuclear weapons program. The economy (employment, wages, inflation) is the priority of most Iranians. The primary characteristic of Iranian politics is its intense struggle for power over control of resources and patronage and only secondarily issues of ideology or principle.

While united on the need for regime survival, elites have very different notions of how, and whether, the country ought to evolve and on its international role and orientation. Despite official insistence on a "consensus," this disagreement is clearly manifest in the nuclear issue, which reflects this sharp rivalry.

There is little political mileage to be made domestically in being soft on the nuclear issue. Yet, while both groups have fanned nationalist fervor on the nuclear issue, they have quite different constituencies on which they depend, and different evaluations of the costs and benefits of pursuing the program.

Public opinion is deceptive on the issue: supportive of Iran's "rights" but not keen to pay economically or politically from any confrontation with the international community. A degree of skepticism is evident among the more educated about the regime's intentions as well. Aware of this, the regime has made no effort to promote debate or discussion on its approach to the nuclear question. Framing the issue as one of "rights," "denial," "double standards," and "dictation," the regime has played on the sense of victimhood and historical grievance among the populace. This, however, can both constrain and make more difficult any compromise, or freeze, that may be necessary.

The nuclear issue could be the defining issue for Iran's future domestic and external evolution. Elite divisions and different conceptions of how Iran sees its future and how it should relate to the world, turn on the resolution of this issue. Any settlement that rewards the hardline, confrontational elements will have serious ramifications in the domestic power struggle and Iran's future course. At the same time, dropping the refrain of "regime change" would certainly make it easier for those opposing current policies to do so without the stigma of being foreign agents.

Let us consider the Iranian discourse with the several illustrative quotations that follow.

> "The motives and goals of Iran's mullah government have been even harder for U.S. intelligence agencies to understand and predict than Saddam Hussein's were."[1]

> "We want to relieve this nation of the burden of hundreds of years of humiliation. This nation is proud and powerful but it has been kept behind."[2]

> " ... [T]he United States policy has consistently pursued a policy of denying Iran the chance to turn into a major power on the one hand and a regional power on the other .... The political backbone of these [European Union-3] demands deals with the fact that in the contemporary Middle Eastern political structure, Iran does not acquiesce to American wishes.... Iranian acquisition of power is related to the natural talent of Iranians in a fundamentally new way, an Islamic way of life and the logic of Iran's geo-politics and geo-economics."[3]

> "In the last 27 years the Islamic Republic of Iran has always been at the centre point of the political, economic and even military confrontations of the West and at present, Islamic Iran enjoys a geopolitical heavyweight (*sic*) in the region .... The current century is going to be the century of the nations overcoming dictatorial and dependent governments, and it will be the era of face to face clash with the global arrogance."[4]

"If today we insist on having (the) fuel cycle, (it) is because we want to generate scientific creativity and innovation inside the country .... Big powers want to prevent the developing countries from gaining these abilities. Having a nuclear fuel cycle significantly helps a country to reach stable development."[5]

"Today atomic energy is a *religious obligation* because our oil resources will be depleted. We will have to import oil from foreign countries and this will make us economically dependent and consequently politically and culturally dependent on foreign powers."[6]

"Your incentives are definitely not more valuable than nuclear technology .... How dare you tell our people to give up its gold in return for chocolate?"[7]

"They must change their tone of voice. They must change their lexicon. They must speak to nations like equals."[8]

"Could it be that extremists all around see their interests—however transient, domestic or shortsighted—in heightened tensions and crisis? .... we must dare to leave the emotions aside and avoid polluting the atmosphere with the baggage of immediate and long-past history of Iran-U.S. relations."[9]

"The more Ahmadinejad confronts the international community, the more power he may show to his public in the short term but deny Iran a good life among world nations in the long run."[10]

"What good (will) 3,000 centrifuges do when the country is under sanctions?"[11]

"All our income is going to Palestine and Hezbollah."[12]

NUCLEAR AMBITIONS: IRAN'S MOTIVATIONS

It takes determination, commitment, and resources to seek a nuclear capability, something not lightly or absentmindedly undertaken. Because states usually seek such a capability for a number of reasons, disentangling and prioritizing motivation can be deceptive. In the case of Iran, empathetic observers have sought explanations ranging from the country's humiliating experience of imperialism, to past American interventions, to the solitary experience of confronting an Iraq armed with weapons of mass destruction through to the "tough nuclear neighborhood," defined as Russia, Israel, Pakistan, India, and China.[13] The inequality of the Nuclear Non-Proliferation Treaty (NPT) is another supposed reason for this ambition, although the treaty was always clearly discriminatory (however, this may grate against postmodern sensibilities).

Putting aside the official energy explanation and beyond the plausible attribution of psychological and security motives, it is difficult to discern the "real" motivations. This is due to the changing context of such ambitions, the multiple and changing motivations, and the changing cast of characters associated with the project over two decades.

Motivations can be broken down into three overlapping categories:

1) Security
2) Status and influence
3) Domestic legitimacy

Iran had reasons to seek a hedge against Saddam Hussein during the Iran–Iraq war, when Tehran revived its program, and later the U.S. presence in the region gave Tehran cause for seeking some sort of deterrent, especially after "regime change" came into the lexicon of international security in 2002. Presumably it was thought that deterrence could be achieved through the manipulation of uncertainty. Additionally, access to conventional arms was limited (and expensive), so focus on missiles and weapons of mass destruction appeared attractive. An equalizer, if that's what it is, might be seen as a necessary insurance policy. Frustrated nationalism and aspirations for regional influence (or hegemony) were additional reasons for Iranians to seek such capabilities. A nuclear capable state could expect to be listened to more attentively and consulted regularly. Domestically, the regime had run out of steam by the mid-1990s, losing support for its revolutionary model and values. Having failed to deliver the goods economically, where per capita incomes had declined over the past decades, the regime clearly had no "performance legitimacy" on which to fall back. The nuclear program was clearly intended to serve this purpose, to give the regime's supporters the shot in the arm and the regime the faux legitimacy, it now so desperately needed.[14]

Iran's revived program tells it own story. Iran embarked on first re-building the Bushehr plant (a "sunk cost"). Its approach was unhurried, seeking to put a foot in the door of the technology. The program has since been characterized by persistence and incrementalism, the opposite of a crash program driven by a sense of strategic necessity or urgency. Attention was first given to the fuel cycle in 1988 and 1989; the next eight years of Hashemi Rafsanjani's presidency, the era of reconstruction, was one of focus on importing equipment; and following eight years of Mohammad Khatami's era (1997–2005) was a period when the technology was "indigenized." Significantly the program accelerated in 1999[15] when Iran's relations with the United States were less strained and when Saddam Hussein was "in his box" and under inspections. The rhythm of the program corresponds with Iran's opportunities internationally—with assistance from China and later Pakistani scientist A.Q. Khan and his nuclear black market program—and its own progress in mastering the technology. The program reflects no clear or consistent rationale other than a determination to achieve a capability. The program is itself the rationale.

What of the officially stated energy rationale as motivation? It is true that nuclear energy is making a comeback as a clean source of energy with fewer adverse effects on climate change. Diversification of energy sources is also a prudent response for a country with a growing population and domestic consumption that cannot rely on indigenous resources forever. Iran's explanation for the quest for the full fuel cycle, that it would make it self-sufficient for energy and put it in a position to compete economically in supplying enriched fuel for global demand, is much weaker. Iran does not have indigenous uranium and will still be dependent on imports. Enrichment facilities make no sense for Iran at this stage and will not do so until it has a dozen or so reactors. Tehran's sense of urgency and insistence on this *as soon as possible* makes no economic sense and raises the question whether there is another more sinister motive. (Similarly the refusal to consider suspension seriously also raises concern.) There is further the issue of Iran's secrecy and cat-and-mouse games with the International Atomic Energy Agency (IAEA) and its deliberate cultivation of ambiguity regarding "joining the nuclear club."[16] None of this would be necessary if the program were indeed motivated by an above-the-board energy rationale. It is clear that by its insistence on its "rights" (i.e., its right to peaceful uses of nuclear energy as a signatory under the NPT) and its definition of these rights to include enrichment as well, Iran seeks to use the gap in the treaty to go as far as possible *within the treaty* to achieve a capability to produce fissile material, which could have weapons use. It seeks a weapons option, a virtual capability, for the moment.[17]

Since the program is supposed to be about future energy requirements, it is clear that its security rationale has not been discussed. Allusions to the "nuclear club" have become a code for nuclear weapons. But how a nuclear capability would affect Iran's security and what sort of nuclear capability Iran ought to strive for, probably have not been carefully or systematically considered, much less publicly discussed.[18]

Iran's stated aims are, at a stretch, conceivable but barely plausible and certainly not credible in light of other evidence. Iran's desire "to have its cake and eat it too" may or may not be uniquely an Iranian cultural characteristic. (Similarly Iran is not alone in its negotiations in "selling the same carpet twice." Consider the phenomenon in the West regarding music from records to cassettes to CDs and the same with films from video cassettes to DVDs.) But it is worth noting that while the reactor part of the program was public knowledge, the enrichment part was not, until exposed in mid-2002. It is only then that the rationale was expressed.

If Iran's motives for nuclear technology are various and shifting, and the program has been mostly in low gear, how determined is Iran to acquire a nuclear capability? Has a definitive decision been made? Is such a decision reversible, or if not made, sensitive to costs? Would security assurances help?

Iran's program has been undertaken for general reasons, as much motivated by status and influence as by concrete security concerns. The vague assumption seems to have been that getting your hands on such a capability (however defined) would somehow transform your relationships to your advantage. But this clearly is not the case. As I wrote in early 2002, "Nuclear weapons may appear to give a pleasing symmetry to Iran's relations with Israel or the U.S., but the reality would be quite different. Acquiring such weapons would put Iran into a different league of risk and reprisal, and this would not necessarily leave it with enhanced security."[19]

It seems unlikely that a definitive decision has been made. The nature of the program[20] and Iran's diplomacy (since 2003) suggest a decision to push and wait for the reaction, rather than blunder on regardless. A generalized deterrent and the desire to cast a regional shadow, can, in extremis, wait. Of course Iran would have liked to have created a fait accompli that it still periodically claims in various steps of the cycle. Yet absent the overriding security urgency, the decision to go toward a nuclear capability appears flexible in principle and is susceptible to being delayed or even reversed. But for this to happen, the Iranian leadership will have to believe the costs of continuing will outweigh the costs of stopping its program. This, in turn, will depend on the ability of the international community credibly to threaten, and if necessary implement, sanctions that bite. "Unacceptable costs" for the Iranian regime are defined as measures that threaten its control of power, hence measures that generate significant discontent on "the street." This is because public opinion is not as united on this issue as sometimes depicted. And the political dynamics of Iran are not all supportive of current policy.

POLITICAL DYNAMICS

A monolithic, determined Iran with clear goals and a coherent policy presents one kind of a challenge. A country with contending groups with competing ideas of how the country should be organized and what orientation it should have externally, is quite a different matter. I will argue that, while agreeing on their common interest in maintaining the Islamic republic, these groups contend for power and differ on whether Iran should become a normal state or revive its revolutionary élan by a return to the first principles of the revolutionary era. For both, the nuclear program is a source of political legitimacy, but the groups differ on both tactics and strategy, that is, on how Iran should behave and negotiations should be conducted, and on the ultimate aims of the program. If one group sees it as a bargaining card to secure Iran's legitimate interests and enables it to move to normalization in a globalized world, the other sees it as an equalizer, enabling Iran to continue its revolutionary activities in opposition to the West. Very roughly, the two groups correspond to those of the pragmatic conservatives (accommodationists) and the ideological conservatives (confrontationalists). Clearly the reformists and many of the regimes are faltering supporters and critics fall closer to the first than the second group. The nuclear issue is thus a reflection of a much greater schism in the regime, including the more important questions of power and domestic policy. How it is resolved may determine the fortunes of the two groups and the future orientation of Iran.[21]

Political competition has sharpened in the two decades since the time of Ayatollah Khomeini, the supreme clerical guide of the 1979 revolution. As the society has become younger, and revolutionary appeals falter and are less relevant to the daily needs of an expectant population; and as the world has become more connected and less insulated, the standard formulae of more piety, commitment, and state control have lost their appeal. Political accountability and popular sovereignty have replaced the revolutionary discourse of the earlier era. Daily needs, inflation, employment prospects, and the price of food and fuel take precedence in the minds of many Iranians to slogans.

Political reaction to this change in society, which implicitly challenges the system, has been uneven. The reformist era promised much materially but was unable to enact economic reforms, while making some advances in civil liberties and normalization abroad. The conservatives have reversed both advances but are stuck with an economy that still depends on oil. More broadly, the response of the two groups can be defined as the difference between those accepting privatization and globalization and those wanting state control and denouncing globalization as an American plot. The one sees economic engagement internationally as necessary and inevitable as a way of attracting foreign investment and getting Iran's economy moving, and this implies normalization with the international community. The other approach sees international engagement as a sellout of the revolution's principles and the beginning of the end for the regime. It prefers to redouble the nation's commitment to autarchy and state control. These approaches are ideal types but highlight the broad differences among the various factions. The two approaches rely on very different domestic constituencies and envisage and strive for very different conceptions of Iran.

POLITICAL RIVALRY

These differences of approach have existed for some time but have become more pointed since the arrival of President Mahmoud Ahmadinejad, in July 2005. The regime has a way of permitting and exploiting the coexistence of two different conceptions of Iran, at the expense, very often, of policy coherence. For however intense the power rivalry among the elite, the fact that they share a common destiny within the Islamic Republic conditions their behavior (as Khatami showed, ultimately preferring to hang together lest they hang separately).

Iran's leadership and its associated elites have not lost sight of the primary issue affecting their survival—domestic politics. Here expediency is the name of the game: whatever works to continue the regime.

Again and again domestic considerations have driven foreign policy stances, whether in subordinating or promoting revolutionary stances.[22] Political rivalries dominate perceptions and reports of international affairs.[23] It is through this prism of domestic politics and rivalries that the nuclear issue should be viewed.

The nuclear program, especially its secret components, has been the "baby" of a small group of people, among whom Hashemi Rafsanjani is the most prominent. One assumes that the heads of Iran's Atomic Energy Organization and the chief members of the Supreme National Security Council have had knowledge of the program, possibly even being consulted on it. In addition, elements of the Islamic Revolutionary Guard Corps (IRGC or *Pasdaran* in Farsi) have been responsible for the security of installations. Until mid-2002 there was little discussion and no indication of a debate about the program, nuclear weapons or current or future strategy.[24]

To be sure, the regime's leaders, to keep the people mobilized and motivated, played on Iran's sense of grievance and ambition. The combination of a sense of victimhood and frustrated status could keep an otherwise restive populace focused on foreign threats and slights. The regime's leaders found it useful to manipulate the perception of historical injustices, and to maintain the siege mentality that followed from this sense of embattlement.[25] This could divert attention from the regime's manifest shortcomings, while the quest for status internationally might compensate for the legitimacy deficit at home. Meanwhile, the covert program continued with little fanfare or controversy.

All this was changed in mid-2002, when revelations about Iran's undeclared activities put Tehran on the defensive. This had two immediate consequences: the nuclear program became a public and important political issue, not least domestically. Divisions among the elite quickly surfaced. Hassan Ruhani, the long-serving Secretary of the Supreme National Security Council was given overall charge of the dossier (until June 2005). He had a safe pair of hands, was a pragmatist and was well versed in international affairs.

His inclination was to negotiate, to reassure the international community, without giving up Iran's purported "rights" under the NPT. He accepted application of the Additional Protocol and suspension of enrichment for the duration of negotiations. Throughout these negotiations, Ruhani was the target of criticism and complaint from the ideological conservatives led by *Keyhan* newspaper. Ruhani insisted on the need to keep good relations with Europe and stressed the economic costs of pursuing policies detached from the realities of international relations.[26] His critics sought a policy of defiance and confrontation, including if necessary withdrawal from the NPT.

Iranian leaders orchestrated a campaign depicting the nuclear issue as one of rights and denial, and Western objections to enrichment as a means of keeping the country backward. "To justify its position at home, the regime has again played the political trump card of Iranian nationalism and has cast its defiance as principled resistance to a discriminatory effort inspired by the United States to deny advanced technology to Iran."[27]

The fanning of nationalism and the sense of entitlement on the nuclear issue substituted for the debate on nuclear energy and enrichment that never took place. Little space or information was given for such a debate, which was discouraged. Once the issue became a "national" issue (quite apart from a nationalist one) it became difficult to argue for flexibility or compromise. Ruhani himself was on the defensive throughout the period of his negotiations, with his most difficult critics being in Tehran, rather than in Brussels or Paris.[28] Again and again Ruhani supporters were accused of being "defeatists" and practicing "appeasement." In "nationalizing" the issue, not only was the subject made sacrosanct from criticism, being dealt with only in emotive terms, but externally, defiance and confrontation were assured. "Discrimination," "double standard," "nuclear apartheid," and "selective nonproliferation" became the slogans justifying this stance. Some officials went further arguing the issue was not really about nuclear weapons, but about "respect."[29]

Once President Ahmadinejad came into office he made the nuclear issue one of the bases of his appeal to populism, threatening at once the clerics and the vested interests of the establishment, while freezing out the diplomats.[30] Criticism of this approach has been muffled; the pragmatists were not seeing the nuclear program as a winning issue domestically at least as long as the patent failure of Ahmadinejad's confrontational tactics was not palpably clear (and the verdict on that still remains open).

In many ways the most illuminating way to see the nuclear issue is through the lens of domestic politics. The domestic power struggle over resources and power is still the main issue in Iran. The nuclear issue is one—albeit critical—aspect of it. The quest for status and influence, natural enough for a great nation, is also about diverting pressures externally and substituting for a defective and faltering legitimacy by a regime aware of its contradictions. The fanning of nationalism on this issue, and the pandering to the sense of historical victimhood is political opportunism at its most conspicuous. The cynical use of embattlement to stifle discussion and stimulate outrage also pushes abroad responsibility for incompetence or worse. Finally, political competition on how to pursue Iran's nuclear aspirations, through negotiation or confrontation, is also a product of a domestic power struggle where hard-liners seek to depict their foes—the pragmatists—as lacking principles, naïve, and defeatist. For their part, the pragmatists, point to the incompetence and recklessness of the ideologues.

A few examples illustrate this. Factional differences account for the differences on whether Iran should consider suspension of enrichment and how it should address the international community on the subject. Ruhani's suggestion to *Time Magazine* reflects the differences, substantive and attitudinal.[31]

A conservative critique of Ruhani included the following propositions: the enemy was not being trusted; self-criticism was tantamount to criticism of Khomeini; and (referring to the war with Iraq) "we went to war to fulfill our obligations and *results are secondary* (emphasis added)." If Ruhani's advice were followed, the newspaper asked: "would the enemy still fear Iran's power and grandeur today?"[32]

Perpetuating the myth of unity on this issue is the claim (or perhaps accusation) that any difference publicly aired encourages the West "to take advantage of the lack of unity among Iran's leaders."[33]

Yet former President Khatami, reflecting the actual lack of unity, pointedly declined to comment on Ahmadinejad's letter to his U.S. counterpart, noting that he was not informed of the planning of the letter "or the expectations behind the letter," or indeed, "what the system's strategy is on negotiations with America."[34]

In September, former President Rafsanjani released a letter written by senior Revolutionary Guard commander Mohsen Reba, to the political leadership in mid-1988, arguing that Iran could only win the war (with Iraq) if it had more men, funds for arms, and access to new arms including laser and atomic weapons. On receipt of the letter, the pragmatic Khomeini decided to end the war by accepting UN Security Council Resolution 598, which he had formerly spurned. Rafsanjani's release of the letter was much criticized by the hard-liners, who recognized in it the disguised warning that Iran could be heading toward an equivalent disaster with Ahmadinejad's nuclear diplomacy. At the same time it drew attention to Khomeini's pragmatism and to how the nuclear issue has been used by hard-liners to sidetrack their political opponents.[35]

PUBLIC OPINION

If the elite are divided, the public is no less so. It serves the regime to talk about the "consensus" behind the program. It suited the pragmatists, when negotiating, to argue that the nuclear program was a national one, not dependent on personalities or factions or government changes. The famed consensus that is said to characterize policy decisions, however, is somewhat more complicated. On one level it is a form of self-protection for the elite, implying *collective decision making and collective responsibility*. Thus once a decision has been made, the elite are all in it together, with little room for opting out or exploiting mistakes or setbacks. This provides an insurance policy for contentious questions like reversing Khomeini's injunction against ties with Saudi Arabia, or in future, opening relations with the United States or reversing course on the nuclear program.

The concept is nonetheless deceptive, for the default position on national security issues has been hard-line, as was clear in the Khatami period when the President was marginal on security issues. It also begs the question whether the Supreme Guide follows or forms the prevailing consensus. Especially as differences in approach have leaked out, the Guide has been upstaged by a populist president speaking over his head to the mobilized faithful.[36]

Indeed, Ahmadinejad has made the nuclear issue *his* issue, taking the question of "Iran's rights" to Iran's most outlying provinces, fanning it shamelessly and making it a nationalist and populist issue that reduces the regime's margin for maneuver.

On one level there *is* a national consensus on Iran's nuclear program. It is a source of pride and Iranians resist dictation from outside as to what they can and cannot have. There are few, if any, dissenters from the proposition that Iran ought to have access to advanced technology, be treated with respect and equality, and have its interests taken seriously. The nuclear issue has become the equivalent of the oil issue in the 1950s, a question of national rights and independence.[37] At this level it *is* a unifying platform for the regime, which, as noted, fully exploits it.

Beyond this level of generality however, this unity fractures. Next to nationalism, is the demand for economic development. But Iran's nuclear program tangibly threatens Iran's economic development, probably the principal issue for most Iranians.[38] Given the gap between state and society, support for the program would be carefully conditioned too, if the proposition that it might help in the consolidation of the current regime were added to a question in the poll.[39]

Despite the official polls that suggest some 80 percent of the populace is supportive of the program, we are not told the wording of the question eliciting such overwhelming support. What is clear is that there has never been an informed debate about the energy rationale in the context of alternative policies and options. Certainly such a broad debate has not been encouraged, least of all when the program was started. Where support and consensus clearly fades is over the price Iranians are willing to pay for the continuation of the program in terms of sanctions, loss of confidence in investment, capital flight, and estrangement from the international community.[40]

Iranian public opinion was neither a driver nor a constraint on the development of the program until 2002. Since then the nuclear issue has been energetically depicted as a national issue. Public opinion has been invoked as an important consideration by both factions; as a reason for pursuing the program regardless by the hard-liners, and as a factor that must be considered carefully by the pragmatists. The latter see the danger of pursuing a confrontational policy and its associated costs as likely to weaken the regime. In manipulating the issue the regime is now to some extent captive of public opinion. Depending on the inclination, the conservatives, appealing to a largely fundamentalist constituency, see themselves constrained by public opinion from retreat; and the pragmatists (appealing to a more middle-class constituency) see the risks of a high-speed economic collision if the current course is pursued, with consequent damage to the regime.[41]

The nuclear issue has been used as a partisan issue by the supporters of Ahmadinejad, implicitly acknowledged by Ruhani in quotations, such as the one at the beginning of this chapter. The nuclear issue could be a key issue in the struggle for power and the defining issue for contemporary Iran. The differences between the two inclinations discussed go to the heart of Iran's future: how Iran ought to evolve domestically, what kind of relationship it should have with the international community, and what sort of foreign orientation Iran should have. Should Iran settle down as a normal state, or continue its aspirations as an exemplary revolutionary state countering the West and the existing international order? While Iranians support a nuclear program, this does not extend to nuclear weapons. The regime's elite support a nuclear option but with very different aims. The pragmatists seek an option as a bargaining card to have leverage in a grand bargain with the United States, to secure Iran's "legitimate" interests and as a step toward normalization. The hard-liners see a nuclear option as an end in itself, an equalizer that will force the world to acknowledge Iran's power and accept it on its own terms. How the current dispute ends will influence these outcomes in one direction or the other.

The regime is sensitive to power and will make any compromise necessary for survival. So far it has not been convinced that it will have to pay an unacceptable price for its policies. Once convinced, reversal will take place.

Western policy needs to ensure that the hard-liners do not emerge successful from their confrontational tactics and use this to consolidate their power and continue their course. At the same time, talk of regime change should be dropped as well. Cultivating the Iranian public with information and in redefining the prevailing narrative to one that puts the onus on the irresponsibility of an opportunistic regime, rather than the denial of technology to the Iranian nation, should be the consistent message from the international community.

NOTES

1. James Fallows, "Will Iran Be Next?" *The Atlantic Monthly*, December 2004.
2. Ayatollah Ali Khamene'i Islamic Republic of Iran News Network, June 4, 2006, on *BBC Online*, June 5, 2006.

3. Ali Larijani, Speech at Middle East Center, Tehran, October 27, 2005. Reprinted in *Journal of European Society for Iranian Studies*, 2006, 125-131.

4. General Yahya Rahim Safavi, Islamic Revolution Guard Corps commander in chief. Iran Web site, May 9, 2006, p. 1, in *BBC Online*, May 11, 2006.

5. Dr. Hossein Faqihiyan, Director-General of Nuclear Fuel Production Co., and Deputy of the Atomic Energy Organization (AEO). In daily newspaper, *Farhang-e Ashti*, May 4, in *BBC Online*, May 10, 2006.

6. Ayatollah Makarem-Shirazi, text of report in newspaper *Siesta-e Ruz*, May 6, in *BBC Online*, May 10, 2006. (emphasis supplied).

7. Mahmoud Ahmadinejad, quoted by Nazila Fathi, "Iran Snubs Europe's Nuclear Plan," in the *New York Times*, May 18, 2006.

8. Ahmadinejad speech broadcast by Iranian TV June 3, in *BBC Online*, June 4, 2006.

9. Hassan Ruhani, "Iran's Nuclear Program: A Way Out," *Time Magazine*, May 9, 2006. Ruhani has recently made very clear that divisions within the elite on the nuclear issue stem from "divisions and disagreements [that] are far wider and deeper than what the ordinary members of the public can see." They stem from very different priorities: Iran's national interests versus Iran's revolutionary Islamic pretensions, what he calls differences on "certain fundamental issues and premises." This is as clear and authoritative a statement as can be imagined confirming the fact that different approaches to the nuclear issue reflect much broader differences on Iran's evolution and role in the world, noted in the text. Ex-Nuclear Chief criticizes "ideological" impact on foreign policy," *E'temad* Web site, Tehran July 23, 2006, in *BBC Online*, July 25, 2006. (Ruhani repeats that a suspension of enrichment, without renouncing the right to it, in exchange for technology, was a step forward but that "certain circles incited and upset public opinion" by depicting it as a sellout.)

10. Professor Hossein Salimi, quoted by Ali Akbar Dareini, "Not All Iranians Back President's Rhetoric," http://www.managing-the-atom.org/irannews/85/not-all-iranians-back-presidents-rhetoric.

11. Mohsen Aminzadeh, former Deputy Foreign Minister, in *Aftab-e Yazd*, May 6, 2006, quoted in *BBC Online*, May 7, 2006.

12. Quoted in Michael Slackman, "In Iran's Streets, Aid to Hezbollah Stirs Resentment," *The New York Times*, July 23, 2006, http://nytimes.com/2006/07/23/world/middle east/23iran.html?ei=5087%OA&en=4. Accessed on July 24, 2006.

13. A recent example is the House of Commons, Foreign Affairs Committee, and "Foreign Policy Aspects of the War against Terrorism," Fourth Report of Session 2005–2006, July 2, 2006, 116.

14. For a more elaborate discussion see the author's, "Does Iran Want Nuclear Weapons?" *Survival* 37(1) (Spring 1995), 86–104, and "Whither Iran?" Adelphi Paper No. 342, (Oxford: London, IISS, 2002). See also Mohsen Sazegara "The Point of No Return," Policy Focus no. 54 (Washington Institute, April 2006), 7, 10, 29.

15. For this periodization see Hasan Ruhani, interview with *Fars News Agency*, May 12, 2006, in *BBC Online*, May 14, 2006. For more detail and background see this author's *Iran's Nuclear Ambitions* (Washington, DC: Carnegie Endowment, September 2006).

16. See my *Iran's Nuclear Ambitions*. For a succinct and penetrating analysis of Iran's programme see Mark Fitzpatrick, "Assessing Iran's Nuclear Programme," *Survival* 48(3) (Autumn 2006), 5–26.

17. For a similar analysis see "Does Iran Want Nuclear Weapons?" 99 and "Whither Iran," 76–78.

18. Iranian officials in denying weapons intent sometimes point to the regional costs, the difficulty of matching Israel or the United States, and religious impermissibility of using such weapons. Whether these have been taken into account in private discussions is less clear.

19. "Whither Iran," 75. In 1995 I wrote "While an asymmetric strategy or minimal capability may deter the United States from coercive diplomacy, such a small or embryonic capability would not immunize Iran from any punishment or allow it to behave as it pleases with no risk of a response." "Does Iran Want Nuclear Weapons?" 95.

20. See Alexander Montgomery, "Ringing in Proliferation: How to Dismantle an Atomic Bomb Network," *International Security* 30(2) (Fall 2005), 153–187, especially 166–168, 176–178, 185–186.

21. For a similar view see Kenneth Pollack, "Iran: Three Scenarios," *MERIA* 10(5) (June 2006), 73–83.

22. For example the hostage crisis (see Mark Bowden, "Manipulative Mullahs: Playing to the Home Crowd," *International Herald Tribune*, May 6, 2006) and the Salman Rushdie affair. The Ayatollah "drank poison" to end the war with Iraq, because the war was beginning to be unpopular domestically, see Shahram Chubin and Charles Tripp, *Iran and Iraq at War* (London: Tauris, 1988).

23. Mohammed Ayatollahi Tabaar, "The Beloved Great Satan: The Portrayal of the US in the Iranian Media since 9/11," *Journal of European Society for Iranian Studies*, (2006), 63–78.

24. Writing in 1995 I noted that "There is no debate in Iran about "going nuclear" or about the place of nuclear weapons in current or future strategy." Nor was the doctrine discussed. See "Does Iran Want Nuclear Weapons?" 86, 99.

25. For a further discussion see my "Iran's Strategic Predicament," *The Middle East Journal*, 54(1) (Winter 2000), 10–24. I noted the ideology of confrontation and a sense of grievance and victimhood which led to an "unhealthy kind of self-absorption"; the attribution of responsibility for the nation's failings to foreign conspiracies and the brittleness of the regime's legitimacy, which could no longer depend on the "unqualified acceptance of a credulous population, [and] is now subject to 'performance legitimacy.'" This, I argued, would be the precondition for playing a more influential role in world affairs. For embattlement and the diversion from domestic problems see "Whither Iran," 110.

26. For examples and references see *Iran's Nuclear Ambitions*.

27. Shahram Chubin and Robert Litwak, "Debating Iran's Nuclear Aspirations," *The Washington Quarterly* 26(4) (Autumn 2003), 99.

28. Senior Iranian officials connected to the negotiations told me that Ruhani lasted as long as he did "only because he wore a turban." (Geneva, May 2005).

29. Javad Vaeidi, Deputy for International Security in the SNSC defined the dispute as "as much about earning respect for Iran as about developing nuclear power." Quoted by Michael Slackman, "Tehran Rebuffs US on Talks," *International Herald Tribune*, June 2, 2006, 1, 8.

30. For indicative reports see Gareth Smyth, "Iran's Intellectuals Left in Cold by Populist President," *The Financial Times*, June 21, 2006, 7; and Gareth Smyth, "A

year on, Ahmadinenjad still draws the crowds—and irritates the US," *The Financial Times*, June 24/25, 2006, p. 7

31. *Time Magazine*, May 9, 2006. Ruhani suggests a suspension, scope to be defined, without renunciation of the right to enrichment. See also Sadegh Zibakalam, "Don't Think Iranians are United on the Nuclear Issue," *Daily Star* (Beirut), May 8, 2006. http://www.dailystar.com.lb/article.asp?edition_id=10&categ_id=5&article_id=24230

32. Qasem Ravanbaksh, "Don't Make a Mistake, the Enemy Cannot Be Trusted," *Partow-e Sokhan* (Qom) Web site, April 26, 2006, in *BBC Online*, May 10, 2006. It is but a short step from here to Ahmadinejad's apocalyptical thinking: "Why should an Iranian president engage in pragmatic politics when his assumption is that, in three or four years, the savior will reappear? If the messiah is coming, why compromise?" Mattias Kuntzel, "Ahmadinejad's Demons," *The New Republic*, April 24, 2006, p. 23.

33. Hoseyn Shariatmadari, a notable hard-line journalist enjoying close relations with the Supreme Guide, in *Keyhan BBC Online*, May 15, 2006.

34. Sayyed Mohammad Khatami, *Aftab-e Yazd* Web site, May 11, 2006 in *BBC Online*, May 13, 2006.

35. For a useful and accessible summary of this episode see Najmeh Bozorghmehr, "Nuclear Row Sparks Echoes of Iran's Brutal War with Iraq," *The Financial Times*, October 26, 2006, p. 5. See also Rasool Nafisi "The Khomeini Letter: Is Rafsanjani Warning the Hardliners?" The author notes that the incident "reveals the diversity of views on the nuclear issue." http:www.iranian.com/RasoolNafisi/2006/October/Nuclear /index.html.

36. See "Whither Iran?" and Bernard Hourcade, "Iran's Internal Security Challenges," in W. Posch (ed.), *Iranian Challenges Chaillot Paper 89* (Paris: Institute for Security Studies, 2006), p. 57.

37. A comparison suggested by Frederic Tellier, "The Iranian Moment," Policy Focus no. 52 (The Washington Institute: February 2006), p. 30. And Ahmadinejad wants to be the new Mossadeq.

38. See "The Iranian Moment," pp. 15, 23; Naghmeh Sohrabi, "Conservatives, Neoconservatives and Reformists: Iran after the Election of Mahmud Ahmadinejad," Middle East Brief no. 4 (Crown Center, Brandeis University, April 2006).

39. As Ray Takeyh suggests in "Iran's Populace Largely Opposes Nuclear Program." Interview by Bernard Gwertzman, March 2, 2005, CFR online March 7, 2005. See also Michael Herzog, "Iranian Public Opinion on the Nuclear Program," Policy Focus no. 56 (Washington Institute, June 2006), 4–5.

40. See especially "Debating Iran's Nuclear Aspirations," pp. 104–107; "Iranian Public Opinion on the Nuclear Program"; see also Mahan Abdin, "Public Opinion and the Nuclear Standoff," *Mideast Mirror* 1(2) (April/ May 2006).Full article available at http://www.mideastmonitor.org/issues/0604/0604_3.htm. A recent Zogby/Readers Digest poll reports that 41 percent of Iranians put reforming the economy before having a nuclear capability (27%). It also reveals a country divided on many issues, July 13, 2006. http://www.zogby.com/news/ReadNews.dbm?ID=1147. See also Mehdi Khalaj, "Ahmadinejad's Popularity One Year on," Policy Watch no. 1125 (Washington Institute, July 20, 2006)

41. Chen Kane, "Nuclear Decision Making in Iran: A Rare Glimpse," Middle East Brief no. 5. This is a stand-alone eight-page paper available at http:// www.brandeis.edu/centers/crown/publications/Mid%20East%20Brief/Brief%205% 20May%202006.pdf. (Crown Center, Brandeis University, May 2006). The author notes how the negotiators under Ruhani, and by extension the leadership, were sensitive to public opinion on the nuclear issue: while supportive of Iran's "rights," they were very sensitive to the issue of the economic "costs."

4

The Inexorable Momentum of Escalation

Alexei G. Arbatov

The international crisis unraveling around Iran's nuclear program invokes a scary historical analogy of the uncontrolled chain of events which culminated in the First World War. Today, as nearly a hundred years ago, nobody wants a war and everyone recognizes that it would precipitate horrible consequences. Like then, multiple actions of governments and domestic political groups, each having reasons and arguments to claim a just cause, result in an irresistible slide down to war. There are numerous attempts to resolve a conflict through diplomacy, but the search for a compromise is again and again overtaken by technology and actions by various unsatisfied players. It is still to be seen who would perform the role played by Gavrilo Princip, who assassinated Archduke Franz Ferdinand of Austria in 1914, and whether this person will initiate a fatal triggering move in Tehran, Washington, Tel-Aviv, or somewhere else. But in the emerging political environment there appears to be no shortage of contemporary surrogate candidates.

It is true, in contrast to 1914, that a war over Iran would be unlikely to escalate into a truly global conflagration; the military, political, social, and economic inhibitions are today infinitely stronger than they were a century earlier. However, the international implications of such a war would still be dramatic and long-lasting, possibly affecting world security more than any conflict since 1945. Among those consequences would be the emergence of a "black hole" of violence and chaos across a huge space from Palestine to the Hindu Kush, with a high probability of destabilization in the adjacent regions of Transcaucasia, the Arabian Peninsula, Central Asia, and South Asia. The major source and route of the world's oil supply would be badly hindered. The explosion of international terrorism and the further proliferation of weapons of mass destruction would probably make the events of the late 1990s and early 2000s pale in comparison. The final collapse of nonproliferation regimes and a deep and long-term fracturing of major power relations would undermine their cooperation on energy security and other aspects of world order. Except for the two world wars, the international community has not encountered a conflict on such a scale in modern history.

The three largest actors shaping the current drift to war are: (1) the technological evolution and conceivable intentions of Iran; (2) the state of the nonproliferation regime and the interactions of key nations; and (3) the differing views and priorities amongst the states and institutions involved in the Iranian crisis.

IRANIAN CAPABILITIES AND INTENTIONS

There exists a vast pool of data on the Iranian nuclear program and detailed accounts of the sequence of events leading to the present crisis. The crisis commenced in June 2003, when the International Atomic Energy Agency (IAEA) reported on Iran's failure to comply with nuclear safeguards under the Nuclear Non-Proliferation Treaty (NPT) and called on Tehran to "freeze" its uranium enrichment project near the city of Natanz. For the purposes of this chapter it will suffice to mention two important points about the extent of Iran's program and the nonproliferation mechanisms of the IAEA.

Firstly, the Iranian nuclear energy program still falls short of the one planned and started under the Shah with full U.S. approval and Western technological assistance, including a full nuclear fuel cycle consisting of uranium conversion and enrichment, used nuclear fuel reprocessing and plutonium separation, and light-water and heavy-water reactors. Iran is fully entitled to a full nuclear fuel cycle under the NPT, if need be with foreign assistance, provided that all materials and facilities are under IAEA safeguards (Articles III and IV). A number of nonnuclear NPT signatories have full or partial fuel cycles, including Japan, Germany, the Netherlands, Brazil, Argentina, and South Africa.

Secondly, there are formal claims by the IAEA of Iranian noncompliance with the safeguards agreement (foremost, secret construction of an enrichment complex at Natanz and the purchase of centrifuges from Pakistan) and some suspicions of prohibited military activities. But no hard facts on violations of the NPT per se have been discovered, despite unprecedented IAEA inspection operations during 2003–2005. In this sense, the South Korean government's confession of having produced some quantities of weapons-grade uranium and plutonium in 1982 and 2000, was a bigger and more direct NPT violation than the charges against Iran.

Of course, with Iran there is also indirect evidence of a military nuclear program. For instance, there is Iran's development of long-range ballistic missiles (the It-3ER with a 2,000-kilometer range and the Iranian variant of the BM-25 missile with a range up to 3,000 kilometers), which because of their poor accuracy would be senseless without nuclear warheads. Other suspicious activities include, but are not limited to, the construction of a heavy-water production facility and heavy-water research reactor at Arak and the acquisition of nuclear warhead manufacturing blueprints.

However, all this is not enough to accuse Iran of a formal breach of the letter of the NPT; after all, these activities may be dismissed as purely scientific endeavors or theoretical projects to hedge for possible future security threats: the ability to "break out" is not the same as possessing a particular capability. Many nonnuclear states develop ballistic missiles for various purposes and conduct all kinds of research in nuclear technologies. Tehran persists in assuring the world of the exclusively peaceful nature of its nuclear programs and its willingness to abide by the terms of NPT and cooperate with the IAEA once accusations against it are revoked.

As for Iranian material capabilities to produce weapons-grade nuclear uranium, opinions vary widely. Provided that there is no covert military nuclear program, according to an official U.S. assessment, the present operational facility and limited number of P-1 centrifuges in Natanz would be able to provide a sufficient amount of weapons-grade uranium for several explosive devices only after several or more years following any decision to switch to production of highly enriched uranium. If Iran deploys 3,000 more powerful P-2 centrifuges (which may now even be in production) this lead time will shrink dramatically to less than a year. In the event that Iran deploys a full industrial-scale setup of 54,000 P-2 centrifuges, for which the Natanz facility was built, the time would shorten to a matter of weeks.

Unofficial assessments by Russian experts suggest that the amount of time Iran would take to produce weapons-grade material would be roughly 30 percent longer than U.S. estimates in all three of the aforementioned cases. In addition, it is important to remember that whereas producing, deploying, and putting in operation 3,000 P-2 centrifuges would require two to three years, deploying 54,000 centrifuges might take ten to fifteen years.

Along the parallel track of plutonium reprocessing, the time estimates are less definite. Completing construction of a heavy-water production facility and heavy-water 40-megawatt reactor in Arak, commissioning a spent fuel reprocessing plant, and accumulating sufficient quantity of weapons-grade plutonium would probably require ten to twelve years. Manufacturing a plutonium-based, implosive-type deliverable nuclear warhead would present yet another difficult problem, which the Democratic People's Republic of Korea (the DPRK or North Korea) seemingly has not yet resolved after many years of technical efforts. However, having much larger economic and intellectual resources and relying on possible outside assistance (e.g., from Pakistani scientists) Iran may master this technology with greater success.

Tehran's intentions are even more difficult to assess than its technical programs. A complicating factor is that there are various groups and views in Iranian clerical, state civilian, political, military, and industrial elites. Their interaction is producing the resulting policy, which fluctuates within a changing domestic and external environment. There is no doubt that the Iranian nuclear program goes far beyond what would be a cost-effective energy project (especially in view of Iran's limited deposits of natural uranium). In addition, its missile program and other discovered and suspected endeavors, cast serious doubt on Tehran's official claims of purely peaceful intentions. Paired to its inflammatory declarations addressed to Israel and the United States and open support for some organizations using terrorism (foremost Hezbollah), the final goals of its nuclear program may be extrapolated to quite frightening dimensions.

However, giving Iran the benefit of the doubt, there is no hard evidence of its full-steam development of a military nuclear program. Most Iranian projects may be explained by peaceful plans. Some nonnuclear NPT member states have uranium enrichment and plutonium separation facilities while having little or no natural uranium deposits on their territory. Some have heavy-water plutonium-producing reactors or even breeder reactors, and others are developing long-range or space-based missile systems.

Hence, on the basis of available information about Iranian technological developments, it is impossible to demonstrate with a high degree of certainty that Tehran has taken a final decision "to go nuclear." Nonetheless, it is quite plausible that Iran is determined to keep such an option open by developing its nuclear energy projects, foremost the full nuclear fuel cycle. The determination to develop a full nuclear fuel cycle, with a matching number of light-water and heavy-water reactors, is a common denominator in the arguments of all influential clerical, political, military, and industrial groups in Iran. Some of those may wish to go further than that, and manufacture nuclear weapons; others may intend to stop short of that goal and simply retain such a capability as a powerful lever in its foreign policy, without incurring all the consequences of actually crossing the nuclear threshold. Whatever the secret "grand design" and whenever it is adopted, it may well be opposed by dissenting groups and might well be revised in future for better or for worse, under the influence of shifting circumstances.

A final decision by Iran to cross the Rubicon and become a nuclear weapon state may take place in the coming decade, between 2010 and 2020. This decision will be affected by various domestic and external events. This conclusion leaves a possibility of preventing Iran from eventually acquiring nuclear weapons or even achieving a robust material capability to pursue this option with a short lead time.

AMERICAN POLICY ON IRAN

The adamant U.S. position regarding the unacceptability of Iran's acquisition of nuclear weapons is hard to disagree with, taking into account the nature of the regime, the likely regional consequences, and the implications for global proliferation.

It would also be wrong to argue that the United States has drawn no lessons from its recent experience in nonproliferation politics. After the debacle in Iraq, Washington has been more cautious in dealing with Iran. Whereas the decision to intervene in Iraq had been taken by the Republican administration well in advance (apparently the summer of 2002) of the actual military attack in 2003, few in Washington appear keen on the prospect of military action against Iran. It looks like the United States really hopes to find a peaceful solution. Moreover, American policy is moving away from the unilateralism that characterized its policy during 2002–2003. In recent years, it has been encouraging Europe and Russia to pursue their policies of bargaining with Iran; in June 2006, the United States joined Russia, China, Britain, France, and Germany with a multilateral package proposal. Besides, the United States is emphasizing actions through legitimate international institutions and within the framework of international law (namely, the IAEA and the United Nations Security Council).

Despite these positive developments, American policy on the issue of Iran's nuclear program is still handicapped by double standards, insufficient recognition of its past mistakes, and the absence of clear priorities in its overall foreign policy.

First of all, it was the United States that made Iran the regional power it is now. In parallel with the fast growth of Iran's energy exports, economy, population, and military power, the U.S.-led military action in the region has shifted the regional balance of power by removing Iran's two closest enemies: Taliban rule in Afghanistan and Saddam Hussein's regime in Iraq. Moreover, another Iranian rival, Saudi Arabia, has lost much U.S. support because of its connections with Al-Qaeda, while President Pervez Musharraf's regime in Pakistan has been seriously weakened by both military operations in Afghanistan and Iraq. Whether American actions were justified on the basis of fighting a greater "evil," the United States has to digest the fact that its actions have brought about realpolitik consequences, foremost among them the unprecedented rise of prestige, relative power, influence, and ambitions of Tehran. Washington officials made a major strategic miscalculation by treating Iran in the same category as North Korea, whether as a "rogue state" or as a member of an "axis of evil."

Secondly, U.S. allegations of an Iranian military nuclear program are largely compromised by military operations in Iraq, which had been justified by similar suspicions about the nuclear program of Saddam Hussein. The failure to discover should be taken as seriously when it makes similar allegations about Iran. At the same time, with the United States bogged down in its occupation in Iraq and its resources generally overstretched, Washington's threat to use force against Iran looks far less impressive to Tehran. In fact, the United States remains vulnerable to potential Iranian retaliatory actions, should it undertake military strikes on the facility at Natanz or other nuclear facilities. This vulnerability makes it highly unlikely that the United States would be able to confine its possible military action against Iran to an air and missile raid and thereby avoid bloody fighting on the ground (to say little about other Iranian responses, including the possible Iranian oil shipment interdiction in the Persian Gulf).

Thirdly, official American accusations of Iran about violations of the Nuclear Non-Proliferation Treaty and its alleged plans to eventually withdraw from the NPT, following the "North Korean precedent," look quite hypocritical in view of America's own nuclear policy in recent years. In particular, in 2002 the United Sates created a precedent of its own by withdrawing from the Anti-Ballistic Missile (ABM) Treaty, which led to the demise of two Strategic Arms Reduction Treaties (START 2 and 3) and an agreement delineating tactical from strategic missile defenses. The U.S. Senate, and then a Republican administration, rejected ratification of the Comprehensive Test Ban Treaty (CTBT) and declared the Fissile Material Cut-off Treaty (FMCT) as unverifiable. The United States reemphasized nuclear deterrence as a basis of its security, integrating it with conventional precision-guided weapons and antimissile systems and proceeding with the development of new nuclear arms. Taken together, this self-assured posture of "new realism" in Washington, that amounted to a reneging on the disarmament obligations of nuclear-weapon states under NPT Article VI, precipitated an unprecedented diplomatic fiasco during the NPT review conference in 2005.

In this region, U.S. political and military support for nuclear states that are not signatories to the NPT (namely, Israel and Pakistan), coupled with the initiation of nuclear cooperation with another nuclear power outside of the NPT (India), raise serious questions about U.S. allegiance to the cause of nonproliferation. In another region, the willingness of the United States to join other major powers in negotiating with the DPRK—despite its open withdrawal from the NPT and declaration that it possesses nuclear weapons—makes American threats of sanctions and military action against Iran for violations of safeguards and alleged intentions (despite Iranian persistent claims of purely peaceful nuclear plans and programs) look more heavily biased against the regime in Tehran than against nuclear proliferation.

Last but not the least, if halting an Iranian nuclear program is the highest foreign policy priority of the United States (besides disentangling from the Iraqi quagmire), its other policies are in stark discord with that agenda. For instance, if Washington is so interested in Moscow's closer cooperation on

Iran in the UN Security Council and in direct negotiations with Tehran, it is quite a questionable American policy to simultaneously encourage the enlargement of the North Atlantic Treaty Organization (NATO) to the former Soviet states of Ukraine and Georgia. It is not a question of "right and wrong" (Ukraine has a right to join NATO, although some public opinion polls have shown as few as 12 percent of its population in favor of joining); rather, it is a question of how much cooperation U.S. officials expect from Russia over Iran when the United States seems to be going out of its way not to help Russia in an area of great significance to Moscow. It is just as unrealistic to expect such cooperation while attacking Moscow and disregarding its clearly stated and very strong interests in post-Soviet territory.

This is all the more so because Russia is acquiring a new sense of self-assurance related to its economic upswing, huge oil export revenues, and expanding cooperation with China, India, the Muslim world, and Latin America—all while the U.S. global position has weakened. In short, instead of fighting for what neoconservatives may consider "the right cause" all over the world (which is put under heavy doubt by many others) Washington should decide its policies in a more realpolitik manner: for example, does America want to keep Iran from uranium enrichment as long as possible or does America want to admit Ukraine into NATO as soon as possible?

RUSSIAN DILEMMAS

The basic position of Russia was formulated by President Vladimir Putin during his visit to Israel in April 2005. He said that just enhancing IAEA safeguards over Iran's peaceful nuclear program was not enough; Iran had to *abandon plans for the development of a full nuclear fuel cycle and submit the rest of its peaceful nuclear facilities under IEAE safeguards*. In support of this position in 2005, Russia reached an agreement with Iran on the withdrawal of spent nuclear fuel from Bushehr nuclear power plant to Russia for reprocessing; although thus far unsuccessful, Russia has tried to win Tehran's consent on launching a joint venture on an international uranium enrichment center on Russian territory, which would provide a guaranteed supply of low-enriched uranium for Iran's nuclear energy industry.

In 2007 at least, Russia supported the United States and the European Union (EU) "troika" (Britain, France, and Germany) in demanding a full cessation of uranium enrichment process at Natanz, the resumption of comprehensive IAEA inspections and monitoring at this complex, the ratification by Iran of the 1997 Additional Protocol, and full cooperation with IAEA investigations of alleged past Iranian violations of safeguards.

Despite this international policy alignment, Moscow's current position in 2007 was somewhat different from what President Putin expressed in April 2005. In particular, the cessation of Iranian enrichment activities is envisioned as a temporary measure, introduced only for the duration of time required for the IAEA to sort out its problems with Iran's past compliance with safeguards. After that, apparently, Russia would be happy to consider having Iran develop a full nuclear fuel cycle in line with NPT Article IV and under IAEA safeguards.

Most importantly, Russia insists that all controversies must be settled "within the framework" of Iran's relations with the technical agency the IAEA, rather than through UN Security Council sanctions. Moscow demands that all issues be resolved exclusively without the use of force and Russia (together with China) prefers any UN Security Council resolution not to invoke Chapter VII of the UN Charter, which could countenance sanctions and even the use of force. This posture has weakened the U.S. policy of pressure on Iran.

This international weakness, in addition to other factors, makes Iran's leaders perceive that they are negotiating from a position of strength and can challenge Washington with some immunity, while gaining popular support at home and in the Islamic world. Whatever the final goals of Iran, the Russian and Chinese positions provide Tehran with great freedom in its diplomatic and rhetorical maneuvering. Iran exploits this opening by throwing up smoke screens while making consistent progress in crossing one after another technical threshold toward the ultimate development of its nuclear program, perhaps hoping that one day the world will simply accept it as a fait accompli.

At first blush, Moscow's position on Iran looks contradictory. After all, Moscow demands that Iran give away something very dear to it, while simultaneously removing all the tough levers that could help bring about such a concession in the first place. At closer scrutiny, however, Moscow's posture is easy to explain. There is no doubt that Russia does not want Iran to acquire nuclear weapons, both for security and political reasons. Moreover, Russia is not interested in Iran's development of a full nuclear fuel cycle—not just for security reasons, but also for its own commercial considerations (after all, Russia is interested in selling LEU or nuclear fuel to Iran). However, for the Kremlin, the real issue is the following: what measures (and sacrifices in other policy interests) are acceptable in order to achieve the stated goals despite Iranian determination to develop nuclear fuel cycle for whatever purposes?

The fact is, that in contrast to the United States, Russia has huge political and economic interests in relation with Iran. The latter is one of the main recipients of Russian peaceful nuclear technology and arms sales. Also, Iran is seen as a geopolitical counterbalance to the expanding influence of Turkey, the United States, and Islamic "Wahhabism" in South and North Caucasus and Central Asia. Finally, Iranian oil and gas resources (fourth and second largest in the world, respectively) are a lucrative target for Russian future investment.

Hence, virtually all the Russian political elite and strategic community (including the executive and legislative branches of federal power) would exclude the use of economic sanctions or military force to prevent Iran from developing an experimental uranium enrichment capacity (i.e., the presently limited number of operational P-1 type centrifuges in Natanz) under full IAEA safeguards and squarely within the provisions of NPT. Moreover, the position of the Russian elite on this subject may differ from that in the United States or Israel, but it is apparently quite close to the views of EU "troika," the IAEA, China, and India.

Furthermore, an overwhelming majority of the Russian elite would also object to the use of sanctions or military force to deny Iran an enhanced enrichment capability under IAEA safeguards and within the NPT framework (3,000 or 54,000 P-2 centrifuges), despite the estimate that such a capability will get Iran to within a few years or even weeks of nuclear weapons potential.

In this connection, many Russians would refer to a number of NPT nonnuclear weapons states that have such capacity without any problems: Japan, Germany, the Netherlands, Brazil, and Argentina. True, all those states are close allies or partners of the United States, but this does not mean that Russia cannot treat its partners in the same way, even if some of them are disliked by the leadership in Washington. And it is not lost on Russian experts and politicians that the present Iranian nuclear program is close in its scale to the one started in the 1960s under the Shah, with active U.S. assistance. The American policy on Iran is commonly perceived in Russia as designed not against nuclear proliferation, but against the Iranian regime, and on that Moscow believes it is entitled to its own policy tastes.

Finally, there is the hypothetical question about what Russia would do in the event that Iran made a clear decision in the future to opt for a nuclear weapon. On this, the Russian elite would be divided. Still, the majority would prefer peace with a nuclear Iran than war with a disarmed Iran. Proponents of this view would point at nuclear Israel and more recently at nuclear Pakistan, supported by the United States, despite the scandalous disclosures associated with Pakistani scientist A.Q. Khan's nuclear "black market." In addition, most Russians see the U.S. overture on nuclear cooperation with India, after for years opposing such cooperation with non-NPT states, as another reason not to go to the other extreme with Iran. The U.S. decision is seen as a victory of U.S. geopolitical and economic policy considerations, but at the cost of undermining the NPT. Similarly, many in Moscow would consider that Russia is entitled to its own foreign policy priorities, which in some cases may be higher than the goal of enhancing NPT.

Interestingly enough, a minority within the Russian political and expert community, which would go along with the U.S. use of military force to prevent Iran from following in the footsteps of the DPRK, comprises more than liberal political elements. The liberals would take this view out of concern about Russia's cooperation with the West and out of fear of Islamic radicalism's access to nuclear weapons. But some hard-liners would also endure, if not support a U.S. military operation, for quite different reasons. They would welcome it as a promise of the complete demise of American power through getting bogged down in a vast conflict zone. Also, they would be counting on the additional rise in energy export prices as a consequence of war and the long-term removal of the Persian Gulf states, including Iran, as Russia's competitors in the world supply of oil and natural gas. The current posture in Moscow over the Iranian nuclear crisis is the sum of the above considerations and interests, which are promoted by various state agencies and political and economic groups in Russia. Demanding the immediate cessation of Iranian enrichment activities, Russia is following its own economic and security interests and is demonstrating cooperation with the United States (and the West in general) on nonproliferation. By opposing UN sanctions and the U.S. use of military force, Moscow is accommodating its interests in cooperation with Iran and in avoidance of the imminent economic, political, and security damage that would be brought about by war. In this way Russia is also indirectly forging a united front with China, India, and many other countries in opposing a unilateralist and arbitrary American policy of force, permeated with double standards and the disregard for other nations' differing interests and views.

As with any policy embodying a complicated compromise of various interests and competing goals, the Russian course has been only partly successful. It has made war less likely, or at least postponed it for some time; it also may have somewhat slowed down—but certainly not stopped—Iran's gradual movement toward achieving a full nuclear fuel cycle.

THE POSITION OF OTHER STATES

Of all the nations involved in the Iranian nuclear crisis, Israel is by far the most vulnerable (being already within the range of Iranian missiles) and the most scared by the prospect of a nuclear-armed Iran (which might use those weapons or provide them to terrorists). Tehran's support for terrorist organizations and provocative statements against Israel make things worse. At the same time, in contrast to its act of bombing the Osirak Iraqi nuclear plant in 1981, Israel is not capable of mounting such a raid against Iranian nuclear infrastructure because of its scale and its distance from Israeli bases. Attacks on Iran's nuclear facilities would most probably make Israel an immediate target of retribution by Iran, Hezbollah, and terrorists. Apparently Israel cannot count on its antimissile systems to defend it against Iranian It-3ER missiles. As much as it hopes for a peaceful resolution of the crisis, Israel would most probably urge the United States to take military action if Iran moved forward with a massive expansion of its uranium enrichment capacity. In the case of war, Israel would render the United

States full military support and possibly be the principle among very few members of a new "coalition of the willing."

The European Union—in particular, Britain, France, and Germany—would find themselves within range of Iranian follow-on ballistic missiles (the BM-25 type). Europe would find it unacceptable if those missiles could be armed with nuclear warheads.

However, Europe is more interested in a peaceful solution than is the United States, because of its larger interest in energy cooperation with Iran and its greater fear of the political, social, and economic consequences of a major war in the Persian Gulf. Beginning in 2004 the "European troika" or EU-3 became most active in proposing economic and political incentives to Iran, in exchange for halting its full nuclear fuel cycle; for some time it seemed that success was within reach. However, Europe without the United States cannot give Iran security guarantees (as the Iraqi war has demonstrated). Meanwhile, Iran has taken various steps—including starting again its uranium conversion in August 2005 and enrichment in February 2006 and generally defying the IAEA—and thus the position of the EU-3 has toughened and moved closer to that of the United States.

It seems that the European Union would be grudgingly ready to agree to a substantial expansion of Iranian enrichment capacity (3,000–5,000 P-2 centrifuges) under IAEA safeguards. But it would not tolerate a full-scale enrichment capability (50,000 centrifuges) and would feel obliged to at least politically support U.S.-led military action.

As for the IAEA, its position would probably be somewhat different. Having less political motivation as a UN international institution, it would possibly go for a full-scale Iranian enrichment and reprocessing as long as it stays within the safeguards system, provided that Iran ratified the 1997 Additional Protocol to exclude any secret undeclared activities. However, any suspected violations would be immediately reported to the UN Security Council with the expectation of severe sanctions.

China's position is close to Russia's and apparently even more tolerant toward Iran. Having quite a pragmatic foreign policy, Beijing has a much greater interest in Iranian energy, given that Iran accounts for 18 percent of China's oil imports. China has never been a particularly enthusiastic partisan of the NPT and its institutions; it joined the NPT only in 1992 and Nuclear Suppliers Group in 2005. Moreover, it seems that China is much less concerned than other states by the prospect of Iran acquiring expanded enrichment and reprocessing capability or even manufacturing nuclear weapons and ballistic missiles with ranges covering China's territory. Neither is Beijing particularly concerned about Tehran's support for some terrorist organizations. Hence, China will not support a UN Security Council resolution authorizing sanctions against Iran for its past safeguards violations; is may not even support a resolution should Iran proceed with a full nuclear fuel cycle program, withdraw from the NPT, or even openly acquire nuclear arms. Still, China would try to avoid being alone in veto-ing such a resolution and in the absence of a Russian veto would rather abstain.

IS THERE A WAY OUT OF THE *DAEDALIAN* LABYRINTH?

There is no easy political solution or a quick technical fix to the Iranian nuclear crisis. Too many controversial issues and conflicting interests are involved; too complex is the intersection of global and regional security is-sues; and too fast is the political and technological dynamics of the situation. Nevertheless, it is possible to imagine a realistic peaceful resolution of the crisis, which would require action at several levels of policy and diplomacy.

Directly with respect to the Iranian nuclear program, a solution could tech-nically work as follows:

- Tehran agrees to freeze enrichment activities in Natanz for the time re-quired by the IAEA to sort out all questions about Iran's alleged past safeguards violations.
- Iran would then have the right to go on with experimental enrichment at Natanz, not expanding it to full industrial scale (no more than 500 P-1 centrifuges or 200–300 P-2 centrifuges). The work at the Arak heavy-water production plant and heavy-water reactor should be stopped. This would keep Iran many years from a weapons-grade uranium production capability, but it would provide some face-saving by allowing elements of a full fuel cycle, which Iran claims to be its legitimate right as an NPT member state.
- Violation of this agreement and the beginning of massive enrichment by implication would lead to UN Security Council consideration and reso-lution under Chapter VII of the UN Charter, with a high probability that no permanent member of the Security Council would veto a resolution on sanctions.
- The Bushehr complex should be expanded to as many light-water re-actors, as Iran would be willing to buy. Other nuclear facilities and experimental projects would be permitted under IAEA control.
- Iran would become a shareholder and party to a multinational uranium enrichment enterprise with EU, Russian, and Chinese participation. It would be based outside Iranian territory and provide a guaranteed supply of low-enriched uranium (or fabricated fuel) for nuclear power plants in Iran and other states refraining from building a full nuclear fuel cycle.
- Used nuclear fuel would be transported from Iran for reprocessing and safe storage abroad (as envisioned by the Iranian-Russian agreement of 2005).
- Iran would be involved in and benefit from the U.S.-supported Global Nuclear Energy Projects on new safe nuclear energy technologies.

- Iran would ratify the 1997 Additional Protocol and sign a new export-control condition, which might state that all materials and facilities received under the provision of NPT Article IV, would be returned or eliminated under IAEA supervision in the event of a hypothetical withdrawal from the NPT.
- All potential Iranian nuclear exports would be placed under the Nuclear Suppliers Group and IAEA export control regimes.
- Iran should join the Missile Technology Control Regime and abide by its terms.

As may be seen, this package of agreements implies considerable concessions from Tehran, including many which are at present rejected by its leaders. In order to facilitate a policy change by Iran, other powers involved should make their contribution to a broader set of accommodations:

- The United States should provide negative security guarantees to Iran (either in a bilateral or a multilateral framework with other powers), restore diplomatic relations, and render economic and technological assistance (such as with the Global Nuclear Energy Projects).
- The EU would provide promised investment in natural gas extraction and liquid gas technology and help with Iran's accession to the World Trade Organization.

Last but not the least, to ensure that Iran softens its nuclear posture, great powers should seriously enhance the coordination of their policies with respect to nuclear disarmament and nonproliferation efforts:

- There should be a U.S.-Russian and NATO-Russian informal understanding on some crucial issues (e.g., as long as Ukraine stays out of NATO, Iran will not have industrial uranium enrichment capacity). This would ensure a tougher position from Moscow on possible UN sanctions in case Iran violates the agreement on enrichment limitation.
- There should be a revitalization of the NPT process through implementation of some of the thirteen initiatives of the year 2000 NPT review conference; in particular, the United States and China should ratify the Comprehensive Test Ban Treaty and move toward the conclusion of a verifiable Fissile Material Cut-off Treaty.
- The United States and Russia should proceed with a new strategic arms limitation dialogue, including revitalizing the Joint Data Exchange Center, concluding an agreement to sustain the verification and transparency regime after the expiration of START-1 in 2009, and signing a treaty on reducing combat readiness of parts of their strategic nuclear forces.
- The United States should start—or at least create a credible impression of starting—a substantial withdrawal of its troops from Iraq. Tehran would

have to contemplate the prospect of being bogged down in a civil war in Iraq and in a confrontation with neighboring Arab nations over the legacy of Saddam Hussein. This would make Iran more vulnerable to outside pressure and manipulation. This may change its attitude toward accommodation with the other six nations involved in the search for the way out of the *Daedalian* labyrinth that is the Iranian nuclear question.

PART II

North Korea

5

The Trouble with North Korea

Patrick M. Cronin

The trouble with North Korean conduct, so much of which is inimical to regional and domestic peace and prosperity, is the degree to which it operates outside of boundaries and norms of the existing international state system. Whether one considers its expanding nuclear capabilities as a former signatory to the Nuclear Non-Proliferation Treaty (NPT), or its extensive range of illicit operations such as counterfeiting and drug trafficking, or its appalling human rights record, North Korea occupies a peculiarly promiscuous position in international security. In contrast to Iran, North Korea, formally known as the Democratic People's Republic of Korea (DPRK), is a poor, centrally planned economy. It has a homogenous population of 23 million people, about one-third the size of Iran. Yet like Iran it is amongst the most troublesome countries in the world.[1]

Since the division of the Korean Peninsula as a consequence of the Second World War, North Korea has been led by only two men: Kim Il-sung and his son, Kim Jong-il. North Korea remains self-isolated from much of the world, and the government is one of the most opaque on earth.[2] Astonishingly little, for instance, is known for sure about North Korea's nuclear program. There are no reliable first-hand reports that even a single nuclear weapon exists, and yet it is possible that North Korea possesses as many as a dozen or more bombs. The failed quest to find Iraqi weapons of mass destruction has deepened cynicism of such intelligence. Clearly North Korea, like Iran, has been working on a nuclear weapons program for decades. It was only in 2005, however, that North Korea declared that it was a nuclear weapon state. Its nuclear test in October 2006, although less than fully successful, strongly suggests that North Korea possesses at least a rudimentary nuclear threat. What is known for certain is that North Korea has managed to flout the directives of the United States and other powers and survive despite predictions that it could do neither.

Also well known are the long-standing and plentiful conventional and special forces of North Korea. The Korean People's Army (KPA) boasts more than 1.1 million troops—not quite as large as the world's preponderant military power the United States (which has 1.5 million active forces), but double the size of Iran's armed forces. The Army alone has 950,000 soldiers in its ranks and another 600,000 in the reserve force. Nearly 18,000 artillery pieces under the army's command ensure that South Korea's capital, Seoul, is inescapably in the line of fire in the event of any conflict. In addition to active naval and air forces, the KPA inventory comprises a Special Purpose Forces Command of 88,000 forces, including 10 sniper brigades, 17 reconnaissance battalions, and 9 brigades of light infantry. North Korean advisors, meanwhile, are engaged in a dozen African countries. Hence, even if North Korea's impoverished state means that its forces are poorly equipped to sustain a long conventional military battle, they are large and deadly and ready to strike high-value assets in at least Korea and Japan.[3]

COERCING NORTH KOREA

Since North Korea decided to bolster its nuclear program after the end of the Cold War, the United States has twice attempted coercive diplomacy to stop it: first in 1993–1994 with partial success, and then again from 2001 until 2007, when the United States relinquished its extensive demands and settled for a step-by-step process. In both instances, the U.S. goal has been to stop North Korea from developing nuclear weapons and to give up any that it had developed. In the first nuclear crisis, U.S. diplomacy aimed to convince Kim Il-sung to suspend its program to acquire the fissile material necessary to produce nuclear weapons. Washington threatened to impose economic sanctions and to use force if North Korea did not comply with its demands. U.S. actions concentrated on halting North Korea's reprocessing of plutonium embedded in the spent fuel rods that it had extracted from its experimental nuclear reactor at Yongbyon. The crisis began in March 1993, when North Korea in response to a demand by Hans Blix, director general of the International Atomic Energy Agency (IAEA), announced that it intended to withdraw from the Nuclear Non-Proliferation Treaty rather than to submit to the inspection of two suspected nuclear waste sites. By June 1994, the United States and North Korea were on the verge of conflict. North Korea was not budging from its position of refusing full cooperation with the IAEA that was necessary to account for whether it had already reprocessed plutonium, while the United States had issued threats, both publicly and privately, that it would not permit North Korea to develop nuclear weapons and was prepared to use force if diplomacy failed.

The crisis turned from the path of war toward resolution when former President Jimmy Carter, on his own initiative, went to Pyongyang in June, committed the United States to a resumption of talks with North Korea, and told Kim Il-sung that the United States would not go to the UN Security Council to seek the imposition of sanctions, an action that North Korea had declared would be equivalent to an act of war. In return, Kim agreed to freeze North Korea's nuclear program under IAEA monitoring and to begin talks again with the United States. Even though President Carter's actions had not been commissioned by the Clinton administration, it essentially adopted them. On October 21, 1994, the United States and North Korea reached agreement in Geneva on what came to be known as the "Agreed Framework." Each of the two protagonists received something that it wanted. The United States obtained North Korea's agreement to verifiably freeze its known nuclear activity, a commitment to resolve its nuclear past through special inspections (to see how much plutonium it had reprocessed), and an agreement to dismantle its nuclear weapons program. North Korea received direct engagement and negotiations with the United States, heavy oil to solve its immediate energy needs, the promise of future provision of new light-water reactors, the lifting of economic sanctions, and promises of increased aid and trade.[4]

Superficially, the Agreed Framework allowed North Korea a face-saving way to back away from the brink of conflict. But such a judgment is complicated by the possibility that North Korea's leadership may never have thought of itself at the precipice of a crisis. There was also the delicate matter that President Carter's unauthorized intervention was not part of the official U.S. government coercive diplomacy. Finally, there was the still unsubstantiated claim that North Korea cheated on the Agreed Framework by clandestinely pursuing a highly enriched uranium program; that alleged program was announced in 2002 with a high degree of certainty that only five years later seemed to be lacking.[5] At a minimum, the extent to which North Korea had successfully completed a highly enriched uranium facility remained in some doubt in 2007.

Of course, the Agreed Framework can be said to have faltered because of what the United States did and did not do. The United States was far less forthcoming with heavy fuel oil, light-water reactor construction, and a general pathway to normalization and economic incentives than North Korea had apparently expected. There were reasons for this meager follow-through, and in some cases the Clinton administration was at the mercy of Congress for funding and lifting sanctions. Whether this inaction caused the North Koreans to believe that the United States had no intention of meeting its commitments at all, or whether they would have cheated anyway, is not clear. But the faltering implementation of the Agreed Framework eventually would precipitate a second nuclear crisis shortly after the arrival of the second President Bush. Although the North Koreans may have begun a covert uranium enrichment program, they did cease their plutonium reprocessing program for nearly ten years, which means that they had far less fissile material, and therefore far fewer potential nuclear weapons, ten years later than would have been the case had there been no 1994 agreement.

President George W. Bush entered office in 2001 determined to prevent Iraq and Iran from acquiring nuclear weapons and to pressure North Korea to relinquish them. These were the three countries he dubbed the "Axis of Evil" in his second State of the Union address in January 2002. One impact of hard-line policy was to abruptly end the common negotiating approach of South Korea and the United States. One of the achievements of the Clinton administration's handling of North Korea was the concerted attempt by former Secretary of Defense William Perry to align the United States, South Korea, and Japan in a united diplomatic strategy. That strategy was in effect nullified when South Korean President Kim Dae-jung visited President Bush in March of 2001 during the early weeks of the new administration. It became evident at that meeting that South Korea's Sunshine Policy—its engagement strategy for embracing the North—was incompatible with Bush's desire for a "bold approach" that was willing to contemplate regime change should Pyongyang not curtail its nuclear program. As Liru Cui writes in this volume, China saw the trouble with the Korean Peninsula as shifting from a cold war between North and South Korea to a struggle between North Korea and the United States. In this new atmosphere, China was more closely aligned with South Korea in wanting to bring both belligerents to the table. The U.S.-South Korean diplomatic variance also allowed Japan's own special concern—over the status of its citizens that North Korea had abducted in previous years—to sow further division among the three allies dealing with North Korea. These divisions hardly created a cohesive application of external pressure on the DPRK. Diplomacy froze, not North Korea's weapons program. The 9/11 terrorist strikes on America and subsequent interventions into Afghanistan and Iraq pushed the North Korean issue further down the U.S. agenda.

After it had ousted the Taliban regime in Afghanistan and removed Saddam Hussein from power in Iraq, the Bush administration dispatched Assistant Secretary of State James Kelly to confront the North Koreans with the basic choice of disarm or pay the consequences. Although Kelly was a good man for the job—a steady pair of hands with vast experience in the region—he was not authorized by the White House to offer new incentives for negotiation. Pyongyang did not react well to Washington's revised negotiating position—to say nothing of being placed in a camp with Iraq—and during Kelly's meeting in Pyongyang in October 2002, he thought he heard a North Korean confirmation of its alleged covert highly enriched uranium program. While subsequent intelligence would cast at least some doubt on the status of this putative program, it seems probable that North Korea was at least partly bluffing in the face of what it considered intimidation. Even with tepid international support, Washington sought to slap what further sanctions it could find on North Korea. The administration's decision to stop oil shipments, which had been part of the Agreed Framework bargain, proved fatal to the diplomatic bargain that had resolved the first nuclear crisis. To be sure, many had anticipated the Agreed Framework's demise, particularly sometime prior to the finished construction of two light-water nuclear reactors agreed to in 1994. (Providing North Korea or any other would-be proliferator with nuclear technology—even technology more difficult to convert into nuclear weapons—made many in Washington uneasy.) The Korean Peninsula Energy Development Organization (KEDO) that oversaw energy shipments and reactor construction officially suspended its activity in November 2003. North Korea responded by removing IAEA seals at the Yongbyon plutonium reactor, expelling the inspectors, removing the fuel rods from their storage tanks, and then later reprocessing them. North–South talks and a planned joint railroad also fell victim to rising tensions and mutual recriminations between Pyongyang and Washington. A new agreement was reached in February 2007 that called for sealing Yongbyon after operating freely for four years.

The search for what in effect would be a new framework for diplomacy—one that would try to dismantle both the plutonium and uranium enrichment programs—has proved to be elusive. By the spring of 2003, North Korea was hinting at a nuclear deal after quiet talks were arranged in Beijing. Yet, later that year, North Korea was reported to be back reprocessing fuel rods at the Yongbyon reactor. In February 2005, North Korea appeared to proclaim that it was indeed a nuclear state and that the United States would have to deal with it as an equal, thereby marking the first unequivocal public declaration of Pyongyang's intentions; it simultaneously ripped away the ambiguity that China, South Korea, and other countries clung to in the hope that the nuclear program was all a lot of bluff and bluster. Even worse than this step, however, was the ominous statement uttered by Deputy Foreign Minister Kim Gae-gwan, one of North Korea's top officials, that Pyongyang could provide nuclear weapons to terrorist organizations. Coupled with the evidence emerging from Pakistan's debriefing on the transnational nuclear network of A.Q. Khan, that provided apparently incontrovertible evidence that North Korea traded fissile material to Libya in 2001, it also undermined the simple argument of some that a North Korean bomb could be deterred. Perhaps it could be deterred from being launched, but could it be deterred from export into the hands of terrorists without a state?

President Bush insisted that North Korea submit to a comprehensive and verifiable end to all its nuclear programs, while President Kim Jong-il insisted on a host of demands, not the least of which were direct talks with the United States. Washington tried to ratchet up the pressure on Kim Jong-il by establishing the Proliferation Security Initiative (PSI), which provided a coalition of the willing to stop any weapon of mass destruction-related contraband. The PSI was not limited to North Korea but it was aimed primarily at it and Iran to prevent them from proliferating and simultaneously limit their intake of funds from ill-gotten means. Even more important, however, Washington took steps to try and freeze the foreign bank havens for North Korea's illicit assets. These financial sanctions provoked a sharp rebuke from North Korea just at the moment when it looked like diplomacy was gaining traction.

North Korea had eventually agreed to participate in a new multilateral negotiation process, dubbed the Six-Party Talks because of its inclusion of the United States, South Korea, North Korea, China, Japan, and Russia. In September 2005, the Six-Party Talks produced an apparent breakthrough agreement, a diplomatic chapeau analogous to the Agreed Framework eleven years earlier. Most importantly, the accord for ending the impasse committed North Korea to the goal of disbanding its nuclear program. But the talks became almost instantly stymied when the United States led the effort to apply financial sanctions over North Korean currency counterfeiting and other illicit activity. The actions of the U.S. Treasury Department led to a freezing of nearly $25 million in assets in Banco Delta Asia in Macao. The new diplomatic impasse once again extended the duration of the time North Korea could keep reprocessing plutonium and creating more weapons-grade fissile material. The generally accepted estimate had been that the North could have built one or two nuclear weapons based on the fissile material it had produced at Yongbyon in the 1990s; now estimates suggested the North might have quadrupled its small arsenal based on additional reprocessing in 2003–2007.

In the midst of this latest standoff, North Korea decided to amplify tensions in its own way—to escalate horizontally against the ever-tighter squeeze of sanctions and pressure on it to desist from reprocessing. The escalation took the form of missile and nuclear tests. On July 5, 2006, North Korea fired short-range *Scud* and medium-range *No-dong* missiles, as well as one long-range *Taepo-dong* missile which apparently never achieved orbit. Despite UN Security Council sanctions, North Korea proceeded with a historic nuclear test which, though not fully successful, no doubt instructed North Korean scientists in the finer details of achieving a nuclear explosion. At a minimum, North Korea had a crude radiological device; in all probability it seemed closer to a deliverable nuclear-tipped missile.

A great deal of analysis, including in this book, focuses on why Kim Jong-il opted to conduct missile and nuclear tests in the latter half of 2006. Perhaps the favorable diplomatic outcome in early 2007 provides the most cogent answer. But Mr. Kim could not have known then that his saber rattling would be effective. In fact, five factors probably went into his calculus in deciding to launch and test.

The initial impetus was probably a desire to catch up with Iran in the pariah-state proliferators' bidding war for international favors. The firing of a missile capable of striking U.S. territory by an acknowledged nuclear power with enough plutonium for up to eleven bombs sent an unambiguous message to the world: North Korea is a bigger threat than Iran. In this respect, the two separate efforts to avoid global nuclear proliferation are curiously linked. The steady international attentions focused on Iran's accelerated uranium enrichment was drawing more and more attention toward the Persian Gulf and driving down the value of North Korea's arsenal of weapons of mass destruction. The United States and the EU-3 of France, Britain, and Germany had spared little effort to highlight the severity of Iran's actions, and they had engaged China and Russia in negotiations over what to offer and what steps to take at the United Nations Security Council should Iran proceed with a process that could give it nuclear-weapon capacity by 2010.

EU Minister for Foreign Affairs, Javier Solana, had recently delivered to Iran a package of inducements that included a face-saving way for Teheran to continue enrichment on its own soil, albeit with safeguards. When Iran's hard-line President Mahmoud Ahmadinejad was courted at the Shanghai Cooperation Organisation summit in 2006, the slight to President Kim Jong-il must have been palpable. However, if Mr Kim were slighted, it was his own doing: he had boycotted the Six-Party Talks with the surrounding powers. When he finally sent his negotiator to a fourth round of discussions in September 2005, he made headlines. It was at that meeting in Beijing that a ballyhooed breakthrough was reached: North Korea would relinquish its nuclear ambitions in exchange for economic support and a U.S. security guarantee—at least in principle.

This suggests a second factor in deciding to launch the *Taepo-dong-2* missile: President Kim felt reasonably secure that there would be no reprisal. The test suggested that North Korea had pocketed America's pledge not to attack—perhaps interpreting it as a sign of weakness on the part of a diverted, overstretched superpower. However, Pyongyang carelessly forgot about its part of the bargain. In fact, one of the problems with unproductive diplomacy was that North Korea continued to accumulate more plutonium every day, and the unintended consequence of the Six-Party Talks had been to further impel Pyongyang to look like a petulant bully being denied the attention he craves.

After all, North Korea was believed to possess nuclear weapons and Iran only nuclear energy. The fiction of a diplomatic process is that it gave Mr. Kim the equivalent of a theater in which to shout "fire." The initial excitement the pretest drama mustered was the tame statement by U.S. National Security Adviser Stephen Hadley, who said that launching the missile would be a "bad idea." Similarly, the warning from U.S. Ambassador Thomas Schieffer and Japanese Foreign Minister Taro Aso—who said North Korea must stop its "grave and provocative action"—must have seemed no more than an empty threat to Pyongyang. Feeble warnings could only have encouraged Pyongyang to proceed further with preparations for the missile test.

Although Mr Kim may have hoped only to bluff a launch, media coverage of test preparations may have shaped a third aspect of his calculus: withdrawing would convey weakness. The intentions of this "outpost of tyranny," as U.S. Secretary of State Condoleezza Rice once called North Korea, are hardly shrouded in mystery. Unlike the last long-range missile test in August 1998, when Pyongyang jolted the region by firing a *Taepodong-1* missile over Japan and into the Pacific Ocean, this second missile's preparatory steps had been monitored via satellite and broadcast by the media on a near-daily basis for a month.

A fourth factor in the North's saber rattling was likely rooted in North Korea's deep insecurity. It is easy to dismiss the insecurity of foes as propaganda, but insecurity exists nonetheless. Unlike Iran, North Korea was acting more out of weakness rather than strength. A concerted financial clampdown on North Korea's access to millions of dollars had added to the woes of Mr. Kim, whose country's standard of living has fallen far behind that of South Korea. The prospect of being poor, isolated, and without a nuclear insurance policy was too much for Kim Jong-il to accept. Indeed, it was because of Pyongyang's fragility—and the fear of a sudden regime collapse like that which had happened in Eastern Europe—that Seoul had adopted the Sunshine Policy in 1999 and turned away from its long-standing policy of containment and deterrence.

A final aspect of North Korea's calculus may have been a belief that U.S. President George W. Bush would rather have stability than the prospect of another conflict when America was so deeply mired in Iraq. The October 9, 2006, nuclear test was the coup de grâce. In assuming that Mr. Bush needed peace rather than another crisis, Kim Jong-il showed that he knew quite a bit about how the White House made policy. This brinkmanship caused great commotion, further UN Security Council sanctions and, in the end, a volte-face on the part of the United States that allowed the Six-Party Talks to resume with an announcement on February 13, 2007. North Korea forced the United States to blink. To be sure, the United States had been seeking the admirable goal of stopping nuclear proliferation, and there was some solace in the fact that a stern approach had been tried and now the problem was kicked back to multilateral negotiations.

NORTHEAST ASIA AND SECURITY

Since the end of the Cold War, the region has been threatened by an insecure North Korea that has sought to guarantee its survival not by aligning with a major power but by nuclear weapons and long-range missiles. The thus far unsuccessful search to dismantle these systems poses one of the most significant challenges to regional and international peace and security. And the prospects for success in the near term are not bright. The Six-Party Talks have provided a process, but that process has still not managed to put all of North Korea's nuclear programmes on the table. In particular, North Korea appears ready to seal its plutonium reprocessing (again) but it seems equally committed to holding on to other elements of its nuclear program, at least for the time being.

But the issue of nuclear proliferation is not the only challenge to regional security in Northeast Asia. Although North Korea does not enjoy the same central geostrategic position that Iran enjoys in the Middle East, the Korean Peninsula and nuclear proliferation are clearly regional issues affecting all of the neighboring countries. At the same time, the issues of managing Cross-Strait relations, Chinese-Japanese relations, and China's reemergence have also been consistent themes throughout the post Cold-War era and well before, too. More broadly, regional security concerns also include threats from transnational terrorism, conventional conflict, as well as from indirect or untraditional challenges such as energy security, economic upheaval, humanitarian disaster, and disease.

The concept of the nation-state in Northeast Asia today is very much a dynamic rather than a static one. Although globalization has reduced the monopoly of power traditionally associated with the nation-state since the Treaty of Westphalia, the nation state in Northeast Asia suffers from three chiefly internal challenges: physical separation, ideological schism, and socioeconomic barriers. The most fundamental physical divide is the division of the Korean peninsula into two states. Each half of the peninsula is a member of the United Nations, and the two halves are marked by growing disparities in economic power and political freedom. But each is also significantly armed, the Republic of Korea backed by the world's preeminent military power. North Korea, meanwhile, continues to pursue nuclear and missile weapons programs that could rapidly and profoundly affect the future well-being of the region. Even irrespective of weapons of mass destruction, managing the changing relationship between the peoples of the Korean Peninsula remains one of the salient challenges of our time. Korean family ties and nationalism further complicate this picture, as the dominant policy in Seoul aims to bring the two Koreas closer, whereas the surrounding powers, to varying degrees, are more worried about the actions of a North Korean state on its last legs.

But weak states are an equal or greater threat to peace in Northeast Asia. Despite its longevity, the DPRK and its impoverished philosophy of *Juche* could suddenly falter. Self-reliance has failed in every sector of society save weapons of mass destruction, and those weapons do not provide only a tenuous basis for regime survival. The eventual collapse of the current leadership and government and its replacement by a successor may well pose one of the largest challenges to regional security. It seems only a matter of time before the clash of ideologies between North and South force new variations on current ruling philosophies. The ultimate security threat in Northeast Asia in the coming decade, in other words, may be less a nuclear-armed North Korea, than the sudden collapse of the North Korean regime and, in a fit of unification, even possibly the state itself.

Finally, as with the Persian Gulf, Northeast Asia lacks a durable and commonly accepted multilateral security framework. The December 2005 East Asia summit process was an attempt to demonstrate a regional security ethos, but in so doing it revealed the lingering problems preventing such a single, acceptable structure. The main reason is that the dominant Northeast Asia powers, especially China and Japan, simply do not agree on a basic relationship or how to manage their own relations in the region. Each feels the other is attempting to contain its power and expand its own influence. Furthermore, it is still unrealistic to speak of regional security without reference to the critical role played by the United States. While it may be possible to point to a gradual emergence of institutionalism or collective security in East Asia, or even in Northeast Asia (with recent mechanisms such as the Six-Party Talks, which have dealt with North Korea but may attempt to branch out into other issues, as well), the complex triangular relations among China, Japan, and the United States make it difficult to take seriously the concept of regional pan-securitization. Meanwhile, Northeast Asia as a region becomes overly circumscribed when dealing with broader issues such as energy, the environment, and economics—all of which are more easily considered with a wider numbers of actors, from Russia and India to the ASEAN members.

But even as the East Asia Summit process and the Six-Party Talks are no substitute for bilateral alliances for providing regional security in Northeast Asia, the bilateral alliances have also been in flux since 2001. America's regional alliances in the region have started to diverge along two salients: some have grown tighter and some have shown signs of fraying. Alliances balance threatening power, and they are formed when policymakers deem them to be necessary or prudent in support of their national interests. But threat perceptions change with time and circumstance, and one axiom of alliance politics throughout history is that great powers should not allow smaller and small powers to maneuver them into a corner from which there is no way out but to capitulate or to fight. The alliance with the Republic of Korea and the tacit alliance with Taiwan have experienced upheaval in the past decade. In both Seoul and Taipei, opposition parties have replaced traditional ruling parties and shifted approaches to the handling of their biggest security challenge: thus, the Republic of Korea has switched from wanting to deter, contain, and even undermine North Korea to wanting to engage it in a sunshine policy; conversely, under the current Democratic Progressive

Party leadership, Taiwan has opted for a provocative approach to dealing with Cross-Strait relations, an approach that has been more assertive in the direction of independence, with the predictable consequence that China has reacted sharply to what it sees as a gambit to foreclose the possibility of unification. Despite these tensions, both relationships show mixed signs of durability. In South Korea, the Roh Moo-hyun administration, that will leave office in February 2008, had indicated a desire to end the Combined Forces Command and went some way toward defanging the military, notwithstanding a pledged commitment to modernizing but downsizing forces by 2020. Yet Korea also has made progress with the United States on transforming the bilateral alliance and redirecting itself to global security challenges. Relative to the U.S.-Japan-Australian set of security ties, however, the U.S.-ROK alliance has not been strengthened to the same extent; but Chinese-South Korean relations have blossomed in the same period. In short, North Korea poses a long list of troubles, from proliferation and its existing conventional capabilities, from strength and weakness, for direct relations and the impact it could have on alliances and regional security mechanisms.

NOTES

1. Per capita Gross Domestic Product of North Korea, when adjusted for purchasing power parity, is by one educated estimate said to be $1,800, roughly the same as Bangladesh. See The 2006 CIA Fact Book and the 2006 United Nations Human Development Report.

2. For instance, see Jasper Becker, *Rogue Regime: Kim Jong Il and the Looming Threat of North Korea* (Oxford: Oxford University Press, 2005).

3. See the International Institute for Strategic Studies, *Military Balance* (London: Routledge, 2007), pp. 357–359.

4. For a definitive account of the negotiations with North Korea by members of the Clinton administration most directly involved in negotiating it, see Joel S. Wit, Daniel B. Poneman, and Robert L. Gallucci, *Going Critical: The First North Korean Nuclear Crisis* (Washington, DC: The Brookings Institution, 2004).

5. In the Agreed Framework was a provision committing North Korea to implement the North–South joint declaration on the denuclearization of the Korean Peninsula, which explicitly states that neither North nor South Korea will possess nuclear reprocessing and uranium enrichment facilities.

6

Back to Square One on the Korean Peninsula

Sung-Joo Han

The security outlook on the Korean Peninsula remains hazy and fragile, notwithstanding a diplomatic breakthrough in February 2007 over North Korea's nuclear program. The uncertainty and fragility derive partly from the threat of North Korea's weapons of mass destruction, especially its nuclear weapons and missiles, and partly from the fluidity and reshaping of South Korea's more than half-century-old alliance with the United States.[1]

The reversal in diplomatic fortunes arrived only after a protracted five-year nuclear crisis, the second such nuclear crisis since North Korea's nuclear program gained prominence in the early 1990s. In October 2002, both North Korea and the United States announced their intention to abandon the 1994 Agreed Framework that had provided the diplomatic framework for resolving the first nuclear crisis. Perhaps the most contentious period of this second crisis came in 2006, not long after a then-heralded diplomatic breakthrough. But tensions were heating up beneath the surface well before then, including in February 2005, when North Korea officially announced that it possessed nuclear weapons. The overt reaction of the international community to this announcement was neither alarm nor rebuke. Both the United States and South Korea tried to minimize the significance of the statement, ostensibly refusing to play "the North Korean game" of bluff and panicky response. The September 19, 2005, joint statement of the Six-Party Talks led to nowhere even as North Korea continued to operate its 5-megawatt reactor and keep reprocessing the spent fuel the reactor was churning out on a regular basis. The crisis heightened on July 5, 2006, when North Korea test-fired an assortment of missiles—short-range *Scud* missiles, medium-range *No-dong* (also called *Ro-dong*) missiles, and long-range *Taepo-dong* (or *Daepo-dong*) missiles—over the strong objection and warning of its neighboring countries including Japan and China. Although the *Daepo-dong* 2 failed to make orbit, fizzling out shortly after its firing, it was clear that North Korea was capable of posing missile threats to its neighbors, including South Korea, Japan, and China. South Korean fear was as much about the North Korean threat as it was the reaction of the United States and Japan.

Notwithstanding the danger and threat posed by the North Korean nuclear weapons and missiles, South Korea and the United States have been busy dismantling the deterrence system built some three decades earlier in 1978 to counter the North Korean threat: namely, the Combined Forces Command.[2] The Combined Forces Command was intended to prepare for and exercise the wartime operational command of the United States and South Korean armed forces in case war broke out, a mechanism that has served well for deterring North Korea's military provocation and preventing precisely the possibility of such contingencies. The breakthroughs in late 2006 and early 2007 revitalized a diplomatic process and promised a return to some stability, but at the price of a larger North Korean nuclear arsenal than had existed prior to the demise of the 1994 Geneva Agreed Framework.

THE NORTH KOREAN NUCLEAR ISSUE

The second North Korean nuclear crisis that began in 2002 is only recently thought to be on a constructive path. Members of the Six-Party Talks (the United States, China, Russia, Japan, North Korea, and South Korea) signed a joint statement on September 19, 2005, in which North Korea, in principle, agreed to "abandon" its nuclear programs in return for security assurance and economic assistance. However, the "agreement" was long on principles and short on specifics, such as the timing of implementation, what nuclear programs were to be abandoned, and what North Korea would get in return and when. Until late 2006, there was no follow-up, either in the form of a meeting or much less implementation of the joint statement. North Korea had already declared in February 2005 that it possessed nuclear weapons. It had an active program of manufacturing plutonium. An agreement in February 2007 avoided previous goals of complete, verifiable, and irreversible dismantlement in favor of seeking a freeze within sixty days on the Yongbyon plutonium reactor. There was no reference to North Korea's existing nuclear stockpile, other fissile material, or the suspected highly enriched uranium reactor program. As of April 2007, the plutonium reactor at the Yongbyon nuclear facility was once again on its way to being shut down. Unfortunately, while questions remained about other aspects of the North Korean nuclear program, there seemed little doubt that the second nuclear crisis had left North Korea with a more capable set of unconventional armament. Even the February 13, 2007, agreement that ended a diplomatic impasse offered little immediate prospect of coming to terms with these systems. Optimists began to speak of "disabling" rather than dismantling North Korea's nuclear program.

For South Korea, the North Korean nuclear program presents three distinct varieties of danger: first, North Korean nuclear weapons could change the strategic balance on the Korean Peninsula; second, a very strong reaction by the United States and other nations including Japan could lead to an outbreak of war on the Korean Peninsula; and third, North Korean nuclear weapons could touch off an arms race that might spur Japan as well as South Korea to become nuclear-weapon states. Unfortunately, South Korea by itself does not have the means to persuade North Korea to heed its advice to give up its nuclear program in exchange for economic and security benefits. North Korea will only reckon, if at all, with U.S. and Chinese persuasive power, both coercive and remunerative.

Will North Korea give up its nuclear weapons program? Or are all its moves intended to buy time and transfer the blame for failure to achieve an agreement to the other side, that is, the United States? Some believe that the North, as it did in the early 1990s, aims to bargain away its nuclear weapons. Others, however, wonder if Pyongyang is using negotiation simply to buy time to further its weapons development program.

In return for giving up its nuclear weapons program, North Korea demands payoffs such as a security guarantee, economic compensation, and the lifting of international (primarily U.S.) economic sanctions. Echoing a refrain frequently heard from Iran, North Korea also insists on its right to the "peaceful use" of nuclear power, presumably because: (1) it wants to have access to nuclear-generated power; and (2) it provides North Korea with an option for nuclear weapons. Nonetheless, it is not clear at all whether North Korea would actually give up its nuclear weapons—in which it has invested so much and achieved so much—despite the enormous costs and risks. Indeed, it would appear that North Korea considers nuclear weapons essential to guarantee the regime's survival.

In any case, it is highly unlikely that North Korea can be persuaded to resolve the issue with carrots alone. Conversely, the use of sticks or the threat of their use will only strengthen North Korea's resolve to hang on to what they consider the answer to their security problem. In fact, it is likely that North Korea is interested in duplicating the experience of India and Pakistan—that is, in the end, for the United States and others to accept reluctantly but inevitably their nuclear weapon-state status. North Korea does not expect other powers to acquiesce out of friendship, but it may well expect others to accept this accomplished fact because of the lack of viable options.

Will the United States accept the fait accompli of North Korea's nuclear weapons or resort to stronger measures if there is no progress toward resolution of the issue? The George W. Bush administration has been critical of the Geneva Agreed Framework of 1994 that the Clinton administration had negotiated with North Korea. It is opposed to "rewarding bad behavior" and engaging in bilateral negotiations with North Korea. Neither has it been able to draw, much less enforce, a red line that North Korea could not cross, nor set a time limit by which the issue had to be resolved. It is highly likely that because of self-imposed rigidity, the United States has not been able to implement either a flexible or a consistently tough policy. As a result, North Korea has been given the time and leeway to prolong the dialogue process even as it was expanding its nuclear program and arsenal.

The United States may claim that it has been leaving its ultimate response deliberately vague to confound North Korea. On its part, however, North Korea continued to test and challenge the patience of the United States that was deeply bogged down in coping with insurgency in Iraq and whose hard-line policy vis-à-vis North Korea was fully supported only by Japan among the members of the Six-Party Talks. Under the circumstances, North Korea continued to pile up its bargaining chips and leverage, by expanding and improving its nuclear weapons and material as well as its short-range, medium-range, and long-range missiles to carry their warheads. The question boiled down to whether the United States would ultimately change its stance from unproductive rigidity to more practical pragmatism, restrain from the resort to strong (including military) measures if nothing else seemed to work, or accept North Korea's nuclear weapon-state status. Belated consultations, including between South Korea and the United States, resulted in an effort to find the best strategy to deal with the issue (as they did in the earlier crisis of 1993–1994) rather than engaging in a contest over which conviction prevails. But that agreement still represented regression since 2002 because of the expansion of North Korea's arsenal.

What kind of an endgame does China have in mind? Among the countries in the Six-Party Talks, China, which maintains the closest relations with North Korea, seems to have the greatest leverage over Pyongyang. Since 2003, China has been serving as the convener, host, and chair of the Six-Party Talks. China was instrumental in bringing about the joint statement of the six parties in September 2005. And yet China refrains from doing much more than giving friendly advice to North Korea and paying it off with food and energy to come to the talks. China sought to avoid applying any "pressure" on North Korea ostensibly lest it lashed out and became more rigid on the issue. China is reluctant to see the United Nations take strong measures vis-à-vis North Korea, either on the nuclear or missile issue. Before the diplomatic breakthrough with the fifth round of Six-Party Talks, many asked whether China was doing enough, whether it could do more, and what China's interest was with respect to the North Korean nuclear issue. These questions have been muted, at least temporarily, with the resumption of a diplomatic process.

Broadly speaking, China's policy seems to consist of three objectives: 1. to keep North Korea afloat and prevent it from collapsing; 2. to prevent an armed conflict from breaking out on the Korean Peninsula; and 3. to denuclearize the Korean Peninsula. The collapse of North Korea will mean at most the precipitation of an enormous disruption in China's neighborhood with the possibility of millions of North Korean refugees flooding Northeast China. At best, it means the loss of a buffer zone between itself and a unified Korea. A war or an armed clash on the Korean Peninsula would inevitably draw China into the conflict and would serve as a tremendous obstacle to its continued economic growth and expansion. A North Korea armed with nuclear weapons and missiles that can reach every part of China will mean a serious potential threat to China while at the same time it can lead to the rearming in earnest of Japan and the further strengthening the U.S.-Japan military alliance. Unfortunately for China, these policy objectives are not complementary but are actually in conflict with one another. China has to balance these policy objectives as it tries to maximize the chances of their achievement.

Even during the 1993–1994 crisis, when it seemed that China was only marginally involved, China tried to play a constructive and useful role in ways and when it thought it could play. In fact, there were times, like in June of 1994, when China played a decisive role in bringing North Korea back to the conference table and preventing a disaster from ensuing on the Korean Peninsula. Since 2003, China has been playing a much more active and visible role. Even as China has opposed the application of pressure on North Korea, it has often found the United States' (and recently Japan's) hard-line policy a useful excuse to counsel accommodation by North Korea. The rejuvenated diplomatic framework in 2007 ended for the present in a protracted period of disappointment. Until February 2007, North Korea, in effect, had been able to play a version of brinkmanship vis-à-vis China by threatening to be either more reckless if China applied pressure or more of a burden if China withdrew its advocacy of North Korea.

It is not clear, however, what kind of an endgame China envisages and how China plans to bring it about. It is possible that China places greater hope in coping with the issue through a long-term solution, even accepting North Korea's nuclear weapon-state status in the short- to midterm. Combined with North Korea's formidable missile capability and the potential to transfer nuclear weapons and technology to rogue groups or states, such a gradual and mild approach is likely to clash with that of the United States and Japan. For South Korea, which seems to agree more often with China than with the latter countries, such a division of views represents a serious policy dilemma.

It is impossible for South Korean policymakers to be sure whether North Korea will indeed make the "grand bargain" of giving up its nuclear weapons and program for yet unspecified payoffs. However, at least during the initial stages, North Korea's policy will have to be based on the assumption that such a bargain is possible. North Korean willingness to make the bargain has to be tested for as long and much as possible. It has several advantages. One is that, in case such a bargain can be made, the parties will not have to risk crises and conflicts that can be quite damaging and destructive for all the parties involved, especially for South Korea. Secondly, even if it does not work out, it will have the advantage of convincing all the parties involved (except North Korea, of course) that the next approach to be attempted will have to be tougher. Even China has a good chance of coming on board once it is determined that North Korea is not interested in a negotiated settlement. Needless to say, trying a policy that will not succeed has the disadvantage of allowing North Korea the time and opportunity to expand its nuclear arsenal and make its nuclear status even more of an accomplished fact. However, such a risk is relatively a small one compared with the advantages of the alternative approach. In the meantime, South Korea will have to persuade North Korea with whatever leverage it has that it is in North Korea's own economic and security interest to take steps that will lead to a peaceful resolution of the issue.

South Korea also has had dual tasks of encouraging the United States to take a more flexible and pragmatic approach while prompting China to take a more active and forceful approach toward persuading North Korea to agree to resolve the issue and to implement such an agreement. South Korea faces the dilemma of whether it should use "pressure" or coercion as one of the instruments to persuade North Korea to agree to resolve the nuclear problem. On the one hand, the use of pressure runs the risk of breaking off dialogue and contacts with North Korea. On the other hand, excluding such an option in the strategy of dealing with North Korea can deprive North Korea of any incentive to deal with the issue as Pyongyang sees no disadvantage in continuing with its nuclear weapon production. It means that South Korea will have to conduct closer and more active consultation and coordination with both the United States and China. The most important and effective resource in this regard is the ability to come up with ideas and policies that will likely bring the United States and China closer together and make them take a coordinated and effective strategy in dealing with the North Korean nuclear issue. Clearly the new diplomatic framework of 2007 was the result of such close coordination.

What is the outlook on the North Korean nuclear issue? For the moment, the new framework brings a degree of stability and predictability to the Korean Peninsula. North Korea insisted that it would not come back to the Six-Party Talks, much less resolve the issue, unless the United States relaxed its financial squeeze on North Korea, a squeeze prompted by North Korea's counterfeiting of the U.S. dollar and other illicit activities. The United States on its part had been increasing rather than reducing financial pressure on North Korea while showing no intention of entering a bilateral negotiation with North Korea. Especially after the test firing of missiles in July 2006, the United States seemed likely to reciprocate by increasing pressure on North Korea, financially and otherwise. Prior to the February 2007 breakthrough, one could envisage three possibilities, each of them containing elements of danger and uncertainty.

First, North Korea could decide to continue with the present situation while continuing to produce fissile material, increase its nuclear arsenal at the risk of inviting stronger pressure on the North by the rest of the members of the six-party group. Second, North Korea could decide to ratchet up the situation and try the patience of those other countries by, for example, by conducting a nuclear bomb test. Indeed, this is what North Korea did do after the missile tests and before the February accord. The question still remained as to what, if anything, the rest of the world, particularly the United States would and could do, collectively or separately, in response to the continuation and acceleration of North Korea's nuclear program. Finally, North Korea, for the sake of economic assistance and cooperation with key countries, could agree to hold multilateral and bilateral talks with the members of the Six-Party Talks. This is what came about in February 2007 and the subsequent initiation of a sixth round of Six-Party Talks. Fortunately, the United States backed down from its previous demand of comprehensive and immediate denuclearization and instead agreed to a phased negotiation beginning with a return to the shutting down of the plutonium reactor at Yongbyon. The United States also worked to lift the financial sanctions on about $25 million in North Korean assets that had been frozen at Banco Delta Asia in Macao. Under these conditions, North Korea found it beneficial to return to a diplomatic process intended to eventually lead to the cessation of all of North Korea's nuclear programs. Whether such a process can stay on track in the coming years remains an open question.

MISSILE PROGRAM

North Korea's formidable missile capability has been a great source of concern for neighboring countries, including South Korea, Japan, and China, as well as the United States whose close allies and own troops stationed there are threatened. It is estimated that North Korea has more than 800 missiles, including more than 500 *Scud* missiles with a 500-kilometer range, the rest being *No-dong* missiles with ranges up to 1,300 kilometers. The missiles, some of which can be submarine-launched, can carry not only conventional explosives but also chemical weapons (of which North Korea is known to possess 2,500–5,000 tons), biological weapons, and possibly nuclear weapons which the North Korean government claims it possesses. All this is in addition to North Korea's 13,500 units of artillery, many of which can reach Seoul, and which South Korea's defense ministry believes have been deployed against it.

On July 5, 2006, North Korea defied the international community (including pointedly China) by firing an assortment of missiles which included *Scud* and *No-dong* missiles, and apparently one *Taepo-dong* 2 missile, which has a range of more than 3,000 kilometers (and some say up to twice that distance) but which failed to achieve orbit. Why did North Korea launch the missiles and what did North Korea gain and lose with the missile launch? Many in South Korea including the media and the government tend to believe that by launching the missiles, Pyongyang wanted to push the United States to hold bilateral negotiations with North Korea. However, the result has been that it has emboldened the hard-liners in the United States who believe in the futility of negotiation with North Korea and, in fact, turned the United States away from bilateral talks with Pyongyang. It is hard to believe that the North Korean leadership is both reckless and brainless. It is very unlikely that Pyongyang did not anticipate the harshly negative reaction of the United States which was in the short run driven further away from bilateral negotiations with North Korea.

What did North Korea gain as a result of the multiple missile launching? For one thing, Pyongyang was able to demonstrate to the world (and potentially to overseas buyers of the missiles) the apparent accuracy and high quality of North Korea's *Scud* and *No-dong* missiles. Although the *Taepo-dong* missile was a spectacular failure, the failure was quite effectively diluted as it was launched together with several other shorter-range missiles. Furthermore, to the extent that North Korea wished to learn whatever problems and weaknesses it has had with this type of intercontinental ballistic missile, it must have achieved the objective of acquiring the necessary data to improve and perfect the *Taepo-dong*.

Furthermore, North Korea succeeded in changing the main subject of negotiation with the United States when the time came to conduct it. The main concern of the rest of the world became whether it would launch another set of missiles or not rather than whether it possessed them. The missiles thereby became another bargaining chip in trying to remove the financial and other restrictions that the United States was imposing on North Korea related, for example, to its counterfeiting activities.

North Korea had another, perhaps unexpected, gain. The missile launching elicited a South Korean response which was quite apart from that of most other countries, particularly the United States and Japan. The South Korean government took the position that, more than the North Korean missiles themselves, a greater danger to security related to the possibility that countries such as the United States and Japan would overreact and perhaps ignite an armed conflict in the Korean Peninsula. In particular, South Korea reacted angrily when some Japanese leaders held out the possibility of a "preemptive attack" on North Korean missiles, while underplaying the threat that the North Korean missiles posed and showing scant enthusiasm for international measures such as the UN Security Council resolution condemning the North Korean missile launching. In short, North Korea succeeded in breaking whatever solidarity that remained among South Korea, Japan, and the United States as South Korea chose to isolate itself among the three de facto allies.

Nonetheless, North Korea had something it lost as well. Most importantly, its relations with China, its main sponsor and supporter of the last resort, became estranged. Having been embarrassed by its inability to persuade and refrain from the missile launching, China eventually decided to join Russia in supporting a UN Security Council resolution chiding North Korea for its disruptive act, a resolution that was likely to legitimize international measures, financial and otherwise, which would have the effect of sanctioning and restricting North Korea. It is unlikely that China would "abandon" North Korea completely with such measures as cutting off assistance in energy and food. As much as China feels threatened by North Korean missiles and nuclear weapons, it does not wish to see North Korea collapse or led to an outbreak of armed conflict on the Korean Peninsula. However, there was no doubt that China would be less enthusiastic about providing North Korea with economic assistance that North Korea was in dire need of or with diplomatic support in international forums. Under the circumstances, it became difficult even for South Korea to provide as much assistance to North Korea as it probably would have liked. The diplomatic breakthrough saved China for now from being more severely tested about how far it would be willing to go to stop unwanted North Korean behavior.

The North Korean missile launching also resulted in providing Japan with the needed justification to increase its defense capabilities, streamline legal and administrative provisions to become a "normal state," and strengthen its security alliance with the United States. It is not clear whether North Korea anticipated or even cared about such consequences. It might have figured that the militarizing of Japan and hardening of the U.S. attitude toward North Korea were trends that were taking place any way and that additional incentive on the part of either Japan or the United States to turn further against itself would only be of marginal significance. Apparently, North Korea judged that it was more important to perfect and demonstrate its missile capabilities, to enhance its negotiating leverage vis-à-vis the United States, and to intimidate South Korea into becoming more cooperative and accommodating toward North Korea. In all likelihood, North Korea is content that its objectives have been achieved, perhaps even more so with the latest diplomatic framework. The February 2007 agreement brought the situation back to square one; the biggest change was that North Korea had meanwhile strengthened its nuclear and missile program.

So, where does all this lead us to as far as the security outlook on the Korean Peninsula is concerned? North Korea insists, and the current South Korean government seems to believe, that South Korea is not the target of its missiles. Even as the South Korean government of Roh Moo-hyun tried to present a sanguine face regarding the North Korean military threat, and was concerned more about what it considered an overreaction by the United States and Japan, both the missiles and nuclear weapons (possibly in the form of warheads) posed a threat to South Korea as much as to Japan. In fact, whether the South Korean government recognizes and admits it or not, South Korea was placed under notice by the successful demonstration of its missiles and missile technology, as well as of the fact that all parts of South Korea can be targeted by North Korean missiles. Furthermore, it is not a groundless fear on the part of South Korea that Japan, which is most directly threatened by the missiles, would be tempted to react, possibly with the support of the United States, in a way that would disrupt peace and stability on the Korean Peninsula.

Unlike the nuclear issue, however, missiles seem to have no way out of its dilemma, even in theory. In the absence of any international legal instrument or regime, and acceptable compensation, it is very unlikely that North Korea will be persuaded to reduce, much less give up, its missile capability. Like the nuclear issue, however, missiles will require a concerted and coordinated effort of those parties that are threatened by them to deal with the problem effectively and in a peaceful way.

U.S.-KOREAN ALLIANCE AND KOREAN SECURITY

North Korea's nuclear weapons and missiles would be difficult issues to deal with under any circumstances. The difficulty would be doubled if and when there are uncertainties and infirmities with the alliance between the Republic of Korea (variously the ROK or South Korea) and the United States. There are at least three reasons why the more than half-century-old alliance between the Republic of Korea and the United States, which has served as an effective deterrent against possible North Korean attack, began to be shaken. The first is the difference in perception regarding North Korea and different approaches the two countries have been advocating for the purpose of dealing with nuclear-armed and missile-toting North Korea. The second is still fairly widely held anti-American sentiment that the government has not done an effective job of dampening. The third reason why much of the South Korean public began to feel uneasy about the robustness of the U.S.-Korea alliance is the move on the part of the Roh Moo-hyun government, now supported by the George W. Bush administration of the United States, to realize an early transfer of "wartime operational command of the Korean armed forces" from a U.S. commander solely to the Republic of Korea.

As the issue of transferring wartime operational command gained momentum in 2007, it deserves a fuller elaboration. In the wake of the outbreak of the Korean War in 1950, South Korean President Syngman Rhee handed over the control of Korea's armed forces to U.S. General Douglas

MacArthur, the head of the United Nations Command that responded to the North Korean invasion. In 1978, the Combined Forces Command was set up to exercise command of the United States and Republic of Korea forces on the Peninsula. In 1994, Seoul gained peacetime control of its armed forces while wartime operational command was to be jointly exercised by the United States and the Republic of Korea with the U.S. general serving as the commander of the Combined Forces Command. Coming on the heels of plans to reduce U.S. troops by 12,500 by 2008 from a strength of 37,000, the anticipated transfer of wartime operation within a few years caused concern in Korea that it could ultimately mean the dissolution of the Combined Forces Command and weakening of U.S. resolve to defend South Korea and to serve as a deterrent to a possible North Korean attack.

With a strong determination on the part of the Roh Moo-hyun government and the connivance of the United States, the process of transferring back to the Republic of Korea of the wartime operational command proceeded despite strong opposition to the transfer by the defense community, which included former ministers of national defense, leading retired members of the military, and experts who were concerned that the transfer would have what they called a devastating effect on military cooperation between the United States and South Korea.

Those who are opposed to the planned transfer of operational command make the following several points: (1) the Republic of Korea would be far from being ready to exercise wartime command by the expected year 2012; (2) separate commands coordinated by a third body would make the exercise of wartime command inefficient and ineffective; (3) South Korea is not likely to be supplied with necessary intelligence (particularly satellite generated); (4) in case of a contingency, Korea is not likely to be provided with troop augmentation by the United States; (5) the cost of replacing U.S. intelligence, transportation, and logistics capabilities would be simply prohibitive even if the United States agrees to supply the necessary equipment and technology; (6) inasmuch as the transfer has been one of the key North Korean demands for decades, the eventual transfer as well as the debate within South Korea would send the wrong message to North Korea regarding the U.S.-ROK alliance and what North Korea could expect from an armed attack on South Korea; and (7) finally, South Korea would be marginalized as an ally of the United States. A further question was whether the timing—set for 2012— was adequate in view of the planning and preparations necessary for the transfer. Nonetheless, the process of transferring the wartime operational control by the year 2012 was proceeding inexorably as the United States not only responded positively to the South Korean proposal for the transfer but, in fact, also offered a counterproposal to complete the transfer by an even earlier date, 2009. But by March 2007 both sides seemed settled on a target transfer date of 2012, thereby pushing the issue onto political successors in both Seoul and Washington.

The Roh Moo-hyun government defended its policy of seeking an early transfer of the operational command with the following several arguments: 1. it is essential for an independent and sovereign country to have full control of its own armed forces; 2. the United States supports the transfer; 3. the transfer will not weaken the U.S.-Korea alliance or its deterrence and defense capability as the United States is pledged to support to strengthen the ROK armed forces and provide more troops and equipment in case war breaks out in Korea; 4. North Korean military capability has been overestimated while the South Korean military strength has been underestimated; 5. the expense required for the transfer is within acceptable limits; 6. in order to be an equal dialogue partner with North Korea, South Korea should have full control of its own armed forces; 7. the transfer has been sought for some twenty years, hence, the Roh Moo-hyun government is not the first to raise the issue; and 8. if war breaks out and it becomes time to "recover" North Korea, the Republic of Korean armed forces can take control of North Korea and manage the military situation there without intervention of other countries including the United States.

Interestingly, having overcome the initial puzzlement over the Roh Moo-hyun government's willingness, indeed eagerness, to sacrifice the deterrence and defense shield, the United States has become a willing and enthusiastic supporter of an early transfer of the operational command. Why? The decisive element in this equation is probably the strengthening of security relations between the United States and Japan. The United States found in Japan a willing partner who would pick up and fill whatever slack that might result from the rearrangement of the U.S.-ROK alliance. During the Cold War years, alliance with South Korea was important to the United States, in part to counter Soviet expansionism and in part for maintaining a forward base to defend Japan. Today, however, Japan can be depended on as a reliable ally even without the firm support of South Korea or substantial troop presence in Korea. Stationing troops in Korea has become less of a sine qua non for maintaining troops in Japan than it was thought to be even if Japan would become the only country where the U.S. troops are stationed in Asia. Thus, the strategic value of South Korea to the United States has significantly diminished.

In addition, with the transfer of wartime operational command, the United States can expect: 1. greater freedom to exercise "strategic flexibility" (i.e., use of U.S. troops in Korea for regional and global purposes when necessary); 2. opportunities to further reduce U.S. troops in Korea; 3. no more need of U.S. troops to serve as the "trip-wire" against a North Korean conventional attack; 4. reduction of U.S. expenses for defense of South Korea; 5. removal of elements that would cause anti-Americanism in Korea; 6. strengthening of U.S. bargaining position in negotiating conditions for military support of South Korea; 7. increased arms sales to South Korea as it tries to fill the gap left by reduced security commitment of the United

States; and 8. greater freedom to focus on other security issues such as the Middle East. It is understandable why the United States not only supports but is also actively seeking an early transfer of the wartime operational control of the Korean armed forces.

What will the debate on and the apparently premature transfer of wartime operational control do to the security of the Korean Peninsula? It will certainly give a clear message to North Korea that the U.S.-Korea alliance has been weakened and that the combined ROK and U.S. forces in Korea are not going to be as solidly united or closely coordinated as before. In due time, North Korea will feel more at liberty to challenge and intimidate South Korea, what with its superiority in weapons of mass destruction and missiles. At the same time, the United States will feel freer to challenge or put pressure on North Korea by military means, if necessary. In short, South Korea will be spending a lot more for much less security.

Those in South Korea who have been alarmed with the move to transfer the wartime operational control have been dismayed by their government's decision to go ahead with the plan without seeking a consensus within the country. They have been further disappointed with the United States which appeared only eager to reduce the defense and deterrence burden in the Korean Peninsula. Then-U.S. Secretary of Defense Donald Rumsfeld's rush with the matter even led him to state that "North Korea does not pose much of a conventional military threat to South Korea," a statement that seemed designed only to justify the United States's reduction if not withdrawal of security commitment in Korea.

As the tenure of President Roh Moo-hyun was winding down in advance of the December 2007 elections, the U.S.-ROK alliance seemed to be weakening in an inexorable way that would make it impossible to reverse the trend as the United States seemed only too happy to pull its feet out of the Korean morass. Even assuming the February 2007 agreement held together, there was still the likely prospect of reverse salami tactics by North Korea, that is, doling out bits of information, incremental steps on reporting, minor concessions, and eventually, after a long wait, perhaps some disabling of facilities. Except for the South Korean government, which was putting up a brave face in the face of unexpected turn of events and where South Korea had to take up more of the defense and deterrence responsibilities earlier than expected, most Koreans are bracing for the uncertainties of security in the years to come.

NOTES

1. The United States and the Republic of Korea (South Korea) signed a Mutual Defense Treaty on October 1, 1953, which entered into force on November 17, 1954. In the treaty, the parties reaffirmed their desire "to strengthen the fabric of peace in the Pacific area." They further declared their "common determination

to defend themselves against external armed attack so that no potential aggressor could be under the illusion that either of them stands alone." The contents of the treaty are straightforward. Article 1 commits the United States and the Republic of Korea "to settle any international disputes in which they may be involved by peaceful means in such a manner that international peace and security and justice are not endangered and to refrain in their international relations from the threat or use of force in any manner inconsistent with the purposes of the United Nations." Article 2 stipulates that the pair "will consult together whenever, in the opinion of either of them, the political independence or security of either ... is threatened by external armed attack...." Article 3 declares that "an armed attack in the Pacific area on either of the Parties ... would be dangerous to its own peace and safety and declares that it would act to meet the common danger...." But the United States added a further explanation that this article applies only to cases of "external armed attack." Article 4 grants United States military forces land, sea, and air access "as determined by mutual agreement." Article 5 noted that the treaty would be ratified within the constitutional frameworks of each party. Article 6 stated that the treaty would "remain in force indefinitely," although either party could "terminate it one year after notice...." The treaty was signed by Foreign Minister Yung-tai Pyun and Secretary of State John Foster Dulles. The treaty in its entirety is reprinted in the appendices.

2. A combined U.S.-ROK operational planning staff developed in 1968 as an adjunct to the United Nations Command that had existed since hostilities broke out on the Korean Peninsula in 1950. On November 7, 1978, this binational defense team evolved into the warfighting headquarters known as the ROK/U.S. Combined Forces Command.

7

North Korea: Getting to Maybe?

Mitchell B. Reiss

A stock character in children's stories is the well-intentioned but guileless fellow, who, through a combination of naiveté, bad luck, and poor decisions, finds himself in a dangerous situation from which he cannot easily extricate himself. At this point in the narrative, hopelessly outnumbered, surrounded, and out of options, he typically turns to his trusty sidekick (for there is always a trusty sidekick) and confidently exclaims, "Now we have them just where we want them."

One cannot help but recall these stories, and this intrepid character, when reading analyses of North Korea's behavior, especially in the wake of its July 5, 2006, missile tests. A political and diplomatic disaster for Pyongyang, we were assured. North Korea had finally bitten the hand that feeds it, others announced; it was more isolated than ever before. Kim Jong-il has miscalculated, we were confidently told. Compared to these assessments, the cockeyed optimism of our fictional friend seems downright pessimistic.

To be sure, the immediate aftermath of the missile launches appeared to bear out these judgments. China and South Korea publicly condemned the missile tests. Beijing even voted in favor of United Nations Security Council resolution 1695, which criticized the tests, demanded a suspension of all ballistic missile activities, and called on all states to prevent any transfer of technology that could be used for the North's missile or weapons of mass destruction programs; for China, this was an unprecedented public censure of the Kim Jong-il regime. Tokyo and Washington also publicly criticized Pyongyang. The tests no doubt pushed Japan and the United States closer together on security issues, further encouraging Japan's "normalization" on military matters.

However, there is less to this response than meets the eye. Much of this short-term anger, certainly in the region, quickly evaporated, and it is hard to see any long-term damage to core North Korean interests. It is not at all clear that the North has hurt itself. In fact, looking ahead to 2007, it would appear to have emerged ahead of the game.

The UN Security Council resolution was significant largely because of China's public stance against the Kim Jong-il regime, but it was no secret that Beijing was opposed to the missile tests. Indeed, Chinese Premier Wen Jiabao confidently predicted a few days before the tests that they would not take place. The text of the UN Security Council resolution contained no enforcement mechanisms, did not invoke Chapter VII (the basis for the U.S. military action against Iraq) and imposed no real penalties on the North; indeed, those were the only grounds on which China and Russia would sign up to it. Neither China nor South Korea had previously expressed interest in joining the Proliferation Security Initiative (PSI), which would ratchet up the pressure on Pyongyang. That stance has not changed after the North's missile tests. Countries or companies that traded in nuclear and ballistic missile technology with North Korea before the tests will hardly be deterred after the tests because of this resolution.

More importantly, there was no indication that China and South Korea turned off the spigot of energy, food, and other assistance to North Korea. Despite announcing that it would not resume humanitarian aid shipments until the missile crisis had been resolved and the North had returned to the Six-Party Talks, Seoul resumed assistance in the aftermath of severe July floods in the North. South Korean President Roh Moo-hyun indicated his opposition to any further sanctions on North Korea. (This response highlighted South Korea's fears that Chinese influence in the North had reached troubling levels—China is now the North's leading trading partner—and a subtle competition was taking place between Seoul and Beijing to shape the future of North Korea.) And while Japan and the United States made common cause after the July tests, the threat from the North's ballistic missiles was hardly a new one; the two countries were already working closely in the military and security arenas.

North Korea's tests also exposed fissures among the other parties to the Six-Party Talks. Then Japanese Chief Cabinet Secretary Shinzo Abe, the eventual successor to Prime Minister Junichiro Koizumi, and others asserted Japan's right to launch preemptive attacks; he later had to backtrack from these statements in the wake of international criticism, especially from South Korea. Remarkably, Seoul seemed to find Abe's statements more threatening than the missile launches themselves, issuing a strong rebuke to Tokyo: "There is no reason to fuss over this from the break of dawn over Japan, but every reason to do the opposite."[1] And the missile tests also damaged the credibility of the U.S. security umbrella; despite well over a hundred billion dollars invested in ballistic missile defense, doubts were expressed in both Tokyo and Washington about America's ability to intercept the North's missiles.

A fuller examination of the balance sheet of North Korean gains and losses thus arrives at a different tally than the initial analyses. On the plus side, the North was able to break out of its self-imposed missile moratorium and test three different types of rocket (*Scuds* with ranges of 500 kilometers and perhaps even up to 900, *No-dongs* with a range of 1,300 kilometers, and the *Taepo-dong* 2, with a top range of 6,000 kilometers) for the first time since 1998. The test firings were also a demonstration for potential customers; some news reports alleged that Iranian officials witnessed the tests. It may have provided Pyongyang with an extra measure of psychic gratification to know that the multiple launches, at night, reportedly surprised foreign observers.

On the domestic front, the tests may have served multiple purposes simultaneously. A flexing of military muscle no doubt pleased the hardliners in the military of the Democratic People's Republic, the Dear Leader's most important constituency, by strengthening the country's deterrence and defense capabilities consistent with its *songun* or "military first" policy. Interestingly, it may also have satisfied those in the foreign ministry and elsewhere who wished to reengage with the United States in the Six-Party Talks. According to this line of reasoning, only further "provocations" would underscore the urgency of negotiating with Pyongyang and force the United States to adopt a more flexible posture at the negotiating table. Voices inside South Korea, as if on cue, responded to the tests by calling on the United States to redouble its efforts and accommodate the North in the Six-Party Talks.

While it may be impossible to divine the internal machinations of the Pyongyang regime, there is little question that the tests served as a means to rally domestic opinion more broadly behind the regime by once again playing the nationalist card and belligerently defying the outside world. In effect, the tests were *Juche* with a vengeance. Perhaps most ominously, the missile launches served as a test run to gauge international reaction, and desensitize the international community and especially North Korea's neighbors in the region, to future missile tests and the September 2006 nuclear weapon test.

Regardless of how one evaluates North Korea's gains and losses, it is clear that the other parties to the Six-Party Talks emerged as relative losers, if only because they expressly warned Pyongyang, for weeks in advance, against taking these steps. Once again, North Korea not only ignored their entreaties, but engaged in precisely the behavior it was instructed to avoid. Perhaps the least noted and most astonishing aspect of the entire diplomatic process involving North Korea during the past few years has been the almost complete inability of four of the world's strongest military and economic powers, including three nuclear-weapon states and three members of the UN Security Council—the United States, China, Russia, and Japan—to shape the strategic environment in Northeast Asia. They have proven thoroughly incapable of preventing an impoverished, dysfunctional country of only 23 million people from consistently endangering the peace and stability of the world's most economically dynamic region. This has been nothing less than a collective failure.

SETBACKS FOR THE UNITED STATES

While international relations theorists can debate how this remarkable reversal of the standard measures of power and powerlessness could occur, North Korea's gains have come at the expense, not least, of the United States. Washington has suffered setbacks to its major policy objectives in the region and globally.

First, and most obviously, it has been unable to eliminate the North's nuclear weapons program; in fact, the program has expanded on George W. Bush administration's watch. During the past six years, the North's nuclear stockpile has increased from enough material for an estimated one or two bombs to approximately six to twelve bombs, according to the open literature. The reactor at Yongbyon has been reactivated and until the spring of 2007 was producing enough plutonium, when separated, to make one or two additional bombs per year. Neither America's declared policy of seeking a diplomatic solution through the Six-Party Talks nor the preferred policy of some members of the administration to topple the Kim Jong-il regime had been able to secure this objective.

A second goal has been to manage American alliances, most notably with Japan and South Korea. North Korea has driven Japan and the United States closer, but Tokyo still has misgivings about whether Washington will protect all of its equities in the Six-Party Talks, especially those re- lating to the abducted Japanese citizens. It opened a separate channel to Pyongyang, with Prime Minister Koizumi even holding two summit meet- ings there, much to the dismay of hard-liners in Washington. Relations between Seoul and Washington have declined in recent years, with many observers in both countries openly worrying about the long-term health of the alliance. And while much of this friction has to do with the genera- tional torch being passed to a younger and more self-assured cohort of South Korean leaders, the fundamental difference lies in differing approaches to the North. As long as South Korea remains integral to maintaining the United States as a Western Pacific power, Washington needs to work out a modus vivendi with Seoul over how best to manage its competing approaches to the North.

A third goal is to preserve American status and standing in Asia and here, once again, the Bush administration has suffered some setbacks. Although sound reasons exist for the Six-Party Talks format, with China serving as host and mediator, the perception that Washington has delegated or outsourced its North Korea policy to Beijing has taken hold and diminished its stature while burnishing Beijing's. More broadly, Washington's inability (and to some, its perceived unwillingness) to address competently a significant national security threat—recall that North Korea is a charter member of the original "axis of evil"—has further tarnished American prestige in the region.

Finally, since the start of the nuclear age, the United States has been the foremost advocate of the global nonproliferation regime. Yet its efforts to halt the spread of nuclear weapons have suffered from Pyongyang's expelling International Atomic Energy Agency (IAEA) inspectors and flouting the Nuclear Non-Proliferation Treaty (NPT), with little discernible price to be paid. Further, there increasingly appears to be a connection between North Korea and Iran that transcends a commercial relationship; it appears that Tehran is borrowing pages from the North's playbook on how to manipulate the international system to evade UN Security Council sanctions and make a dash for a nuclear weapons capability. At a time when the nonproliferation regime is under assault from a number of different quarters, Pyongyang's continuing defiance signals that countries can violate international law and build a nuclear stockpile at little cost.

While a nuclear deal with North Korea would have promoted multiple U.S. foreign policy goals, the real failure of U.S. diplomacy in the Six-Party Talks during the past few years has not been its inability to reach an effective agreement with North Korea. *The real failure has been Washington's inability, after several years of on-again, off-again negotiations in Beijing, to learn whether North Korea is actually willing to surrender its nuclear weapons program, and if so, at what price.* The United States has been unable to clarify North Korea's intentions in the Six-Party Talks, which has handicapped its ability to realize America's other policy goals in Northeast Asia and around the world.

BARGAINING WITH AN OPAQUE REGIME

This is not to gainsay the difficulty of dealing with North Korea. The regime is a very difficult target to penetrate; North Korea has often been called the longest-running intelligence failure in American history. While its intentions are almost always opaque, it is dispiriting to contemplate the extent of our ignorance about the regime's capabilities. The litany of questions we do not have answers for, or do not know as clearly as we would like, includes the following:

- What is the amount of plutonium that North Korea possesses?
- Has it been able to use this material to assemble nuclear weapons, and if so, how many?

- What is the location of the plutonium or any nuclear weapon?
- What is the physical size of any weapon? Have they been miniaturized to fit on the ballistic missiles currently in the North's arsenal? Or can they only be delivered across the Demilitarized Zone (DMZ) by oxcart?
- What is the precise state of the enrichment program?
- Has the North transferred any technical knowledge, fissile material, or nuclear weapons to third parties? And would we know if it had?

None of these questions presents an insuperable obstacle to negotiating with Pyongyang, but they should provide some perspective concerning the magnitude of the challenge of negotiating with North Korea.

It is far from clear how much this challenge would be tempered if Washington would talk one-to-one with Pyongyang, as urged by many of the Bush administration's critics. There are a host of nontrivial issues associated with bilateral talks that are often overlooked. During the discussions between the United States and North Korea that led to the October 1994 Agreed Framework nuclear deal, Seoul and Tokyo quickly grew to resent their national security equities being negotiated by Washington without their presence and direct participation. Bilateral talks also made it easier for Pyongyang to exploit this asymmetry and pit the allies against the United States. And at various points in these talks, almost always when an impasse had been reached, usually South Korea but also Japan, from time to time, pressured the United States to make additional concessions to appease the North. These dynamics would certainly be present today in any extended bilateral negotiations between the United States and North Korea. Moreover, Washington would face added pressures from China and Russia if they believed their interests were being compromised in bilateral negotiations between the United States and the Democratic People's Republic of Korea (DPRK or North Korea).

For the United States, then, there is a potentially significant downside to any bilateral negotiations with the North. The upside is harder to see. Presumably, the main purpose of bilateral talks would be for the two parties to exchange positions and ideas directly, without the presence of the other parties. Yet there is little, if anything, Washington would wish to share with Pyongyang that it had not already discussed with its allies, South Korea and Japan, and perhaps also with the Chinese and Russians. The same logic applies to North Korea. Are the North Koreans really going to share proposals with the Americans that they would withhold from the other parties, especially since any proposal that is discussed would eventually have to be shared with the others? Pyongyang's demand for bilateral meetings clearly lies outside any traditional logic of negotiating an agreement. For North Korea, for whom status is all-important, the optic of it sitting across the bargaining table from the United States would represent a significant propaganda victory.

None of these arguments is reason enough for the United States not to negotiate directly with North Korea, but they should give pause to those who think that even a fundamental shift in Washington's approach toward negotiating directly with Pyongyang would automatically yield agreement or not create its own problems.

So is there any chance that the February 2007 breakthrough in the Six-Party Talks will be realized and lead to a reduction of tension and nuclear capabilities on the Korean Peninsula? The answer to that question depends on changing both the procedural style and policy substance of the Six-Party Talks.

THE PROCEDURE AND SUBSTANCE OF TALKS

The process by which negotiations are conducted cannot guarantee success, but they can either impede or facilitate it. The Six-Party Talks are currently plagued by numerous procedural shortcomings. Most obvious is the reluctance of North Korea to even come to the bargaining table, only emerging from its shell after many months of cajoling, flattery, and outright bribery by some of the other parties. Sadly, given the duration and extent of these efforts, it sometimes seems as if the sole objective of the Six-Party Talks is to get Pyongyang simply to show up.

But even after North Korea takes it seat at the table, past practice does not inspire confidence that the parties will be able to conduct business. To date, the negotiations have been overly scripted and far too brief. Typically, the delegations parachute into Beijing for two or three days where they recite formal talking points, then disappear for another six months or so before they repeat the process all over again. This format makes it impossible to even begin a serious negotiation. Candid, intensive, and extended discussions are the only way to probe the other side's intentions to learn if a deal is possible, and if so, at what cost.

Should these procedural difficulties be overcome, Washington would still need to assign a senior official expressly for these negotiations. An Assistant Secretary of State, no matter how experienced and talented, cannot devote himself full-time to this issue and still fulfill his other responsibilities throughout Asia and the Pacific. This matter of personnel is related to the larger question whether the United States, distracted by events in the Middle East and elsewhere, has the requisite political willpower to invest the time, energy, and resources to explore in a serious and sustained manner whether progress can be reached before the second Bush term expires.

Fundamental questions of substance also need to be addressed. For North Korea, the threshold question is whether it is willing, at any price, to abandon its nuclear weapons program, return to the NPT and permit wide-ranging international inspections. Does Kim Jong-il believe he can safeguard his regime—deter threats or coercion from outside actors—without nuclear arms? Expressed differently, does Kim believe he stands a better chance of sustaining himself in power if he abandons nuclear weapons, receives external economic assistance, and starts to integrate his country into the broader regional economy? Pyongyang has so far not needed to answer these questions; indeed, it may not yet know the answers.

For the United States, the threshold question is whether it can establish a clear hierarchy of policy preferences for North Korea. In other words, can it tolerate the perpetuation of the Kim Jong-il regime in return for a nonnuclear North Korea that nonetheless retains ballistic missiles and a large conventional military, and that continues to repress its own people?

To be sure, the Bush administration's declared policy is to negotiate a diplomatic deal at the Six-Party Talks that codifies a change in regime behavior. Yet Pyongyang may be forgiven for wondering if the administration's intentions are really regime change. Official documents such as the 2002 Nuclear Posture Review, which identified North Korea in its contingency war plans, and the 2002 National Security Strategy, which elevated the importance of preemption in U.S. foreign policy, along with numerous presidential addresses, suggest a desire to eliminate the Kim Jong-il regime. These statements are bolstered by less scripted but perhaps more revealing comments such as President Bush's admission to Bob Woodward that he "loathes" Kim Jong-il, his comment that if his options in Korea "don't work diplomatically, they'll have to work militarily," and Vice President Dick Cheney's admonition that "we don't negotiate with evil, we defeat it." Given this ambivalence, can the Bush administration reassure Pyongyang that it is prepared to live with a nonnuclear North Korea? And if it can, would Pyongyang believe it?

In September 2005, it appeared as if these questions had been answered affirmatively and the contours of an agreement had been reached. On September 19, 2005, the six parties signed a joint statement reaffirming that the goal of the talks was the "verifiable denuclearization of the Korean peninsula in a peaceful manner." The North Koreans pledged to return to the NPT and allow IAEA inspections. The United States stated that it had "no intention to attack or invade the DPRK." Other provisions contained incentives for all the parties, but most especially North Korea, and covered economic cooperation, energy assistance, including nuclear energy and normalizing diplomatic ties.

In retrospect, the joint statement appears to have been initially oversold as a diplomatic breakthrough. Within forty-eight hours of its being signed, both the United States and North Korea offered differing interpretations of the text, and even though a follow-on meeting took place two months later, the parties merely used that occasion to repeat previously held positions.

Reviewing the diplomacy of the past few years, it appears that the parties to the talks rank differently the danger posed by a nuclear-armed

North Korea. No doubt all of North Korea's neighbors would prefer to see it without a nuclear weapons program. In fact, they have repeatedly stated that a North Korea with nuclear weapons is "unacceptable." Yet, aside from the United States, the other parties appear willing to accept a nuclear armed North Korea, even if Pyongyang conducts a nuclear test.

These different assessments of the threat relate directly to the negotiating strategies the parties have been willing to employ. Ideally, a negotiating strategy contains both incentives for behavior one wishes to encourage and penalties for behavior one wishes to discourage; they should complement each other. Because the parties to the Beijing talks view the threat from North Korea differently, however, they differ in their willingness to offer incentives and impose penalties on Pyongyang.

Consequently, one lesson from these negotiations is that North Korea has paid virtually no price for its intransigence. The negotiations are all "carrot" and no "stick," to use the language of the Agreed Framework negotiations during the early 1990s. It is the absence of any tangible dis-incentives, or the prospect of any disincentives, for North Korea that has handicapped the negotiations.

Specifically, if the number one goal of the Kim Jong-il regime is survival, any negotiating strategy must aim to influence that core objective. One way is to *promote regime maintenance* through the incentives offered in the September 19, 2005, joint declaration. But another is to *threaten regime survival* by reducing, even eliminating, energy and food assistance, and subjecting the regime to further isolation, if it refuses to negotiate seriously and resists a nuclear deal. Otherwise, why should North Korea change its ways? For Pyongyang, muddling through is far preferable than undertaking the wrenching policy changes denuclearization would entail.

Since China and South Korea have the greatest economic and diplomatic interaction with North Korea, they have an essential role to play in crafting a more robust approach. To date, they have preferred an incentive-based approach, with transfers of energy, food, and other assistance to the North Korean regime. Yet this seems to have bought Beijing and Seoul little influence, only massive ingratitude. Still, they continue to provide assistance unconditionally; indeed, President Roh Moo-hyun in early 2006 stated in what he believed to be an off-the-record comment that the South would continue to assist the North no matter how provocatively or unhelpfully Pyongyang may behave.

As suggested by their responses to the July 5, 2006, missile tests, there appears to be no circumstances under which Seoul and Beijing would reappraise their virtually unqualified engagement and adopt more coercive strategies against Pyongyang. Their behavior reveals the "dirty little secret" of Northeast Asian politics—no one in the region favors Korean reunification anytime soon. China and South Korea, and to a lesser extent Japan and Russia, have been are reluctant to use their leverage in ways that might stress further the North Korean regime for fear it might cause the country to implode.

Notwithstanding the emotional attraction of a reunited Korea, South Korea knows that its extraordinary high standard of living—the Organization for Economic Cooperation and Development (OECD) currently ranks it the tenth wealthiest country in the world—would be jeopardized were it to absorb 23 million poor cousins from the North. It would set back South Korea by at least a generation, maybe longer. China, Japan, and Russia all believe their influence on the Korean peninsula would decline after reunification or that a single Korean nation would pose a greater economic and military threat. They share a view similar to that of France toward Germany during the Cold War—we like Germany so much, Paris declared, that we're glad there are two of them. All of these parties fear a collapsed North Korea more than one that is nuclear-armed.

North Korea, of course, has the most to lose. Reunification promises no bouquets; it would mean the end of the Kim Jong-il regime. Only the United States, the country most distant from the region, is willing to pressure Pyongyang through policies like the Proliferation Security Initiative, the Illicit Activities Initiative, and economic sanctions, but these tools are insufficient to collapse the regime.

THE LONG ODDS AGAINST SUCCESS

The odds favoring a diplomatic resolution of the North Korean nuclear program—as opposed to just a process or any agreement—remain long. The United States would need to resolve its policy ambivalence and reassure Pyongyang of its willingness to live with a nonnuclear North Korea. North Korea would need to keep returning to the negotiating table, decide it could abandon its nuclear ambitions and start to integrate itself into the larger regional community. China and South Korea would need to demonstrate a willingness to use, or threaten to use, sticks as well as carrots, against North Korea to help shape its behavior. Other myriad procedural and policy objections would also need to be overcome.

Even if we were to make the heroic assumption that all these policy and procedural changes would take place, as some have suggested with the February 13, 2007, accord, there would remain the thorny issue of implementing any deal. And no issue will be more complex and contentious in any final agreement than assuring the complete, verifiable dismantlement of the North's nuclear program.

Again, there are both procedural and substantive aspects to this issue. Procedurally, North Korea would want to structure any agreement so that it could delay, for as long as possible, having to relinquish its nuclear secrets. (A precedent along these lines that is favorable to Pyongyang already exists under the terms of the 1994 Agreed Framework nuclear deal.) Largely because of North Korea's abrogation of that agreement, the United States would insist that Pyongyang produce its fissile material and any nuclear bombs and related technology up front, before it received any economic, energy, or other benefits. In short, the issue here is how one structures the process to determine who goes first.

Substantively, how would the international community have confidence that the North's entire nuclear weapons program had been fully captured? In broad terms, there are two ways to construct a verification and compliance regime. The traditional way is for a country to make a "correct and complete" declaration of its nuclear facilities and materials and then allow international access to these locations. This approach places a large responsibility on the inspection agency to locate the North's nuclear inventory and ferret out any facilities or materials that North Korea did not disclose. This would be a daunting task in any society, but it is especially burdensome given the obsessive secrecy of North Korea, its propensity to dig tunnels, and its past record of cheating on international agreements. It is also unclear whether this approach would ensure success in uncovering the entire program. The number of inspectors needed, estimated to be in the hundreds, and the amount of time required to comb North Korea, would prove highly problematic for the IAEA. The level of intrusiveness required is also likely to be a nonstarter with North Korea.

An alternative approach would place the initial burden of responsibility on North Korea to produce not just a list of its nuclear facilities and materials, but also the actual materials and related technologies. In other words, Pyongyang would be obligated to deliver all of its fissile material, any nuclear weapons, and any plutonium or enrichment technology for the IAEA's inspection and auditing, before it is removed from the country. What North Korea provided would be assessed against intelligence estimates to account for any discrepancies. This approach would probably not eliminate all questions over the North's nuclear arsenal, but it promises to capture at least the majority of the program and reduce the scope of any subsequent disagreement. If the verification debate can be reduced to a few grams worth of fissile material rather than three or four bombs worth, then confidence in any long-term compliance program, which will be needed in any case, would be that much higher.

THE DISTANT GOAL OF VERIFICATION

We are a long way from having to worry about the details of a verification and compliance scheme for a denuclearized North Korea. Several years of Six-Party Talks have yielded little. The high point of this process was the September 19, 2005, joint statement, after which the parties were unable to build upon the pledges in that document. Then the February 13, 2007, breakthrough offered a greater promise of stable negotiations. Serious negotiations, which had seen to be retreating into abeyance after the missile and nuclear tests of 2006, once again resumed. But the question remained in 2007 as to whether they would actually produce disarmament.

Only the most myopic or naïve observer could believe that we now have North Korea "right where we want it." North Korea may have between six and twelve nuclear weapons and was until April 2007 producing enough plutonium for one to two additional bombs per year. It continues to advance its strategic position without paying any significant price. The strategic positions of the other parties to the Six-Party Talks, on the other hand, continue to erode. None is safer or better off today than it was a few years ago.

The challenge of reversing this slide and negotiating a nuclear deal with Pyongyang should not be underestimated. Even with goodwill and sincerity, significant obstacles exist. Only when the other parties to the Six-Party Talks undertake a fundamental reassessment of the costs and benefits of their current policies will there be a chance to prevent Pyongyang from becoming the next member of the nuclear club.

NOTE

1. For instance, Jung Tae Ho, spokesman for President Roh Moo-hyun, said, "We will strongly react to the arrogance and senseless remarks of Japanese political leaders who intend to amplify a crisis on the Korean Peninsula with dangerous and provocative rhetoric such as 'pre-emptive strike.'" See Cho Sang-Hun, "Seoul Assails Tokyo on Pre-emption," *International Herald Tribune*, July 11, 2006. See http://www.iht.com/articles/2006/07/11/news/missile.php.

8

Security and the Korean Peninsula: China's Role

Liru Cui

China's role regarding security on the Korean Peninsula will be determined by three factors. First, China's role will be internally derived by the guiding principles of its foreign policy as well as the domestic elements that go into influencing and making China's foreign policy. Second, China's role on the Korean Peninsula will be affected by international factors, including regional and global security and the policies of relevant countries. Third and finally, China's role will be determined by the dynamics of the first two factors, that is, trade-offs and considerations between domestic and international perspectives of the Korean Peninsula.

For years under the Cold War system, dominated by the United States and the former Soviet Union, China normally adopted a noninterventionist policy toward its immediate neighbor, the Democratic People's Republic of Korea (the DPRK or North Korea). China rarely reacted to North Korea unless there was a clear national interest at stake. Even Chinese involvement in the 1950–1953 Korean War was a passive military reaction to what was perceived in China as a grave security threat from the United States. China never succeeded in, nor has it been capable of, incorporating the Korean Peninsula under its sphere of influence.

In the early 1990s, when the Soviet Union collapsed and the Cold War ended, Russian influence on the Korean Peninsula began to fade away; China, however, managed to maintain its traditional friendly ties with the DPRK, thereby increasing its influence on the Korean Peninsula. Along with its increasing economic strength and flourishing foreign relations, China cast a greater influence over the surrounding areas. However, the noninterventionist policy remained intact until the end of the twentieth century, concomitant with the first North Korean nuclear crisis.

In October 2002, a nuclear crisis reoccurred on the Korean Peninsula and an escalation in tensions between the United States and North Korea put the entire region at risk. In order to safeguard peace and stability in Northeast Asia and continue the smooth development process of China itself, China accepted the joint proposal of other concerned parties and began a process of mediation that became enshrined in the Six-Party Talks (to include China, the United States, North and South Korea, Russia, and Japan).

From August 2003 through April 2007, China hosted six rounds of the Six-Party Talks in Beijing as the key mediator of the DPRK nuclear crisis. Such unusual Chinese diplomatic action, not seen for decades, has received a great deal of attention and appreciation from the international community. China has thus become an important player in the affairs of the Korean Peninsula. This chapter focuses on China's role in dealing with the major powers and North Korea, especially over the nuclear issue.

FUNDAMENTALS

The issue of the Korean Peninsula is a relic left over from the Cold War. The nub of the problem centers on two actors, the United States and the DPRK. Problems between the United States and North Korea could only be solved by face-to-face dialogue between the two countries. However, the lack of trust between the countries has severely impeded serious dialogue. Generally, the DPRK has demanded direct dialogue as "necessary," while the United States, operating from an equal level of distrust, has held direct dialogue at arm's length on the grounds that it is "useless." This impasse provided the key opening for China, which was able to identify a role of bridging these differences by helping to orchestrate the Six-Party Talks.

After the belligerent countries signed the Korean Armistice Agreement in July 1953, ending open hostilities without a formal peace accord, China withdrew all its troops from the Korean Peninsula.[1] Throughout the Cold War era, despite the special amity between China and the DPRK, tactical military confrontation between the United States and North Korea persisted as an extension of the global U.S.-Soviet rivalry. After Sino-Soviet tensions became apparent in the 1960s, and particularly after a Sino-U.S. rapprochement in the 1970s, China and the United States cooperated in countering the Soviet threat and China's role on the Korean Peninsula diminished. By the 1980s, Soviet assistance to the DPRK had surpassed that of China, and Pyongyang viewed relations with Moscow as more important than its relations with Beijing. In the 1990s, the importance of DPRK-Russian relations declined dramatically, because of the collapse of the Soviet Union, the end of the Cold War, and Russia's inclination to improve relations with the United States and Europe. When Russia and China successively established diplomatic relations with the Republic of Korea (the ROK or South Korea), the confrontation on the Korean Peninsula had evolved into a cold war entirely between the DPRK and the United States and South Korea. North–South relations eventually simmered down in response to changes occurring in the domestic politics of South Korea: viz., the Sunshine Policy adopted by the ROK since President Kim Dae-jung came to power and positive responses it elicited from North Korean Labor Party General-Secretary Kim Jong-il. As the policy of Seoul drifted apart from that of Washington, South Korea has turned into a secondary player in the U.S.-DPRK confrontation.

The fundamental policy goal for China toward the Korean Peninsula is to maintain peace and stability. China has adopted two approaches on the diplomatic front in pursuit of this goal: first, to take any actions that will prevent the worst from happening; second, to make all efforts that are conducive to the improvement of the security situation on the Korean Peninsula. China's diplomacy, on most occasions, has been carried out in line with the first overriding objective. However, the first approach often leads and impels China to perform, simultaneously, actions belonging to the second approach, since preventing conflict on the Korean Peninsula requires active engagement. Typical of this active engagement is the role of China in seeking a solution to the second nuclear crisis involving the DPRK. China is mainly playing the important role of strategic balancer in the security situation on the Korean Peninsula. As stated above, since the 1990s China has shifted from a relatively passive role to a more active role. Such a process is consistent with the change in overall Chinese diplomacy, as China has become more engaged in global affairs in the past decade.

CHINA-DPRK RELATIONS: A NECESSARY BALANCE

The traditional relations between China and the DPRK are based on historical ties between the Communist Party of China and the Labor Party of the DPRK, the alliance forged during the Korean War when the two worked together side by side, the 1953 Korean Armistice Agreement signed jointly by both sides and the 1961 Treaty on Friendship, Cooperation and Mutual Assistance between Beijing and Pyongyang. Since the 1980s, the two countries have chosen different roads for economic growth and development, and the political and security interests of the two have changed in accordance with the new international environment and the altered situation on the Korean Peninsula in the wake of the Cold War. Despite these changes, China and North Korea retain a unique or particular relationship. It is difficult to distinguish how much these relations are shaped by history and how much is based on practical considerations. Within the circle of Northeast Asian and Korean studies in China, different scholars have different opinions about the foregoing question, which in itself reflects a new problem facing Sino-DPRK relations. Yet on the policy level, mainstream thinking in China holds that peace and stability on the Korean Peninsula can best be maintained by retaining the traditionally amicable bilateral relationship.

The Berlin Wall collapsed in 1991, which was followed by the unification of East and West Germany, the disintegration of the Soviet Union and eventually the end of the Cold War. However the cold war on the Korean Peninsula survived the demise of the global Cold War. Hostility still lingers along the 38th parallel decades after the 1953 Korean armistice. This is an unbalanced cold war, unlike the confrontation between the two superpowers. On one side is the United States, which enjoys a unique, unipolar role in global affairs. On the other side is North Korea, which has been overshadowed by the economic achievements and elevated international status of the ROK; South Korea has also enjoyed political milestones such as the consecutive establishment of diplomatic ties between Russia and the ROK and China and the ROK, and these have had further political, diplomatic, and psychological effects on North Korea. All in all, drastic changes brought about by the end of the Cold War have cornered the DPRK into an unprecedented situation.

Peace and stability on the Korean Peninsula are directly related to the situation of the DPRK. The DPRK has entered a period of difficulties in political, economic, and diplomatic areas since the 1990s. Pyongyang's isolation inevitably led to the gravest sense of insecurity on the DPRK side since the Korean War. Any country facing such a disadvantageous situation will definitely respond accordingly and different reactions will result in different consequences. Some countries have hoped blindly that changes, even changes in the regime itself, will happen in the DPRK simply under conditions of sufficient external pressure. However, given the mistrust formed by long-term hostilities on the Peninsula, the weaker DPRK is not inclined to put all of its eggs into one basket and suddenly rely on the goodwill of outside powers. In fact, while making certain efforts to improve external relations, the DPRK mainly has taken actions to strengthen its own military confrontational capability or demonstrate its willingness to resist. To some extent, the first nuclear and missile crises were moves by the DPRK to pivot from a passive and reactive role to an active and offensive posture, despite its continuing weakness. No matter how the outside world evaluates the DPRK's actions and policies, the choices of the DPRK are by no means strange; they are instead the logical result of a calculus-based insecure system that exists on the Korean Peninsula.

The end of the Cold War should have been a good thing for peace and security in Northeast Asia. Unfortunately, the strategic imbalance remaining on the Korean Peninsula brought new dangers and thus constituted a major destabilizing factor. Although the Korean Peninsula is no longer the vital front in a U.S.-Soviet confrontation, its geopolitical importance has not disappeared. No matter what, China does not want to see any significant contingencies occurring on the Korean Peninsula. Either economic collapse or political turmoil of the DPRK could trigger turbulence all over the Peninsula and reverberate into China. In this sense, the implication of maintaining the China-DPRK traditional relationship goes far beyond a bilateral framework. This relationship not only has obvious political significance as a kind of continuation of the traditional friendship between China and the DPRK, but also serves as an important remedy for the serious strategic imbalance that persists on the Peninsula. It therefore benefits the stability on the Korean Peninsula and tallies with the interests of both China and the DPRK, as well as the regional interest of peace and stability in Northeast Asia. That is the very reason why China continuously upholds traditional relations with the DPRK.

But we must make it clear that the China-DPRK relationship is above all normal state-to-state relations between two sovereign countries. Their histories have made their respective leaders and peoples particularly sensitive to the concepts of sovereignty, independence, peace, and mutual respect. As a major power, China needs to be cautious. This is partly reflected in the idea that China-DPRK relations are peculiar or unique. Recent developments prove that the ideological factors in the relationship have become increasingly fainter, as the bilateral political, economic, and social discrepancies have widened. In this sense, the China-DPRK relationship is becoming more normal. As for the overall bilateral relationship, no fundamental changes are expected in the foreseeable future unless unilateral changes take place in the DPRK or radical changes occur on the Korean Peninsula. The outside world always believes that China can exert influence over the DPRK by making use of traditional links; in fact, that is largely a fantasy. It does not mean that China has no influence on the DPRK; but China's influence is rather limited. Some people expect China to press on the DPRK by leveraging the bilateral relationship; a few blame or accuse China of playing games. Not only are these views based on a misperception of China-DPRK relations, these interpretations are also naïve with respect to China's strategic thinking behind its foreign policy goals and its opinions about the situation on the Korean Peninsula.

CHINA-ROK RELATIONS: A NEW BALANCING FACTOR

The balanced policy applied to the Korean Peninsula by China is also reflected in the rapid development of China's relations with South Korea since the 1990s. Indeed, looking at the Korean Peninsula from Beijing since the end of the Cold War, the normalization and growth of China-ROK relations is the most notable change in the security landscape. Bilateral ties have been strengthened comprehensively in economic, political, and cultural dimensions since diplomatic relations were established in 1992; China-ROK bilateral relations have become the most envied relationship in East Asia.

First of all, the pace of the development of Sino-ROK economic relations is as incredible as their economic miracles. Seizing the opportunity brought by the economic takeoff of China, the ROK has made use of the complementarity of the two economies and succeeded in turning China into South Korea's biggest export market for commodities, technologies, and capital. Only one year after they established diplomatic ties, China became the third-largest trading partner of the ROK. In 2001, exports to China from the ROK exceeded those to Japan. In 2003, China replaced the United States as the biggest export market of the ROK. In 2004, China grew to become the number one trading partner of the ROK, with a total Korean investment of $17.9 billion spread across 13,200 joint ventures. Bilateral trade volume in 2006 surpassed $100 billion.

At the same time as economic relations have been marching forward, images of China among the ordinary Korean people have also undergone dramatic changes as a result of the end of the Cold War. According to opinion polls, Korean politicians, opinion makers, and the public generally hold a friendly attitude toward China; few openly worry about the so-called China "threat" and more Koreans believe that China, and not the United States, will be the most important country for the ROK in the future. There is also sustained momentum in China-ROK cultural exchanges. For example, there is a stronger desire for studying Chinese than Japanese among Korean students. China has become the third-most popular destination for Korean overseas students, immediately following the United States and Europe.

Rapid advances in both economic and cultural relations have led to the improvement of bilateral political relations as a matter of course. Firstly, Seoul and Beijing expanded their common ground over the Korean Peninsula and Northeast Asian affairs through enhanced bilateral coordination. In April 1996, when the United States and the ROK jointly proposed DRPK-ROK-China-U.S. Four-Party Talks, China responded promptly and positively. Henceforth, China and the ROK have also engaged in concrete cooperation regarding the issue of Taiwan's nuclear waste disposal in the DPRK and the February 1997 defection of Hwang Chang-yop, the man commonly referred to as the architect of North Korea's *Juche* ideology that highlights self-reliance. The Sunshine Policy announced by ROK President Kim Dae-jung, aimed at South–North reconciliation, received vigorous support from Beijing; in return, the Chinese initiative of building a China-ROK cooperative partnership facing the twenty-first century was also echoed by Seoul. In 2003, the newly inaugurated President Roh Moo-hyun reaffirmed the Sunshine Policy after the return of a nuclear crisis in 2002. In July of 2003, China and the ROK jointly declared the goal of building a comprehensive cooperative partnership. President Roh was committed to furthering relations with China, and he endorsed the Chinese position of safeguarding peace and stability on the Korean Peninsula, realizing denuclearization of the Korean Peninsula, seeking a solution of the nuclear issue through dialogue, and addressing the security concerns of the DPRK. In 2005, President Roh even proposed his own Peace and Prosperity Policy and put forth a scheme for Northeast Asia in which Korea would play the role of "balancer." The Six-Party Talks addressing the DPRK nuclear issue, as well as the overall close consultation and coordination between China and the ROK, have served as a vital factor in accelerating a diplomatic framework for the Korean Peninsula.

The great leap in China-ROK relations is a result of the interaction between the evolving international environment and the changing domestic situation of both countries. Tremendous achievements gained from the reform and opening policies of China, and in China's economic development, have produced a positive effect on the surrounding countries. Beijing's guiding diplomatic principle of "peace, development, and cooperation," sincerity in pursuing a good-neighbor policy, efforts in actively managing relations with surrounding countries and pragmatic but creative approaches, have gradually won favor from adjoining countries.

As for the issue of the Korean Peninsula, China insists on observing the five principles of peaceful coexistence; vigorously supports the reconciliation efforts of both the DPRK and the ROK; advocates a comprehensive and balanced solution of the DRPK nuclear issue based on a clear understanding of history; sticks to the unshakable goal of maintaining peace and stability on the Korean Peninsula; and believes that the nuclear crisis should be defused through diplomatic means. China has endeavored to implement these propositions on its own. All of these are somehow understood and accepted by the ROK. As a matter of fact, since a considerable part is actually based on a consensus between the two countries, they are naturally appreciated and supported by Seoul. It is fair to say that among the United States, the ROK, China, and the DPRK—the four most-concerned countries—China and the ROK share the most common ground about the DPRK nuclear issue. Their communication and cooperation during the Six-Party Talks have overshadowed those between the United States and the ROK or China and the DPRK.

It is worth noting that from the perspective of the ROK, closer ties with China are the outcome of Seoul's more independent foreign policy, such as President Roh Moo-hyun's notion of making South Korea a regional "balancer." China welcomes the tendency toward a more independent South Korean policy because it buttresses peace and stability on the Korean Peninsula. Even so, Beijing harbors no illusion that Seoul will put its relations with Beijing on top of the ROK-U.S. alliance. Nevertheless, this trend still has both practical effects upon, as well as far-reaching implications for, the development of the situation on the Korean Peninsula and readjustments of relations among relevant powers.

CHINA-U.S. RELATIONS: SEEKING COMMON GROUND

The relationship between China and the United States has an important bearing on the overall situation on the Korean Peninsula. Relations with the United States is the most important external factor determining whether China will enjoy a peaceful international environment in order to carry out reforms, open up smoothly, and concentrate on economic construction. After the former Soviet Union collapsed, some Americans viewed China as the most menacing potential rival for the United States and hence called for vigilance regarding China. But the United States has vast economic interests in China and needs Chinese cooperation on a number of issues in international affairs. The dominant part of official U.S. policy toward China is in favor of developing relations, while still concealing some tricks guarding against potential challenges from, and confrontation with, China. China refers to this hedging strategy as "dual tactics."

China's development strategy requires a stable and steadily improving Sino-U.S. relationship and is based on the presumption that China and the United States share more common interests than differences. Judging from the experience of the past thirty years, China believes that a framework for peaceful coexistence is possible as long as this relationship is properly managed. Therefore, it is of vital importance that we appropriately deal with critical and sensitive bilateral issues so as to avoid strategic misjudgment and potential scenarios in which the two powers are forced to engage in confrontation. The DPRK nuclear issue belongs to this category.

It needs to be pointed out that there are quite a few people on both sides of the Pacific Ocean holding pessimistic opinions about the future of Sino-American relations. In particular, there is an anti-China force in the United States that is rather fearful of an increasingly strong China. This group persists in believing that the growth and decline of the relative strength and interests of China and the United States are a zero-sum game, in which gains for China can only come at the expense of American power. This faction also sees the essence of the bilateral relationship in terms of competition; cooperation is superficial, temporary, and expedient, in this group's perspective. If the United States wishes to uphold its global interests and leadership role, the school of thought holds, then the United States needs to build up its capabilities to prevent the rise of China and to deter China's strategic plans before China becomes too powerful and poses real threats to the United States. At present, such a school of opinion has considerable influence in the U.S. government and in the U.S. Congress; unfortunately, it impedes potential progress in Sino-U.S. cooperation, including over the DPRK nuclear issue from time to time.

Because of obvious geopolitical reasons, both China and the United States have significant strategic interests on the Korean Peninsula. The uncertain nature of the Sino-U.S. relationship in the post–Cold War era determined that both sides must prepare for the best, as well as for the worst scenario on the Korean Peninsula. Meanwhile, both China and the United States acknowledge that maintaining peace and stability on the Peninsula is congruent with their fundamental interests; hence the safe management of security on the Peninsula should be their common responsibility. Thus to realize a denuclearized Korean Peninsula is not only the common objective of both countries but also an important subject for bilateral cooperation. At a time when there is much effort to find a durable diplomatic solution to the DPRK nuclear issue, cooperation has remained essential, even if both China and the United States have also had to prepare for a range of contingencies.

There are basic differences in the policy priorities of China and the United States with respect to the Korean Peninsula. For the United States, the utmost concern and overwhelming goal is to dismantle the DPRK's nuclear program. Washington officials have focused on this overriding objective. Meanwhile, China, in the process of seeking a denuclearized Peninsula, attaches equal importance to ensuring that peace and stability on the Korean Peninsula will not be disrupted. Thus, from the very beginning, China proclaimed a three-pronged policy: first, to make unremitting efforts aimed at the denuclearization of the Korean Peninsula; second, to firmly oppose the use of force; and third, to adhere to finding a diplomatic solution. Since the DPRK is a sovereign state, its reasonable concerns ought to be acknowledged. The emphasis on preserving peace and stability on the Korean Peninsula refers to avoiding those external direct causes that could lead to turmoil inside the DPRK or force officials in Pyongyang to take desperate action. For this reason, China opposes using external pressure or other means to pursue "regime change" in the DPRK. Similarly, China has been reluctant to push the DPRK nuclear issue before the UN Security Council, or to impose sanctions on North Korea, since these steps would have closed the door to the resumption of diplomacy.

Owing to the differences in their policy goals, China and the United States have naturally advocated different approaches to solving the DPRK nuclear issue. The U.S. diplomatic history witnessed the alternate utilization of carrots and sticks. As for the DPRK nuclear issue, the George W. Bush administration basically gave preference to coercive measures to force the DPRK to give up its nuclear program. Washington's rationale was simple: the United States could not hold direct talks with North Korea because it was untrustworthy and a member of an "Axis of Evil." By joining in the Six-Party Talks, the United States hoped to transform the mechanism into a diplomatic instrument, exerting pressure on the DPRK. China has different considerations. First, China disagreed with Washington's logic. As soon as Washington labeled Pyongyang a member of the "Axis of Evil," the United States injected a notion of "original sin" and that the DPRK should be denied its sovereign rights. Such a conditional starting point deprived the dialogue of a sense of equality. China held, that in order to solve the DPRK nuclear issue, one must recognize the complex background of the issue and treat earnestly treat the reasonable concerns of the DPRK. The profound bilateral mistrust caused by long-term hostility and an increasingly grave sense of insecurity on the DPRK side are undeniable and realistic reasons for problems over North Korea's nuclear program. As the major parties concerned, the United States and the DPRK must conduct direct dialogue so as to solve the DPRK nuclear crisis and reduce tension on the Korean Peninsula. The Six-Party Talks are a platform for dialogue—tailor-made for the United States and the DPRK by China—to address bilateral issues through multilateral means. China also hosted trilateral dialogues, consisting of the United States and the DPRK, in Beijing in April 2003 as a prelude to the Six-Party Talks. But the resumption of the Six-Party Talks in February 2007 was only because of a mutual consent to a more flexible and equal starting point for negotiations.

BE A LOYAL BROKER

The basic standpoints, policy goals, and the unique position of China with reference to the DRPK nuclear issue have defined China's role as a loyal broker. China is one of the three signing parties of the armistice agreement, the closest neighboring country of the Korean Peninsula, with which it shares a common border, and the founding member of the Four-Party Talks, addressing the first round of the DPRK nuclear crisis. What is more, China has incorporated the major concerns of the United States, the DPRK, the ROK, Russia, and Japan into its own standpoints and policy goals.

The fact that the United States and the DPRK—the most directly concerned two parties—failed to conduct direct dialogue due to the extreme distrust between them, constituted not only the main reason for China to play the role of the honest broker but was also the key obstacle to the Six-Party Talks. China persisted in believing that despite their conflicting positions and deep distrust, there was still common ground between Washington and Pyongyang. The February 13, 2007, breakthrough in resuming the Six-Party Talks provides new impetus to discover and exploit this common ground and build a process of expanding consensus. Between August 2003 and April 2007, China hosted in Beijing six rounds of Six-Party Talks. During the talks and throughout the whole period, China played an active role as a loyal broker and worked together with all sides to facilitate dialogue between the United States and North Korea, discussed various schemes to solve differences, deepened mutual understanding, and identified the sticking points of particular issues and the potential steps forward to make progress. The most outstanding achievements have been the Joint Statement delivered at the end of the fourth round of Six-Party Talks in September 2005, and the new framework of February 2007. The

2005 joint declaration, based on the draft proposed by China, outlined the following provisions:

- The DPRK is committed to abandoning all nuclear weapons and existing nuclear programs and returning, at an early date, to the Nuclear Non-Proliferation Treaty (NPT) and to International Atomic Energy Agency (IAEA) safeguards.
- The United States affirmed that it has no nuclear weapons on the Korean Peninsula and has no intention to attack or invade the DPRK with nuclear or conventional weapons.
- The DPRK stated that it has the right to peaceful uses of nuclear energy. The other parties expressed their respect and agreed to discuss, at an appropriate time, the subject of the provision of light-water reactors to the DPRK.
- The directly related parties will negotiate a permanent peace regime on the Korean Peninsula at an appropriate separate forum.

Although different parties may interpret the above provisions in their own way, it is indeed a significant achievement to confirm the commitments in an official document. It is true that both the United States and the DPRK made respective compromises. The international community generally believed that the Six-Party Talks had renewed hope for a diplomatic resolution of the North Korean nuclear crisis and gave credit to China for its successful diplomacy.

It is true that the DPRK nuclear issue is still unresolved. The phase two discussion of the fifth round of the Six-Party Talks was put in abeyance after October 2005. On July 5, 2006, the DPRK disregarded the warning of the international community and outrageously test-fired seven missiles, suddenly reviving tensions. The UN Security Council unanimously adopted Resolution 1695, demanding suspension of all related ballistic missile activity and urging the DPRK to return immediately to the Six-Party Talks without precondition. China also voted for the resolution. Unfortunately, the DPRK rejected the UN resolution. China also supported further UN action—UN Security Council Resolution 1718—following North Korea's October 2006 nuclear weapon test. Many observers interpreted China's support for these resolutions as a signal of policy change. This trend in Sino-DPRK relations and the future role of China regarding the Korean Peninsula, have drawn worldwide attention.

But China has no reason to change its policy goals concerning the DPRK nuclear issue since it tallies with the fundamental interest of all relevant parties. It is inevitable that the DPRK partly resented China's votes, but China-DPRK relations did not undergo significant change because of them. China persevered in promoting the Six-Party Talks and on February 13,

2007, a diplomatic breakthrough ended the impasse and eased tensions once again. Peace and security can best be maintained by making use of the Six-Party Talks to find a lasting settlement to the DPRK nuclear issue.

NOTE

1. The Korean Armistice Agreement was signed on July 27, 1953, ending three years of war. The signatories were: the United Nations Command, which represented sixteen U.N. member states that had committed troops to Korea under U.N. Security Council resolutions of June 27 and July 7, 1950; and the military commands of North Korea and China. The South Korean (ROK) Government refused to sign, although it declared that it would not obstruct implementation of the pact.

9

Engaging the United States and China: North Korea's Missile and Nuclear Tests

Narushige Michishita

On July 5, 2006, the Democratic People's Republic of Korea (DPRK or North Korea), launched seven ballistic missiles, including several *Scud* and *No-dong* missiles and one *Taepo-dong* 2 missile, in the Sea of Japan. While the *Scud* and *No-dong* missiles were successfully launched, the *Taepo-dong* 2 apparently failed to fly as designed. Then on October 9, 2006, only two months after the missile tests, North Korea conducted a nuclear test. This chapter examines these unprecedented tests and their implications for regional security.

LESSONS FROM THE JULY 2006 MISSILE TESTS

There are several analytical points that can be drawn from the July 2006 missile test. First, it involved the largest number of missiles that the North Koreans have launched in any single day. In May 1993 they launched three *Scuds* and one *No-dong* over two days. In August 1998 one *Taepo-dong* 1 was launched solo, without accompanying missiles. In this sense the July 2006 missile launch was a combined and expanded replay of the 1993 and 1998 missile launches to test the missiles' technological maturity and impress the United States, Japan, and other concerned nations.

A second notable aspect of the missile test relates to the direction in which the missiles were fired. The *Taepo-dong* 2 seems to have been launched to the east in the direction of Hawaii, as was its shorter version in 1998. The *Scud* and *No-dong* missiles flew over the narrow corridor between the

Russian Far East and Hokkaido, unlike the May 1993 tests in which they were launched in the direction of Tokyo. One can infer from this trajectory that the North Koreans sought to avoid bringing the situation too close to the brink by once again testing missiles over Japan. The difference between the different tests is that in 1993 the *No-dong* was still in the experimental stage; now it is fully operational and deployed in large numbers. A launch of operational missiles toward the Japanese capital, even if they fell well short of the target, would have created an extremely dangerous situation. It is, in this context, interesting that the North Korean official news agency reported about three weeks after the missile launch that the, "DPRK launched missiles only after airspace, land and waters of the sea had been confirmed to be completely safe from them. Their launches, therefore, hurt neither ships nor civilian planes nor anyone."[1] In this sense, at least, the 2006 missile launch was controlled and "limited."

The flip side of the coin, however, is that North Korea has reserved the option to further escalate the situation by launching missiles toward highly populated areas, such as Tokyo, in the future. In April 2003 North Korea warned that, "Japan should behave with discretion, clearly mindful that it is also within the striking range of the DPRK."[2] It should not be surprising if North Korea uses the same rhetoric again. The option of conducting future tests over Japan would have the merit—from North Korea's perspective— of being able to escalate tensions without conducting another nuclear test, which would be deemed even more provocative. Moreover, if North Korea were to launch only *No-dong* missiles, it might be difficult for Japan and the United States to detect and prepare for such a test.

Third, North Korea did not characterize the *Taepo-dong* launch as an attempted satellite launch as it did in 1998. Just after the missile launch, North Korea's Ministry of Foreign Affairs announced that the "missile launches" were "part of routine military exercises staged by the KPA [Korean People's Army] to increase the nation's military capacity for self-defense."[3] The North Koreans can still claim that the *Taepo-dong* 2 had carried a satellite, since the Ministry announcement did not specify which missiles they were characterizing as "missiles." But the change in its tone was apparent, and it was consistent with the change in the characterization of their nuclear program. In the 1990s, North Korean officials insisted that their nuclear program was a peaceful one and that they had neither the intention nor the capability to develop nuclear weapons. However, in October 2003 it was announced that they had switched their peaceful nuclear program "in the direction of increasing its nuclear deterrent force" in order to "cope with the situation created by the U.S. hostile policy toward the DPRK."[4] Then, in February 2005, the Foreign Ministry announced that North Korea had "manufactured nukes for self-defence."[5] North Korean officials have clearly defined the development of both nuclear weapons and missiles as part of their effort to "bolster [a] deterrent for self-defense."

Fourth, the successful launch of *No-dong* missiles had significant implications for the security of Japan, given the fact that some 200 operational *No-dongs* appear to have been deployed. The *No-dong* is launched from a mobile transporter-erector-launcher, and thus it would make a hard target to destroy on the ground. Given the difficulties that would be involved in trying to neutralize the missiles on the ground prior to the launch, Japan has decided to accelerate the deployment of ballistic missile defenses. Unless one has robust intelligence and a targeting-and-ground-attack capability, then defense is a reasonable choice for dealing with mobile ballistic missiles like the *No-dong*.

Fifth, the *Taepo-dong* 2 is less of an immediate military threat than the *No-dong* or *Scud* given its technological immaturity and its inability to be fired from mobile launchers. Deployed in relatively primitive fixed silos, the *Taepo-dong* missile would be a vulnerable system, easily at risk of preemption in a crisis or war. As a result, accidents caused by technical problems are a more immediate danger than damage caused by deliberate strikes. In fact, given the failure of the *Taepo-dong* launch, the missile could well have landed in Japan and caused collateral damage, including accidental deaths. Moreover, if the missile were directed toward Hawaii as some reports had suggested, its debris could even have landed in the islands. Like the *Taepo-dong* 1 launch in 1998, the *Taepo-dong* 2 posed a limited but real physical threat to Japan and, to a lesser extent, the United States. The *Taepo-dong* 2 launch would have had different implications depending on what kind of payload it was carrying. If it had been fitted with a reentry vehicle, rather than an artificial satellite, the test would have been deemed a much greater threat.

Sixth, since the *Taepo-dong* missile is a vulnerable system, its significance does not lie with its military utility but with its political-diplomatic utility as a weapon of fear and as a bargaining chip. Its significance comes from the psychological impact that it has the potential to reach the Continental United States. One caveat, however, is that precisely because it could be preempted with relative ease in the event of a crisis, the North Koreans might be tempted to use it before it were destroyed. Deployed in fixed silos, the *Taepo-dong* would be a destabilizing, dangerous system.

Finally, before July 2006, some speculated that the North Koreans might launch the *Taepo-dong* 2 toward Alaska or major cities in the Continental United States. However, a launch in the direction of Los Angeles was never likely because the missile would have flown over the vicinity of Vladivostok, Yuzhno-Sakhalinsk, and Petropavlovsk-Kamchatsky. If launched in the direction of Washington, DC, it would have flown over Chinese territories, Khabarovsk, Siberia, and Toronto. Such a launch could have resulted in a crisis involving not only the United States and Canada, but also Russia and China. North Korea was not likely to be willing to take on such additional risks.

THE OCTOBER 2006 NUCLEAR TEST

North Korea conducted a nuclear test on October 9, 2006, but the magnitude of the explosion apparently fell well short of expectations because the chain reaction must have stopped before it was half way completed. While the test marked a major step forward in North Korea's nuclear development, it also clearly showed that North Korea remains a long way from possessing credible and operational nuclear weapons.

Second, even the imperfect nuclear explosion posed a major threat to the security of the region in general and to South Korea and Japan in particular. Both countries are within the range of *Scud* and *No-dong* missiles, which could be used to deliver a nuclear warhead. Thus the nuclear test, combined with the successful launch of these short-range and medium-range missiles, had significant implications for the two countries.

Finally, because of the limited nuclear explosion, North Korea's nuclear status remains disputed. North Korea calls itself "a responsible nuclear weapons state,"[6] while the United States, Japan, and South Korea do not recognize it as such. The room for different interpretations of North Korea's nuclear status provides opportunities and challenges. It provides opportunities in the sense that we can argue that North Korea has still not crossed the threshold to become a nuclear weapon state; but it poses challenges in the sense that it will certainly complicate a process of negotiating an end to North Korea's nuclear programs.

NORTH KOREA'S POLICY OBJECTIVES

The most important diplomatic objective of North Korea's missile and nuclear tests seems to have been to get the United States and Japan back on the engagement track by giving an impression that the North Korean leaders were irrational, unpredictable, confused and, left to their own devices, dangerous. In the past ten years, it has become clear that the North Korean leaders are much more rational than once believed. Under such circumstances, to attract the attention of neighboring countries, the North Koreans had to escalate their actions and make their neighbors think that they were "crazy" after all.

The North Koreans surely had no illusions as to the negative reaction they would receive from the international community, particularly the United States and Japan. Their calculation seems to have been that despite the negative reactions in the short run, continued escalation of the situation would eventually bring even the United States and Japan back to the negotiating table. Past cases, such as the March 1993 announcement to withdraw from the Nuclear Non-Proliferation Treaty (NPT), the August 1998 missile launch, and the January 2003 announcement again to withdraw from the NPT, all eventually led to negotiation. In light of the

February 13, 2007, agreement to resume the Six-Party Talks, perhaps the North Korean calculus was not in error.

By launching missiles and testing the bomb, the North Koreans might have attempted to distract Japanese public attention away from the abduction issue. Since Kim Jong-il acknowledged in September 2002 the involvement of North Korean agents in the abduction cases, "the North Korea issue" in Japan, except for policymakers and analysts involved in military and strategic affairs, has become that of the abduction issue, and not the nuclear or missile issue. In fact, North Korea had invited Japanese journalists to Pyongyang to take a look at "evidence" of the deaths of the Japanese abductees, including Megumi Yokota who had become for many Japanese a symbol of North Korean perfidy. The Japanese media, invited to report on the abduction issue in July 2006, ended up covering the missile launch.

It is widely accepted now that the North Koreans did not inform the Chinese of the missile launch in advance of the event. At the time of the nuclear test, they did so, but only at the last minute. This failure to communicate an important event in advance almost surely offended North Korea's comrades in China. Of course, given North Korea's policy objective of delivering an international shock, it was only natural that Pyongyang kept quiet about what was to happen.

First, both North Korea and China have long sought to encourage the United States to seriously negotiate a deal with North Korea. But the United States had not responded positively to the overture and, instead, urged China to take the lead, engage North Korea, and bear both political and economic burdens. The Chinese then claimed that their influence over North Korea was severely limited and that the nuclear issue would not be solved without serious U.S. engagement. In this context, it was understandable for North Korea to attempt to demonstrate how the Chinese could not stop it from acting ruthlessly, and suggest that only the United States could do the job. The Chinese leaders certainly lost face, but such a consequence was consistent with their claim that they did not have much influence over North Korea. The Chinese leaders must have understood what the North Koreans were trying to accomplish, and the return to diplomacy orchestrated by China in early 2007 suggested that they had used the heightened crisis atmosphere after the tests to reinitiate diplomacy.

Second, there seems to have been a new element in North Korea's diplomacy: namely, the use of brinkmanship vis-à-vis China. Faced with the rapidly increasing economic and human interactions with China, North Korea has become increasingly concerned about the detrimental consequences of a close bilateral relationship with a modernizing China. For instance, North Korea had become deeply dissatisfied with the way China was managing a joint Chinese-North Korean glass factory and natural resource extraction project. The North Korean government insisted on running these activities in a socialist manner. North Koreans are interested in increased economic cooperation with China, but they are worried about the growing Chinese influence over economic affairs in their country.[7] In addition, they seem to have been frustrated by the Chinese decision to let the North Korean bank accounts in Macao be shut down, and by the slow Chinese effort to convince Americans to lift the financial "sanctions." By conducting the missile and nuclear tests in the face of Chinese objections, the North Koreans might have been expressing their determination to defy excessive Chinese influence over their internal affairs. If this speculation is correct, North Korean diplomacy entered a new era via the exercise of brinkmanship with its closest traditional ally. Of course, North Korea has long maintained an ultra-realist policy of playing one actor against another vis-à-vis the United States, China, Japan, and South Korea, driving a wedge in their relationships whenever possible.

Some analysts contend that the missile tests were intended to demonstrate missile capabilities to potential customers and, in fact, Iranian representatives were in North Korea for the July 5, 2006, launch. However, arms sales is probably not one of the primary reasons for the tests, if only because the missile and nuclear tests were intended to invite uproar in the international community, which in turn would make it difficult for potential customers to buy advanced weapons from North Korea.

There are several possible reasons why North Korea conducted the missile and nuclear tests in the second half of 2006. First, midterm elections in the United States were to be held in November, and a divisive policy debate was expected to take place between Republicans and Democrats in the weeks running up to the election. In fact, some Democratic members of Congress and foreign policy advisers were starting to argue that the Bush policy toward North Korea had failed and that direct U.S.-DPRK talks were needed to address the nuclear and missile issues. The North Koreans might well have hoped that the missile and nuclear tests would fuel such a debate within the United States. On June 21, North Korea's official Korean Central News Agency (KCNA) reported that, "Voices accusing the U.S. administration of its Korea policy and calling for DPRK-U.S. direct talks for a solution to the nuclear issue are growing louder in the U.S. political circles these days." The report from Pyongyang went on to cite the pro-negotiation argument set forth by former U.S. Deputy Secretary of State Richard Armitage and Senator Joseph Biden, among others.[8]

Second, the European Union (EU) made a package proposal to Iran regarding its nuclear program in June 2006. The proposal indicated the EU's willingness to provide light-water reactors to Iran in return for Iran's pledge to freeze its nuclear program. The proposal had a lot in common with the 1994 U.S.-DPRK Agreed Framework. Although North Korea remained silent on this proposal, it might have thought that the same kind of deal could be struck with regard to its nuclear program.

Third, the missile and nuclear tests were a way for North Korea to express its defiance to the freezing of its foreign assets in Macao's Banco Delta Asia and the Bank of China; the strengthened law enforcement measures were ostensibly aimed against North Korea's illegal activities such as counterfeiting, but North Korea viewed them as financial sanctions in the midst of a nuclear negotiation. However, the relationship between the ends and means in this regard was not very clear. It was easily anticipated that the missile launch would encourage the United States, Japan, and even China to strengthen their efforts to crack down on North Korea's illicit activities. In fact, these countries moved to increase pressure on North Korea immediately following these events. Some interpreted the North Korean actions as desperate attempts to circumvent the strengthened sanctions on the part of the United States and other countries; but it was more likely that the North Koreans assessed that they could put up with increased pressure when they conducted the missile and nuclear tests. Otherwise, these actions would have been self-destructive. In sum, the North Koreans had decided to escalate in the short run to ease pressure on it in the longer run. In their calculations, the missile and nuclear tests were the first step to force the United States and Japan to come back to a posture of engagement and not regime change.

Finally, related to the previous point, the North Korean leaders might have decided to conduct the missile and nuclear tests to consolidate domestic unity. On October 20, 2006, eleven days after the nuclear test, "more than a hundred thousand servicepersons and citizens from all walks of life" were mobilized for a rally at the Kim Il-sung Square to hail the "historic successful nuclear test."[9] And the North Korean authorities have reportedly been using the nuclear test to make the people take pride in their country and their leaders. Since the North Korean government embarked on economic reform in 2002, free-market economy has been growing rapidly in the country. As the people of North Korea have become more self-reliant and less dependent on the government, they have become less respectful of the government and their leaders, particularly Kim Jong-il. The gap between the government and the people seems to have been growing. The missile and nuclear tests may well have been aimed at filling this widening divide between the government and the people in North Korea.

REGIONAL RESPONSE

After the missile launch, Japan was quick to submit a draft resolution condemning North Korea to the United Nations Security Council that invoked Chapter VII of the UN Charter. Although the United States and Japan strongly condemned the missile launch, they eventually accepted a Chinese demand to drop reference to Chapter VII—which would have made implementation mandatory and not voluntary on UN member states. As a result, the UN Security Council Resolution 1695, without mentioning

Chapter VII, called on member states to prevent missile and missile-related items, materials, goods, and technology from being transferred to or procured from North Korea; it also called on states to prevent the transfer of any financial resources in relation to North Korea's missile or weapons of mass destruction programs. The United States and Japan conceded to the Chinese demand, but obtained a binding resolution, which they could use when they wanted to increase pressure. The resolution did not automatically lead to sanctions, but it paved the way for strengthening the Proliferation Security Initiative (PSI) and provided a pretext for intensifying the pressure in the future. In addition, the resolution would discourage potential buyers and sellers, be they states or nonstate actors, interested in doing business with North Korea. Preventing such transactions in the first place is always better than dealing with them after the fact, and this was indeed the idea underpinning preventative measures like the PSI.

After the nuclear test, the UN adopted Resolution 1718 on October 14, which invoked Chapter VII and called on all member states to take action, including the inspection of cargo to and from North Korea to prevent illicit trafficking in nuclear, chemical, or biological weapons. However, these sanctions were not aimed at harming the North Korean people or even at overthrowing the North Korean regime. They were aimed specifically at stopping or at least slowing down North Korea's weapons programs. In this sense, they are not general sanctions, but "smart" sanctions aimed specifically at North Korea's destabilizing behavior. At the same time, Resolution 1718 demanded North Korea return to the Six-Party Talks to work toward the implementation of the Joint Statement of the Six-Party Talks issued in September 2005.

Despite the strong rhetoric, the United States and Japan only moderately strengthened their pressure on North Korea after the missile and nuclear tests. They continued to crack down on North Korea's illegal activities and those who attempted to provide North Korea with nuclear or missile-related materials and equipment. But they neither significantly increased pressure nor imposed drastic sanctions. There were several reasons for this. First, the United States and Japan feared that putting too much pressure on North Korea could have encouraged China and South Korea, which were deeply concerned about possible instability in North Korea, to side with or even help North Korea survive the pressure. The division between the United States and Japan on the one hand and China and South Korea on the other would require a balance to be struck between applying pressure on North Korea and keeping the outside powers united in their approach.

Second, it was the Bush administration's policy not to react positively to provocation. North Korea had always attempted to draw attention from the United States and the international community with bad behavior. It coerced to negotiate and reconcile, especially with the United States. These tactics worked fairly well, partly because we did not know how rational or irrational the North Koreans leaders, and particularly Kim Jong-il, were. The Clinton administration hedged against worst-case scenarios by engaging in bilateral negotiations with them. But matters had changed. In the past ten years, it had become clear that the North Korean leaders were far more rational than previously believed. Despite all the aggressive rhetoric, North Korea had refrained from any physical attack on Americans since 1981, when North Korea launched surface-to-air missiles at a U.S. SR 71 reconnaissance aircraft (which they missed). North Korea had ended its active interactions with foreign terrorist groups.[10] In recent years, Kim Jong-il had met all of the top leaders of major concerned countries except the United States. Kim's frequent international exposure had demonstrated that however idiosyncratic his aims might be, he was a calculating and rational actor.

As a result, the situation had been created where the United States and other parties could relatively safely assume that North Korea would not take self-destructive actions, such as using nuclear weapons or exporting nuclear weapons to third parties, let alone terrorist groups. This had two opposite effects on North Korea. On the one hand, the North Koreans had become people with whom one could do business. This is why the United States signed the Agreed Framework in 1994 and Secretary of State Madeleine Albright visited North Korea in 2000. Even the Bush administration decided in February 2007 that it could or should negotiate with North Korea without resorting to tougher sanctions, not to mention "preemption." On the other hand, the United States had become more relaxed than before in dealing with North Korea. In 1994 the United States planned a preemptive strike against North Korean nuclear facilities at Yongbyon when Pyongyang started to unload 8,000 spent fuel rods, which supposedly contained enough plutonium for several nuclear weapons. A decade later, in 2003, the United States had not even filed a case in the UN Security Council when North Korea started reprocessing the same spent fuel or after it declared the possession of nuclear weapons.

Third, the United States sought to use this opportunity to delegate to China the diplomatic leadership for engaging North Korea, while Washington and Tokyo focused on the containment of North Korea. In fact, China's ability to engage North Korea has improved significantly in the past ten years, and it is capable of playing the leading role in engagement policy toward North Korea. When North Korea announced its withdrawal from the NPT in 1993, it was only four years after the Tiananmen incident. China's future was still unpredictable. Some argued that China would grow into a strong and rich nation, while others contended that it might disintegrate due to mounting political and socioeconomic pressure. China was busy taking care of its interests, and did not have room to make a substantial commitment to North Korea.

Today, China's rise has become a solid assumption on which major powers base their foreign and security policies. China takes a strong leadership role in organizing and convening the Six-Party Talks, which it helped to establish in 2003. Since 2000 trade between China and North Korea has grown annually by an average of 30 percent, contributing to an estimated 3.5 percent annual growth rate for the North Korean economy. In 2005, China's trade with North Korea totaled $1.3 billion, up from $488 million in 2000.[11] In October 2005, when President Hu Jintao visited Pyongyang, China and North Korea signed the Agreement on Economic and Technological Cooperation.[12] China has become the most important external partner for the North Korean economy.

U.S. policy toward North Korea in the 1990s was one of direct engagement based on bilateral talks and agreements. It became, until 2007, one of indirect engagement combined with containment, in which diplomatic leadership was delegated to China. Ten years ago, the United States was the only player capable of credibly engaging North Korea. Now, combined with South Korea's active engagement policy, which has become much more robust in the past ten years, China can credibly engage and manage North Korea. Under such circumstances, the United States has felt less obligated to directly engage North Korea. In this context, while the United States supports the Six-Party Talks and talks to the North Koreans in that framework, it had become reluctant until February 2007 to play a more active diplomatic role. North Korea's policy objectives and military-diplomatic conduct did not dramatically change on either July 5 or October 9, 2006. However, the strategic environment surrounding it had changed dramatically in the past ten years.

NORTH KOREA'S POLICY OPTIONS

As a result of the changed regional environment, North Korea could not achieve its objective of inviting strong reaction, that in turn could lead to serious and meaningful talks with the United States. At first, the missile and nuclear tests created a political environment in the United States in which it was more difficult for its leaders to negotiate a deal with North Korea. Policy options available to North Korea remained the same as before: North Korea could make a "strategic decision" to abandon nuclear weapons, or it could keep muddling through with help from China and South Korea. By early 2007, with American compromises over financial sanctions and a more incremental approach to nuclear negotiations, North Korea returned to the Six-Party Talks with only an initial commitment of shutting down its plutonium reactor. Thus, the escalation did spur negotiation with the United States, while leaving all of North Korea's options on the table.

In the coming years, it will be interesting to see whether the North Koreans stay on a diplomatic path, a path of muddling through, or opt for a more aggressive path. In the late 1990s, more than two years after the *Taepo-dong* launch, they neither escalated the situation by launching missiles, nor made a "strategic decision" to normalize relations with the United States in response to the active engagement policy suggested by a "Review of United States Policy Toward North Korea: Findings and Recommendations" (commonly referred to as the Perry Report after former Secretary of Defense William Perry).[13] After the extremely active bilateral U.S.-DPRK talks, exemplified by Secretary of State Madeleine Albright's visit to Pyongyang, North Korea in the end relented.

In 2006, the North Koreans must have reactivated their nuclear and missile diplomacy without any illusion that it would produce positive results in a short period of time. It was only the beginning of a long process. When they launched the *Taepo dong* 1 in August 1998, two and a half years remained in President Bill Clinton's term in office. When they launched missiles in July 2006, two and a half years remained for President George W. Bush's term in office. North Korea's sense of timing remains the same as in the 1990s. What changed was not North Korea but the United States; and thus in February 2007 Washington backed off its earlier approach and accepted a China-brokered deal that allowed the resumption of the Six-Party Talks.

North Korea's long-term objective seemed all along to achieve something akin to the 1994 Agreed Framework between the DPRK and the United States. Short-term escalation was the preferred North Korean path to both arrangements. When North Korea escalates, it also demands that the United States engage in serious bilateral talks. The United States responded in the 1990s; the United States again responded after 2006. The joint statement on February 13, 2007, allowed the parties to return to a September 2005 diplomatic framework; matters did indeed seem to come full circle. Every time North Korea uses provocative actions, it uses other countries' actions or inaction as an excuse. North Korea would still have been able to wait out the Bush administration and negotiate a bilateral deal with the next, preferably Democratic, administration from a position of strength; by the end of George W. Bush's term in office, North Korea would have further built up its nuclear and missile arsenal. As it stands in the spring of 2007, North Korea has de-escalated the crisis after having improved its nuclear and missile weapons programs.

In the coming months and years, should diplomacy again falter, North Korea can also take various types of actions to escalate the situation and raise tensions. It could again launch missiles, embark on additional construction and operation of its nuclear facilities, and test nuclear bombs. Or it could violate the Northern Limit Line—a quasi-maritime borderline between the North and the South—by naval ships and fighter aircraft, conduct armed demonstrations in the Joint Security Area in Panmunjom, or actively cross the Military Demarcation Line—the North–South border since the end of the Korean War–in the Demilitarized Zone. It might also threaten U.S. reconnaissance aircraft or Japanese and South Korean vessels and aircraft operating in the Sea of Japan. In short, North Korea will retain any number of ways to heighten tensions in the future should it deem it necessary to do so.

Finally, one caveat should be made. The North Koreans are a voracious user of surprise, both negative and positive. While surprising us with missile and nuclear tests, they might be preparing to surprise us with positive diplomatic actions. Given the domestic situations of its neighbors, South Korea might be the most attractive target for such an initiative. The two Koreas held a summit meeting precisely one year after a North–South naval clash reportedly killed several tens of North Korean sailors in June 1999. While we watch out for negative surprises, we have to do the same with positive ones.

FUTURE PROSPECTS

In the years ahead, there are broadly two different paths that North Korea could take. At one end of the spectrum, North Korea could pursue more actively the strategy of bandwagoning with the United States, and decide to make a "strategic decision" to renounce nuclear weapons. If this happened, U.S. policy would be the single most important factor determining the outcome of North Korea's strategy. Even if North Korea were to make a major concession, it would be useless unless the United States made its own "strategic decision" to accept the policy of solving the nuclear issue at the cost of having to downplay human rights and other issues of concern. At the other end of the spectrum, North Korea could shift its strategic focus away from the United States to China. If North Korea were to do so, it might mean that it would regard China not only as a guarantor of its regime survival but also as its strategic partner as it did during the Cold War. Somewhere in the middle of the two extremes lies the scenario in which North Korea would follow a policy of equidistance toward the United States and Japan on the one hand and China on the other. In yet another scenario, North Korea could let talks carry on with the express purpose of waiting out the Bush administration in order to negotiate a strategic deal with the next U.S. president, preferably one—from Pyongyang's perspective—less interested in preemption, regime change, and sanctions than President Bush.

The United States

Prior to 2007, the Bush administration seemed committed to taking a long-term strategic approach to the North Korea issue rather than a short-term tactical approach. The United States adopted what it called a "bold approach" and demanded that North Korea make a "strategic decision" about its nuclear program.[14] In other words, the Bush policy sought a broader and more conclusive solution to the North Korean nuclear issue than the 1994

Agreed Framework, be it a "strategic decision" or regime change. In order to encourage North Korea to make the "strategic decision," the United States sought to use wide-ranging policy measures such as the PSI and a crackdown on the money laundering, drug trafficking, and counterfeiting of the North Koreans. These so-called "smart sanctions" targeted North Korea's leadership. They aimed to dry up sources of income for the North Korean leadership while minimizing the negative effects on its people.[15] The U.S. Treasury's decision in September 2005 to designate Macau-based Banco Delta Asia as a "primary money laundering concern" was an important example of such a policy.[16] Another example was the passage of the North Korean Human Rights Act passed by the U.S. Congress in October 2004.

Before 2007, one problem with this bold approach was whether indirect pressure would produce the desired results within a reasonable amount of time. Based on North Korea's escalatory actions in the latter half of 2006, it is widely assessed that the Banco Delta Asia case indeed significantly affected the North Korean leadership. But the case can now be made that North Korea abandoned the Six-Party Talks in the autumn of 2005 in response to the financial sanctions, escalated in the latter half of 2006 with missile and nuclear tests, and then accepted a more limited U.S. overture to return to Six-Party Talks in February 2007. The sanctions had an impact, but the United States compromised by accepting an immediate goal of lowering tensions and resuming talks and putting aside its longer-term goal of a more comprehensive agreement. Instead, all sides returned to a limited, step-by-step approach ostensibly made possible by the releasing of frozen assets in the Banco Delta Asia.

While the United States put additional pressure on North Korea, Pyongyang produced additional fissile material on its soil. In June 2006, it was reported that North Korea might have eight to seventeen nuclear weapons.[17] North Korea's enlarged nuclear arsenal might or might not help diplomacy in the longer run. It could make North Korea more secure to negotiate, but it could just as easily make it less likely that North Korea would ever part with its presumed nuclear arsenal.

Until the 2007 U.S. compromise, Washington had demanded that North Korea eliminate its nuclear program in a short period of time. However, concerned about the loss of its deterrence and bargaining power, North Korea was never likely to readily give up its nuclear program. In addition, both the Bush administration and the Congress remained tough on North Korea, and were more engaged over the situation in Iraq and Iran than over North Korea. More fundamentally, there remains doubt over the ultimate U.S. goal: to encourage the North Korean regime to take positive diplomatic steps toward denuclearization, or to undermine the regime. U.S. policymakers have often appeared divided on this basic point. A grand bargain with North Korea will certainly require a firm decision on the part of both North Korea and the United States.

Japan

In September 2002, Prime Minister Junichiro Koizumi took a bold approach of his own when he visited North Korea and signed the Pyongyang Declaration calling for normalization. But the revelation that the North Korean authorities had actually abducted Japanese citizens and the reemergence of the nuclear issue prevented the two countries from moving ahead with normalization. First, resolving the abduction issue is not easy. For one thing, the North Korean authorities have claimed that some of the confirmed abductees were already dead. The Japanese government demanded convincing evidence of their deaths, but the North Koreans have been reluctant, or possibly unable, to present such evidence. For another matter, in addition to the confirmed abductees, there is supposedly a larger number of unconfirmed abductees. Since it is practically impossible to find out the whereabouts of all of them, Japan and North Korea will at some point have to make a political decision that the abduction issue has been "resolved" or is at least a matter of routine cooperation. However, it will not be easy, particularly for Japanese leaders, to put an end to the highly politicized abduction issue. Second, the reemergence of the nuclear issue in 2002 precluded the option of bilateral normalization without first solving the nuclear issue. Bilateral talks between Japan and North Korea have taken place separately from the Six-Party Talks, but the former cannot go too far ahead of the latter.

In the fall of 2006, one would have predicted that the most likely scenario for the near future would have been for the United States and Japan to stick to a path of "containment" as spelled out in the 1999 Perry Report. Faced with a diplomatic impasse, the two countries might have just continued to take steps to bolster their defense capabilities. In 2005 the United States had deployed fifteen F-117 stealth bombers in the Kunsan Air Force Base in South Korea. In October 2005, the United States and Japan jointly released the Security Consultative Committee Document, entitled, "U.S.-Japan Alliance: Transformation and Realignment for the Future," in which they agreed to improve several specific areas of cooperation, including ballistic missile defense, the PSI, consequence management preparations for responding to any weapon of mass destruction attack, and the joint transportation, use of facilities, medical support, and other related activities for noncombatant evacuation operations.[18] Japan was slated to start deploying ballistic missile defense systems in 2007. The resumption of Six-Party Talks in early 2007 called into question the future extent of tighter containment and stronger defense.

China

Despite its rhetoric that the country is "self-reliant" (the meaning often associated with North Korea's ideology of *Juche*), North Korea has always sought to find patronage among the great powers. In the Cold War period, the Soviet Union and China provided such patronage. After the end of the Cold War, North Korea lost the commitment from these communist friends, and started to seek the alternative patronage of the United States.

After ten years of struggle, North Korea has come to realize two things: one is that the United States might not be willing to provide such patronage; the other is that China, together with South Korea, could become North Korea's new patron. Both China and South Korea have increased their strategic weight in the past ten years and have become willing to make a stronger commitment to the survival of the North Korean regime. North Korea might not be able to balance against the United States in conjunction with China and South Korea; however, it might be able to adopt a policy of equidistance toward the United States and Japan on the one hand and China and South Korea on the other.

There are limits to this option, however. First, North Korea must alter its behavior in order to obtain fuller support from China. China would require North Korea to freeze, or at least slow down, its nuclear and missile development, refrain from conducting in brinkmanship diplomacy and engaging in wide-scale illicit activities, and not take any other actions that might destabilize the region. In fact, the missile and nuclear tests greatly offended and frustrated China. China would loath to see North Korea give ammunition to strengthen the U.S.-Japan alliance and their development of combined missile defense and other defense capabilities. However, without brinkmanship and illicit activities, North Korea's diplomatic influence would be seriously limited and the vitality of its leadership significantly undermined. Moreover, North Korea's economic dependence on China has deepened rapidly. If this trend continues, North Korea's freedom of action will gradually be undercut. In the long run, North Korea should also be concerned about the United States and China cutting a strategic deal to attempt regime change in North Korea.

Second, moving too close to China might make it more difficult for North Korea to normalize its relations with the United States. The United States chose a multilateral forum—the Six-Party Talks—partly because it hoped that China would shoulder the burden of managing North Korea. Heavily engaged in Iraq, Afghanistan, and facing challenges from Iran, the United States welcomed an increased Chinese commitment to North Korea since that would free the United States from the business of engaging North Korea. It may be that the original U.S. hope will be realized. North Korea moving closer to China would also mean that Japan would become discouraged from taking an active engagement policy toward North Korea. North Korea's chance of obtaining substantial economic assistance from Japan might diminish.

Third, related to the second point, China might avoid taking full responsibility for managing an irresponsible North Korea. The Chinese policy has long been that of urging the United States and North Korea to come to a deal and normalize their bilateral relations. China hopes the United States will take care of North Korea as the United States does China.

South Korea

There are also limits to North Korea's option of choosing South Korea as a strategic partner. Although the Roh Moo-hyun administration had been strongly committed to an active engagement policy toward the North, South Korea is still allied with the United States even while that alliance undergoes severe strains. If pressed hard, South Korea could choose the United States and discard North Korea as a partner. In addition, the South Korea's new president, elected in December 2007, may well bring about a change in South Korean priorities. While the engagement policy will likely survive, the tone and nuance of South Korea's engagement of the North is likely to evolve.

NOTES

1. "KCNA Blasts Rice's Outcry," *KCNA*, July 24, 2006, available at http://www.kcna.co.jp/item/2006/200607/news07/25.htm.

2. "KCNA Urges Japan to Behave with Discretion," *KCNA*, April 9, 2003, available at http://www.kcna.co.jp/item/2003/200304/news04/10.htm.

3. "DPRK Foreign Ministry Spokesman on Its Missile Launches," *KCNA*, July 6, 2006, available at http://www.kcna.co.jp/item/2006/200607/news07/07.htm.

4. "DPRK to Continue Increasing Its Nuclear Deterrent Force," *KCNA*, October 2, 2003, as published at http://www.globalsecurity.org/wmd/library/news/dprk/2003/10/dprk-031003-kcna04.htm.

5. "DPRK FM on Its Stand to Suspend Its Participation in Six-party Talks for Indefinite Period," *KCNA*, February 10, 2005, at http://www.kcna.co.jp/item/2005/200502/news02/11.htm.

6. "DPRK Foreign Ministry Spokesman Totally Refutes UNSC 'Resolution,'" *KCNA*, October 17, 2006, available at http://www.kcna.co.jp/item/2006/200610/news10/18.htm.

7. A Japanese journalist who visited North Korea around the time of the missile launch, interview by author, July 18, 2006.

8. "Direct Talks between DPRK and U.S. Urged," *KCNA*, June 21, 2006.

9. "Servicepersons and Pyongyangites Hail Successful Nuclear Test," *KCNA*, October 20, 2006.

10. Press Conference with Australian Foreign Minister Alexander Downer and Deputy Secretary of State, Commonwealth Parliamentary Offices, Richard L. Armitage, December 13, 2002.

11. Lee Young Hun, "Bug-Jung Muyeog-ui Hyeonhwang-gwa Bughan Gyeongje-e Michineun Yeonghyang (Current Status of North Korea-China Trade and Its Impact on North Korean Economy)", Institute for Monetary and Economic Research, February 13, 2006; Ministry of Unification, "Peace and Prosperity: White Paper on Korean Unification 2005" (Seoul: Ministry of Unification, 2005), 54; and

Ministry of Unification, "Trade Volume between North Korea and Japan," March 2, 2006.

12. "Agreement on Economic and Technological Cooperation Signed between DPRK and China," *KCNA*, October 28, 2005.

13. Dr. William J. Perry, Special Advisor to the President and the Secretary of State, "Review of United States Policy Toward North Korea: Findings and Recommendations," October 12, 1999.

14. "North Korean Nuclear Program," Press Statement, Richard Boucher, Spokesman, Washington, DC, October 16, 2002; "President Bush Discusses Iraq," remarks by President Bush and Polish President Kwasniewski in photo opportunity, Office of the Press Secretary, January.14, 2003; and "Dealing with North Korea's Nuclear Programs," prepared statement of James A. Kelly, Assistant Secretary of State for East Asian and Pacific Affairs, Senate Foreign Relations Committee, 15 July 2004.

15. According to David Asher, North Korea's criminal sector may account for as much as 35–40 percent of its exports and a much larger percentage of its total cash earnings. David L. Asher, "The North Korean Criminal State, Its Ties to Organized Crime, and the Possibility of WMD Proliferation," remarks to the Counter-Proliferation Strategy Group, Woodrow Wilson Center, October 21, 2005.

16. "Treasury Designates Banco Delta Asia as Primary Money Laundering Concern under USA PATRIOT Act," JS-2720, September 15, 2005.

17. David Albright and Paul Brannan, "The North Korean Plutonium Stock Mid-2006," Institute for Science and International Security (ISIS), June 26, 2006, p. 1.

18. "U.S.-Japan Alliance: Transformation and Realignment for the Future," Security Consultative Committee Document by Secretary of State Condolezza Rice, Secretary of Defense Donald Rumsfeld, Minister of Foreign Affairs Machimura, and Minister of State for Defense Yoshinori Ohno, October 29, 2005.

Conclusion: Managing Double Trouble

Patrick M. Cronin

Iran and North Korea are pivotal security challenges. Together they amass an arduous array of troubles: flashpoints for war, catalysts for nuclear proliferation, spoilers for alliance management, burdens for weak regional security mechanisms, and wild cards in the deck of major power relations and global institutions. At a minimum, Iran and North Korea hold some of the keys to stability and order in their respective regions. Successfully managing the quandaries they create will be one of the litmus tests for international statecraft throughout the coming decade. How Western and other international leaders manage this pair of countries will, to a large extent, shape the future of regional security in the Middle East and Northeast Asia and perhaps determine the pace of global nuclear proliferation.

THE NEED FOR STATECRAFT AND DIALOGUE

Statecraft, including diplomacy backed by force, has not fared particularly well in coping with this thorny duo during the past ten years. Neither Iran nor North Korea has buckled under the threat of sanction or even force—including veiled references to the possible use of tactical nuclear weapons.[1] In fact, if any country has successfully demonstrated its coercive diplomacy skills, it would appear to be both Iran and North Korea: the former by managing to turn a deaf ear to the remonstrances and sanctions of the UN Security Council, while simultaneously snatching British sailors and plunging deeper into uranium enrichment; the latter by responding to a freeze on some of its foreign holdings, by walking away from multilateral negotiations and launching a fusillade of missiles and conducting a nuclear test. In the case of North Korea, the escalatory steps appear to have been a pivotal factor in wringing a concession from the United States and reinitiating multilateral security negotiations in early 2007.

A security paradox for our time is that complex security problems demand political solutions, but even in our era marked by the information revolution, states cannot muster the political will to sustain direct diplomatic dialogue. Diplomatic surge may be able to find, over time, a peaceful resolution to the challenges of Iran and North Korea; but the United States has not even been interested or able to sustain steady and direct diplomatic contact with each of these countries. The challenge of managing Iran and North Korea is more like a multiday cricket test match than an Olympic sprint: time, patience, perhaps even myriad tea breaks, and a long-term strategic outlook will be essential to the successful handling of relations. This is easier said than done. The United States has difficulty achieving a consistent application of diplomacy. The Clinton administration's Agreed Framework between the United States and North Korea eventually foundered on a lack of political support within the United States for maintaining engagement in the midst of vexatious interpretations of North Korea's actions and inactions. Similarly, the George W. Bush administration's "bold approach" for dealing with North Korea also suffered from a deficit of political backing, albeit mostly in international circles and, then, within the administration itself. Policies for reining in Iran's nuclear programs have also fluctuated in recent years, and attempts at sustained, official, and high-level diplomatic contact between the United States and Iran have proven elusive since the founding of the Islamic Republic in 1979.

If only patience were the answer, then all might be left well enough drifting along. Unfortunately, one of the reasons for America's mood swings has been to make belated adjustments to policy in response to revised readings of the intentions and capabilities of Iran and North Korea. Each of these two countries has its own internal dynamics, security dilemmas, and regional ambitions, and all of these realities combine to create a diplomatic dynamic as complex as chaos theory. In the case of Iran, a specific concern is that the moment for freezing its enrichment program may have come and gone, paving the way for Iran to fashion a covert nuclear weapon even if engaged in dialogue. In the case of North Korea, negotiations are stretched out with great alacrity much like unproductive labor—with great effort over lengthy periods without giving birth.

THE LIMITS OF COERCION

Coercion is an integral part of international diplomacy, particularly the international diplomacy of major powers. History is replete with illustrations showing the high cost of war in blood and treasure. History is equally able to document the failure of diplomacy alone to prevent aggression. These sober facts make clear why policymakers often resort to the middle ground of utilizing diplomacy backed by force, or threats of force short of war, to help maintain peace. Although sometimes effective, coercive diplomacy offers no nostrum for peacefully resolving the acute challenges of international security. After all, if coercive diplomacy were simple for a preponderant military power such as the United States, then the 1991 and 2003 wars in Iraq would have been averted, and negotiations to halt the burgeoning nuclear programs of Iran and North Korea would long ago have shown more tangible results.

Although diplomacy backed by force has punctuated major-state behavior since the onset of the modern states system, the intellectual concept owes a great deal to the clear thinking of the late Professor Alexander George. In particular, George's slender 1991 volume, *Forceful Persuasion: Coercive Diplomacy as an Alternative to War*, addressed the question of how a global, nuclear power like the United States might successfully use limited force and mere threats of force to compel an adversary to retreat from territory that it had occupied, halt military aggression, or in some cases even stand up and relinquish power. The crux of the challenge for the user of coercive diplomacy, thought George, was how to persuade rather than bludgeon opponents into seeing a situation their way and thereby achieve important objectives at reduced costs. The philosophy associated with President Teddy Roosevelt—"speak softly and carry a big stick"—embodies the spirit of coercive diplomacy as a means of signalling, or bargaining, to an opponent the merits of settling disputes without having to wage war. While force is indeed the element that separates coercive diplomacy from mere diplomacy, the concept retains purpose only if force is tacit or threatened to buttress diplomacy; or in some cases the demonstrative use of force can signal the willingness and capacity to resort to full-scale military action, should an opponent not acquiesce.

Coercive diplomacy thus is distinctly different from the two theoretical concepts related to force that characterized most of the Cold War: namely, deterrence, the purpose of which was to dissuade an opponent from taking inimical actions in the first place, and limited war, in which a superpower could use conventional force despite a nuclear stalemate that created a situation of Mutual Assured Destruction between East and West (wars in Korea and Vietnam were the largest proxy wars that fell under this latter theory).

Alas, the theory of coercive diplomacy has been easier to articulate than its practice, at least if America's recent experience with Iran and North Korea are any guide. The United States made little progress between 2001 and the spring of 2007 in getting either Iran or North Korea to abandon its nuclear program. Three factors were responsible for this feckless stalemate. First, Iran and North Korea clung to nuclear programs because they were deemed essential to their security if not survival. Iran and North Korea were being told to compromise on matters of core national interest, whereas the United States and other outside powers had only a varying degree of national interest intertwined with nonproliferation. Second, the Bush administration approached each of these countries with a high degree of ambivalence as to whether it believed in any diplomatic solution or really sought regime change. Only time and circumstance and a far more limited approach to diplomacy managed to bring North Korea and the United States back to the Six-Party Talks. The distrust between Iran and the United States showed no signs of evaporating at the time this book went to press in the summer of 2007. Thirdly and finally, the United States failed to keep a united front arrayed against each of these two powers. Although the Bush administration demonstrated far more pragmatism during its second than its first term in office, it was a pragmatism not just borne of experience but also exhaustion and overstretch brought about by a costly Iraq intervention. It is as if the United States during the first years of the twenty-first century had used up its quota of goodwill and influence and had to buy time, shift policy, and change leaders to position itself for regaining at least some of its leadership in world affairs. Reconciling America's role in the world after President Bush will be a signal challenge for the next occupant of the White House. Allies and international consensus will not guarantee that these troubles vanish; but they will, if used well, provide sustainable means of grappling with them.

... THEN THERE WERE TEN?

Are Iran and North Korea the ninth and tenth nuclear weapon states in the world? When the Nuclear Nonproliferation Treaty was signed into force in 1968, there were five acknowledged nuclear powers: the United States, the Soviet Union, Great Britain, France, and China. Today, there are three other countries known to have nuclear weapons: India, Pakistan, and Israel. Since the early 1990s, one other country has been assumed to possess at least one or two nuclear weapons: North Korea. A nuclear weapon is now within close reach of Iran, should it choose to assemble one. But there is a difference between being able to build a bomb and possessing a nuclear weapon.

Although the prospects are grim, there is the possibility of diplomatic advancement. Iran and North Korea each have complex and mixed motivations for pursuing nuclear weapons. In principle, addressing some of those motivations could well prove to be a milestone toward a negotiated solution to the nuclear question. One potential benefit of the costly war in Iraq may be that Iran and North Korea decide that the threat of American military attack is even less realistic than it might have seemed in prior years. If so, then security guaranties may be easier to provide, especially if supported by other powers in or out of the UN Security Council. Economic motivations are also important. Not only was it the issue of financial sanctions that pushed North Korea to escalate tensions (rather than to watch a slow, turning of the screw ending in its potential demise), but even Iranian domestic politics have been consumed by the relatively poor economy of what should be a more wealthy state. High oil and gas prices have in recent years abetted Iran, with energy exports more than doubling for Iran between 2002 and 2005, according to the World Bank and other sources. A downturn in energy prices arguably might have the salutary effect of making the economy, and not security, the principal concern of Iranians. Under those circumstances, a package of incentives from outside, in exchange for retaining a verifiably peaceful nuclear program, may not be assigned only to the realm of fantasy. Similarly, with North Korea, we now face the possibility of the use of salami tactics in reverse, whereby it will participate in Six-Party Talks while offering only the barest minimal information or concession, and then only at the last possible minute keeping the North Korean nuclear issue on a diplomatic track over a sustained period of time. Yet those talks may well reduce if not eliminate the threat.

Recent experience, however, suggests we will in the short run fail to disarm North Korea's nuclear program and prevent the further emergence of an Iranian program. The consolation is that these states are also beholden to the logic of deterrence. It can be said that nuclear deterrence works better in practice than in theory because of the psychological and political dimensions. For the same reasons, coercive diplomacy is harder in practice than it would seem to be in theory. Most often, coercive diplomacy fails because it entails many actors aligning policies over time against one determined, often authoritarian actor better able to pursue one goal; because the use of force lacks credibility relative to the survival-seeking of a rogue actor; because political constraints on democracies make it difficult to offer sufficient carrots or incentives to make concessions leading to a bargain more palatable and less costly to face; and because of a lack of trust in relations on which bargains are based. Nonetheless, coercive diplomacy can succeed, in principle as well as in practice, especially when the objective is focused and limited, rather than threatening to regime survival; when threats are mixed with incentives to effect a face-saving element; when there is a united front from the international community rather than escape valves offered by other states or actors that make a deal unnecessary; when leaders are persistent in their pursuit of an objective over time—even if the tactics necessarily vary. Above all, however, coercive diplomacy is about particular actors pursuing particular goals, which makes generalizations or ready checklist formulas or prognostications problematic or even dangerous.

THE CHALLENGE TO DETERRENCE

The Cold War experience that averted a nuclear weapon being fired in anger tells us that responsible states understand the dangers of nuclear war, but they by no means guarantee the future nonuse in the light of new nuclear powers like Iran and North Korea. The two countries challenge deterrence in some fundamental ways.

There is no uniquely Persian conception of deterrence. The authors in this volume have noted Iran's assorted motivations, including traditional realpolitik borne of a series of military defeats. The critical imponderable that keeps security planners from sleeping at night is whether the Iranian leadership would ever countenance firing a nuclear weapon in anger or facilitate another actor's ability to do so. Iran is a revisionist power, but this revisionism concerns its status in the international community, not its territorial boundaries. As Shahram Chubin suggests in his chapter, Persian nationalism is historically characterized by a sense of grievance, and a sense of entitlement or destiny. This is matched with an Islamic sense of martyrdom dating back to the revolution; and a strong awareness of the need for self-reliance, modern military equipment, and weapons of mass destruction, stemming from Saddam Hussein's missile and chemical attacks in the 1980s war.

If loose rhetoric led to nuclear war, deterrence would have failed long ago. Even so, it is sobering to consider that the Iranian leadership has made many caustic comments that give rise to concern. Chairman of the State Expediency Council, Ayatollah Rafsanjani, announced in December 2001 that Iran could withstand many nuclear blows, while Israel could only take one. Representative of the Supreme Leader on the Supreme National Security Council, Ali Larijani, declared to the Revolutionary Guard Corps, "We could move to a new technological level which would protect us from the Americans," and President Ahmadinejad has announced, "once we get the technology, we will be a superpower." Beyond these blustery statements related to power are the even more worrisome discourse related to apocalyptic religious visions. The vision of the twelfth Mahdi is only held by a minority, but this minority has been elevated under the leadership of President Ahmadinejad. Adherents believe that the Mahdi will reappear, and that this can be hastened or retarded by human action, and particularly by bloodshed.

It remains premature to speak of an Iranian concept of deterrence, not least because Iran has made no clear decision on whether to seek to convert its nuclear program into a nuclear weapon or arsenal. Nuclear deterrence thus has no formal place in Iranian strategy. Indeed, Iranians mainly discuss deterrence in terms of asymmetric responses or "horizontal escalation"—this means widening the various crises in the Middle East by controlling oil prices, taking hostages, and fuelling the Iraq insurgency. By exploiting strategic ambiguities in the region, Iranian leaders seek to prove that preemption is not the monopoly of the United States. By comparison, they talk less about deterrence with nuclear arms. Indeed, some leaders claim to have issued a *fatwa* against nuclear weapons, although they are also keenly aware that ballistic missiles can bypass the need for logistics, training, and organization that is often lacking in the Iranian military. As Iran accumulates more and more nuclear capability, however, one of the early indicators of a nuclear weapon program may well be a nascent discussion about the concept of deterrence. Iran with nuclear weapons is hardly to be encouraged, but the thought of a nuclear-armed Iran with little concept of deterrence seems equally unnerving.

North Korea's nuclear programs are also challenging traditional notions of the durability of deterrence in Northeast Asia. Northeast Asia is in a process of deep transformation, and this is having dramatic consequences for deterrence in the region. The internal dynamic of the region is changing, and this is accompanied by a sweeping revision of its ties with the West. As with Iran, North Korea's nuclear strategy is more about forestalling attempts to curb its acquisition than any apparent thought to its potential use. The nub of the question here is less the rationality of North Korea, which for all its eccentricities is not seen as impervious to basic deterrence. Instead, a key question is the viability of American extended nuclear deterrence over its allies, Japan and South Korea.

American extended deterrence in the region is focused on three goals: to deter North Korea from proliferating nuclear weapons beyond its borders; to deter them from invading the South; and to deter them from using a nuclear weapon. It is not clear whether North Korea will sell nuclear technology to terrorists, but economic pressures may oblige them to do so. Furthermore, should this take place, it appears that they imagine the United States will do little in response. The problem for the United States is that the onus would be on Washington to document where a given device had originated, which is a very difficult burden of proof.

The Japanese know that acquiring a nuclear weapon would bring far more condemnation and concern than any potential benefit—at least for the foreseeable future. But over the course of a decade even that reasoning could continue to shift. After all, the mood in Japan toward making a strong national security policy independent of the United States shows no signs of abating. It has long been assumed that technically proficient Japan, with its nuclear capabilities and long-range missiles, could under altered circumstances move to fashion a nuclear weapon in a matter of months. More recent discussion on the issue within Japan, where the topic has lost its earlier taboo, suggests Japan's conversion of its civilian capacity into a usable military capability may take far longer than many suspect, perhaps a year or two. In fact, some have likened Iran's current ambition to approximate Japan, although when people invoke the Japan analogy they in fact are referring to a "ready-to-assemble" bomb, rather than simply the raw sinews of nuclear power possessed by Japan. What can be said, is that the strength of the U.S.-Japan alliance prevents the need for Japan to think too seriously about acquiring its own nuclear weapon to guard against mounting proliferation on the Korean Peninsula. But will that logic be maintained if North Korea acquires a more visible and sizable nuclear stockpile?

Meanwhile, South Korea is more comfortable living next to nuclear North Korea than either Japan or the United States. Nonetheless, South Korea may either sense the need for a deterrent of its own, should the U.S.-South Korean alliance falter, or should unification put Seoul in sudden possession of Pyongyang's nuclear inventory. The only truly credible endgame for North Korea's security problem may be reunification in the wake of a North Korean collapse or slow merger. Collapse raises at least three questions: how would China respond? What would be the foreign policy orientation of the new united Korea? And would Korea retain its inherited nuclear capability? It is probable that the South would dismantle its nuclear weapons in the event that it should inherit them, following a collapse of the North Korean government.

The question about the future of the bilateral alliance between Washington and Seoul evokes neuralgia and nostalgia. As the U.S.-Japan alliance has revitalized since the end of the Cold War, the U.S.-South Korean alliance has made only belated steps to reduce U.S. presence and prepare to hand back wartime operational command and control on the Peninsula. Many in South Korea fear a premature handover, if not a rupture in relations, as Sung-joo Han writes in his chapter. Liru Cui also makes it abundantly clear that China and the ROK are likely to continue their tighter set of relations. It remains to be seen what the next occupants of the Blue House in 2008 and White House in 2009 will do to put their bilateral ties in a better state than it has been in the past decade, including thinking about the future of the Six-Party Talks as a potential mechanism for regional security beyond managing North Korea.

Perhaps these concluding fears will not be realized. Indeed, if there is a silver lining on every dark cloud, perhaps an adroit management of these troubles will lead to a regional security architecture and environment that will endure for the decades to follow. Although this volume has focused on the problem of nuclear proliferation, there is a common thread running through the analyses that the solutions must be based on a broader set of political, economic, and military realities, and that the solutions require action on the part of individual nations acting bilaterally and within a multilateral and regional setting. If the United States and other major powers are to work together on a joint regional security project, in either the Persian Gulf or Northeast Asia, it will take time and effort. A credible United States will be essential if the effort is to be taken seriously. But we must recognize where the regions are now, several years after 9/11 and the Iraq intervention: we have multilayered regionalism with a vengeance. The United States can try to halt any new institution that excludes it, but that kind of rejectionism is not apt to earn influence. A more nuanced approach to recalibrating America's role in the world will be to accept the reality of a diversity of efforts with many countries offering their own approaches to reducing the troubles posed by Iran and North Korea. If that means bolstering a larger Arab counterweight to Iran's recent alliance-building with Hezbollah, Syria, Hamas, and even actors in North Africa, then the United States will have to find ways to renew stronger ties with crucial Arab leaders. If it means continuing to allow China and South Korea to play a larger role in Northeast Asia, then again the United States can continue to remain a distant balancer, while simultaneously facilitating the overlapping security structures that may be useful in the future.

NOTE

1. To cite just one instance, see Seymour M. Hersh, "The Iran Plans: Would President Bush go to war to stop Tehran from getting the bomb?" *The New Yorker*, April 17, 2007, http://www.newyorker.com/archive/2006/04/17/060417fa_fact.

Appendices

Maps
Known Nuclear Sites in North Korea and Iran
North Korea and Iran Ballistic Missile Ranges

Chronologies
North Korea Selected Chronology
Iran Selected Chronology

United Nations Security Council Resolutions
UN Security Council Resolution 82 (June 25, 1950)
UN Security Council Resolution 1695 (July 15, 2006)
UN Security Council Resolution 1696 (July 31, 2006)
UN Security Council Resolution 1718 (October 14, 2006)
UN Security Council Resolution 1737 (December 23, 2006)
UN Security Council Resolution 1747 (March 24, 2007)

Selected Agreements, Treaties, and Documents Related to Korea
Korean Armistice Agreement (July 27, 1953)

Mutual Defense Treaty between the Republic of Korea and the United States of America (Signed October 1, 1953)

Agreed Framework between the Democratic People's Republic of Korea and the United States of America (October 21, 1994)

Chairman's Statement After the Second Round of Six-Party Talks (February 28, 2004)

Chairman's Statement After the Third Round of Six-Party Talks (June 26, 2004)

U.S. Treasury Department Press Release Citing Banco Delta Asia for Money Laundering (September 15, 2005)

First Joint Statement of the Fourth Round of the Six-Party Talks, Beijing (September 19, 2005)

Announcement Made by the North Korean Central News Agency Following the October 9, 2006, Nuclear Test

Chairman's Statement After First Session of the Fifth Round of Six-Party Talks (November 9–11, 2005)

Chairman's Statement After Second Session of the Fifth Round of the Six-Party Talks (December 22, 2006)

Joint Statement After the Third Session of the Fifth Round of Six-Party Talks (February 13, 2007)

U.S. Treasury Statement on Banco Delta Asia (March 14, 2007)

Other Agreements
Treaty on the Non-Proliferation of Nuclear Weapons (July 1, 1968)

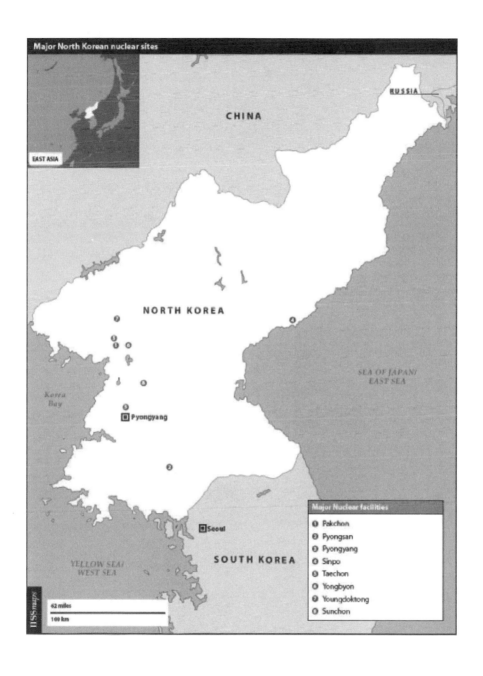

Major North Korean nuclear sites

EAST ASIA

RUSSIA

CHINA

NORTH KOREA

SEA OF JAPAN/
EAST SEA

Korea
Bay

Pyongyang

SOUTH KOREA

Seoul

YELLOW SEA/
WEST SEA

Major Nuclear facilities

❶ Pakchon
❷ Pyongsan
❸ Pyongyang
❹ Sinpo
❺ Taechon
❻ Yongbyon
❼ Youngdoktong
❽ Sunchon

IISS maps

62 miles
100 km

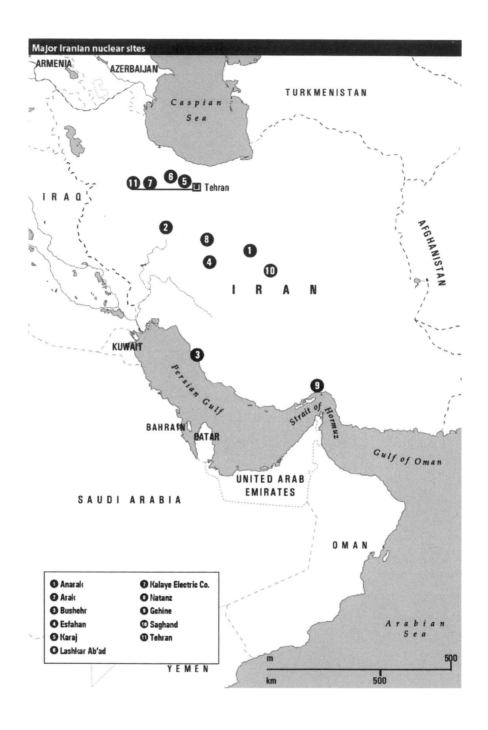

Major Iranian nuclear sites

ARMENIA
AZERBAIJAN
TURKMENISTAN

Caspian Sea

IRAQ

⓫ ❼ ❻ ❺ ▣ Tehran

❷

❽

❹

❶

❿

I R A N

AFGHANISTAN

KUWAIT

❸

Persian Gulf

❾

Strait of Hormuz

BAHRAIN

QATAR

Gulf of Oman

UNITED ARAB EMIRATES

SAUDI ARABIA

OMAN

Arabian Sea

❶ Anarak	❼ Kalaye Electric Co.
❷ Arak	❽ Natanz
❸ Bushehr	❾ Gchine
❹ Esfahan	❿ Saghand
❺ Karaj	⓫ Tehran
❻ Lashkar Ab'ad	

YEMEN

m   500
km   500

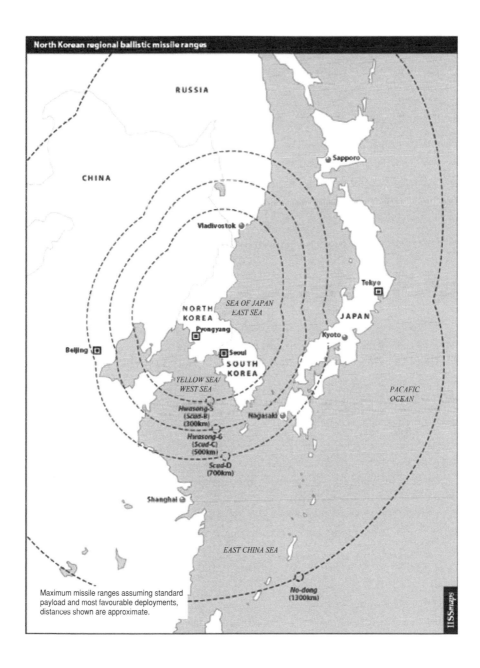

RUSSIA

CHINA

Sapporo

Vladivostok

Tokyo

NORTH
KOREA

SEA OF JAPAN
EAST SEA

JAPAN

Pyongyang

Kyoto

Seoul

SOUTH
KOREA

Beijing

YELLOW SEA/
WEST SEA

PACAFIC
OCEAN

Hwasong-5
(Scud-B)
(300km)

Nagasaki

Hwasong-6
(Scud-C)
(500km)

Scud-D
(700km)

Shanghai

EAST CHINA SEA

Maximum missile ranges assuming standard
payload and most favourable deployments,
distances shown are approximate.

No-dong
(1300km)

IISSmaps

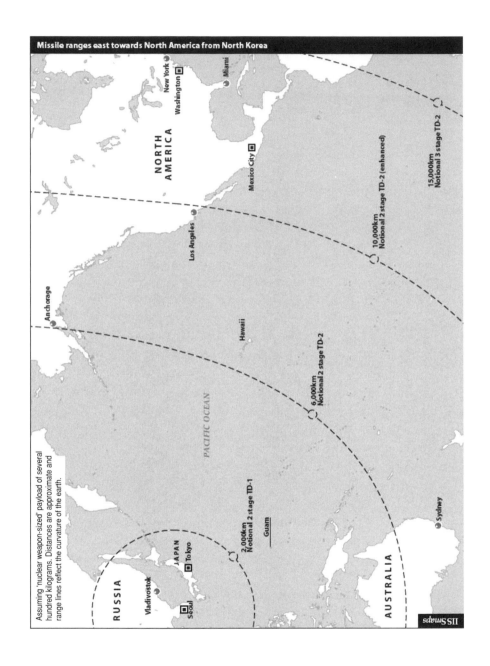

Missile ranges east towards North America from North Korea

Assuming 'nuclear weapon-sized' payload of several hundred kilograms. Distances are approximate and range lines reflect the curvature of the earth.

NORTH AMERICA

RUSSIA

JAPAN

AUSTRALIA

PACIFIC OCEAN

New York
Washington
Miami
Mexico City
Los Angeles
Anchorage
Hawaii
Vladivostok
Tokyo
Seoul
Guam
Sydney

2,000km
Notional 2 stage TD-1

6,000km
Notional 2 stage TD-2

10,000km
Notional 2 stage TD-2 (enhanced)

15,000km
Notional 3 stage TD-2

IISS maps

Iranian Ballistic Missile Ranges

RUSSIA

TURKEY

GEORGIA

KAZAKHSTAN

CYPRUS

ARMENIA
AZERBAIJAN

LEBANON

UZBEKISTAN

ISRAEL SYRIA

EGYPT

JORDAN IRAQ

TURKMENISTAN

KYRGYZSTAN

■ Tehran

TAJIKISTAN

IRAN

CHINA

KUWAIT

AFGHANISTAN

BAHRAIN
QATAR

SAUDI ARABIA

PAKISTAN

UAE

300km *Shahab*-1 (*Scud*-B)

500km *Shahab*-2 (*Scud*-C)

OMAN

YEMEN

INDIA

1,300km *Shahab*-3 (*No-dong*)

2,000 miles

3,000 kilometres

Maximum missile ranges assuming standard payload and most forward
deployment. Distances shown are approximate.

NORTH KOREA SELECTED CHRONOLOGY

September 1945: Japanese forces in Seoul surrender marking the liberation of Korea.

July 1946: Failure of diplomacy between the United States and the Soviet Union regarding the establishment of an interim Korean government.

November 1947: The UN General Assembly adopts a resolution to send a UN Commission to Korea to supervise general elections.

November 1948: Elections are held in southern Korea in May, electing Syngman Rhee; the Democratic Republic of Korea is proclaimed and a new government is formed in North Korea.

January 1949: The United States formally recognizes the state of South Korea and retains forces there; Soviet forces withdraw from North Korea.

June 25, 1950: North Korean forces invade South Korea starting the Korean War.

July 1953: Korean Armistice Agreement signed in Panmunjom, with an agreement on the Demilitarized Zone on the 38th parallel.

October 1953: The United States and the Republic of Korea sign a mutual defense treaty.

1961: North Korea signs treaties of friendships, cooperation, and mutual assistance with the Soviet Union and China.

1977: North Korea signs a trilateral safeguards agreement with the International Atomic Energy (IAEA) Agency and the Soviet Union that brings the IRT-2000 research reactor and a critical assembly in Yongbyon under IAEA safeguards.

1980: The United States detects construction of a new 5MW(e) reactor at the Yongbyon Nuclear Research Centre. The early 1980s see significant expansion of North Korean nuclear activities, including a nuclear reactor, uranium milling facilities, and research and development.

December 12, 1985: North Korea signs the Treaty on the Non-Proliferation of Nuclear Weapons (NPT).

December 31, 1991: North and South Korea conclude the North–South Basic Agreement highlighting their mutual goal of reunification.

January 10, 1992: Signing of the Joint Declaration of South and North Korea on the denuclearization of the Korean Peninsula.

January 30, 1992: North Korea signs a full-scope safeguards agreement with the IAEA. The agreement enters into force on April 10, 1992.

May 26, 1992: IAEA inspections begin. Sample analysis suggests that more plutonium has been produced than has been declared; the United States detects apparent efforts to conceal underground waste sites.

February 11, 1993: The IAEA formally requests special inspection of suspect waste sites.

February 25, 1993: The IAEA Board of Governors gives North Korea a one-month deadline to accept special inspections.

March 12, 1993: North Korea announces its intention to withdraw from the NPT.

April 1, 1993: The IAEA reports North Korea's violation of the NPT to the UN Security Council.

May 11, 1993: The UN Security Council adopts Resolution 825. This leads to negotiations between the United States and North Korea.

May 29, 1993: North Korea tests a *No-dong* missile.

July 8, 1994: Kim Il-sung dies suddenly of a heart attack.

October 8, 1994: Kim Jong-il elected secretary general of the ruling Korean Workers' Party.

October 21, 1994: The United States and North Korea sign the Agreed Framework in Geneva.

March 9, 1995: The Korean Peninsula Energy Development Organization (KEDO) is established to help implement a subsequent agreement to build two light-water nuclear reactors.

1995: The United States would begin providing humanitarian food assistance to North Korea to counter a famine; that aid would reach its high point in 1999 before being scaled back.

December 19, 1997: Kim Dae-jung elected president of South Korea and outlines his "Sunshine Policy" for engaging North Korea.

August 17, 1998: Press reports note suspect nuclear facility at Kumchang-ri.

August 31, 1998: North Korea launches a "satellite" on a long-range *Taepo-dong* 1 missile.

November 1998: Mount Kumgang opens as a special tourist destination in North Korea and a symbol of Kim Dae-jung's Sunshine Policy.

March 17, 1999: North Korea agrees to a U.S. visit to Kumchang-ri in May. The visit shows that the underground structure is not intended for nuclear-related uses.

September 7–12, 1999: North Korea voluntarily agrees to a moratorium on further long-range missile tests. March 7, 2001: President Kim Dae-jung and President George W. Bush meet at the White House; the early meeting highlights the widening approaches of South Korea and the United States in handling North Korea.

June 6, 2001: The Bush administration publishes its "broad agenda" policy toward North Korea.

January 29, 2002: President George W. Bush calls North Korea, Iran, and Iraq an "axis of evil" in his State of the Union Address.

October 4, 2002: North Korean Vice Minister Kang Suk-ju reportedly acknowledges to U.S. Assistant Secretary of State James Kelly that North Korea possesses a uranium enrichment program.

October 16, 2002: The United States announces that North Korea possesses a clandestine highly enriched uranium program.

November 14, 2002: KEDO suspends further oil shipments to North Korea.

December 12, 2002: North Korea announces the restart of its 5MW(e) reactor.

December 19, 2002: Roh Moo-hyun wins the South Korean elections and promises to continue his predecessors' "Sunshine Policy."

December 27, 2002: North Korea expels IAEA inspectors and announces that it will soon complete preparations to resume operations at the reprocessing facility.

January 6, 2003: The IAEA Board of Governors calls on North Korea to allow the return of inspectors.

January 10, 2003: North Korea announces its withdrawal from the NPT.

February 12, 2003: The IAEA reports North Korea's NPT violations to the UN Security Council.

May 12, 2003: North Korea declares that the joint declaration of the denuclearization of the Korean Peninsula, negotiated with South Korea in December 1991, is void.

April 18, 2003: North Korea announces that it is in the final phase of reprocessing more than 8,000 spent fuel rods.

April 24–25, 2003: Three-Party Talks among the United States, China, and North Korea are held in Beijing.

August 27–29, 2003: The first round of Six Party Talks (among the United States, Russia, China, Japan, and North and South Korea) is held in Beijing.

October 2, 2003: North Korea publicly announces that it has successfully finished reprocessing the 8,000 spent fuel rods and is using the resulting plutonium to increase its "nuclear deterrent force."

October 19, 2003: President George W. Bush indicates that the United States is prepared to give written security assurances to North Korea in exchange for a complete, verifiable, and irreversible disarmament.

November 4, 2003: KEDO formally suspends construction of the light-water reactor project for one year.

December 9, 2003: North Korea announces a proposal for a nuclear freeze.

January 22, 2004: A U.S. team visits the nuclear facility at Yongbyon, where they are shown weapons-grade plutonium.

February 5, 2004: The founder of Pakistan's nuclear program, Dr. Abdul Qadeer Khan, admits to having sold gas-centrifuge technology to North Korea, Libya, and Iran.

February 25–28, 2004: The second round of Six-Party Talks is held in Beijing.

June 23, 2004: Third round of Six-Party Talks is held in Beijing. The United States offers North Korea fuel aid if it freezes its nuclear programs.

July 2, 2004: U.S. Secretary of State Colin Powell meets the North Korean Foreign Minister, Paek Nam-sun.

July 22, 2004: The U.S. House of Representatives unanimously passes the North Korean Human Rights Act to improve the human rights conditions of North Koreans.

September 28, 2004: North Korea says it has turned plutonium from 8,000 spent fuel rods into nuclear weapons. Speaking at the UN General Assembly, Vice Foreign Minister Choe Su-hon said the weapons were needed for "self-defense" against "the U.S. nuclear threat."

December 6, 2004: The IAEA estimates that North Korea has reprocessed spent nuclear fuel into weapons-grade plutonium to make four to six nuclear weapons.

December 15, 2004: Production begins in the Kaesong Industrial Complex, a joint North–South economic enterprise that is the centerpiece of South Korean President Roh Moo-hyun's engagement policy.

February 10, 2005: The North Korean Foreign Ministry announces that Pyongyang has manufactured nuclear weapons and that it is indefinitely suspending its participation in negotiations.

May 1, 2005: North Korea fires a short-range missile into the Sea of Japan, on the eve of a meeting of members of the international Non-Proliferation Treaty.

July 12, 2005: South Korea offers the North electricity as an incentive to end its nuclear weapons program.

July 25, 2005: The fourth round of Six-Party Talks begins in Beijing.

September 19, 2005: In what is initially hailed as a historic joint statement, North Korea agrees to give up all its nuclear activities and rejoin the NPT, while the United States says it had no intention of attacking.

September 20, 2005: North Korea says it will not scrap its nuclear program until it is given a civilian nuclear reactor, undermining the joint statement and throwing further talks into doubt.

July 5, 2006: North Korea test-fires seven missiles, including a long-range *Taepo-dong* 2, despite repeated warnings from the international community.

October 3, 2006: North Korea announces plans to test a nuclear weapon in the future, blaming "hostile U.S. policy."

October 6, 2006: The United Nations Security Council issues a statement urging the Democratic People's Republic of Korea (DPRK) not to undertake such a test and to refrain from any action that might aggravate tension.

October 9, 2006: North Korea announces that it has performed its first nuclear test.

October 14, 2006: The UN Security Council passes Resolution 1718, imposing sanctions on North Korea for its nuclear test, reiterates financial sanctions already in place, and calls on keeping luxury goods from North Korea's leaders.

October 27, 2006: Japanese Chief Cabinet Secretary Yasuhisa Shiozaki confirms international consensus that North Korea conducted a nuclear test on October 9.

December 18, 2006: The previously suspended fifth round of Six-Party Talks resume in a second phase. The parties eventually reaffirmed the September 19, 2005, declaration.

January 13, 2007: North Korean official Song Il-ho reportedly tells his Japanese counterpart Taku Yamasaki that North Korea could conduct a second nuclear test depending on U.S. actions.

January 16, 2007: Talks between North Korea and the United States are held in Berlin, Germany.

January 13, 2007: North Korean official Song Il-ho was reported to have told his Japanese counterpart Taku Yamasaki that whether the North Koreans conduct a second nuclear test depends on "US actions in the future."

January 16, 2007: In-between-round talks between North Korea and the United States are held in Berlin, Germany, setting the groundwork for a sixth round of Six-Party Talks.

February 10, 2007: Reports suggests that the CIA estimates in 2002 that North Korea was developing highly enriched uranium may have been over-stated and somewhat less definitive than indicated at the time.

February 13, 2007: The fifth round of the Six-Party Talks conclude with an agreement. Pyongyang pledges to shut down the Yongbyon reactor within sixty days in exchange for 50,000 metric tons of fuel and more to follow the verified disabling of the reactor. IAEA inspectors will be readmitted, and the United States will resume a process of working toward normalization of relations with North Korea.

March 19, 2007: The sixth round of Six-Party Talks commences in Beijing.

IRAN SELECTED CHRONOLOGY

July–August 1968: Iran signs and ratifies NPT.

1979: Iran's Islamic revolution puts a freeze on the existing nuclear pro-gramme.

1982: Iranian officials announce plans to build a nuclear reactor powered by their own uranium at the Esfahan Nuclear Technology Centre.

1996: China and Iran inform the IAEA of plans to construct a nuclear enrichment facility in Iran, but China withdraws from the contract under U.S. pressure. Iran advises the IAEA that it plans to pursue the construction regardless.

August 14, 2002: The National Council of Resistance (NCRI) reveals the existence of Natanz enrichment plant and Arak heavy-water plant.

December 2002: The United States accuses Iran of attempting to develop nuclear weapons.

February 2003: IAEA visits Natanz; Iran promises to put facility under safeguards and consider adopting the Additional Protocol.

June 19, 2003: IAEA issues statement urging Iran not to introduce nuclear material into Natanz.

Early August 2003: EU-3 Foreign Ministers write to Iranian Foreign Minister, offering to begin negotiations to resolve nuclear issue.

September 12, 2003: IAEA resolution calls on Iran to suspend all further enrichment-related activities, implicitly threatening referral to UN Security Council.

October 21, 2003: EU-3 Iran Agreement: Iran agrees to correct past safeguards failures and suspend all enrichment and reprocessing activities.

October 23, 2003: Iran submits to the IAEA what it says is a full disclosure of its past undeclared nuclear activities.

November 11, 2003: IAEA declares that there is no evidence that Iran is attempting to develop nuclear weapons.

November 13, 2003: The United States claims that the IAEA report is "impossible to believe."

December 18, 2003: Iran signs the Additional Protocol to its NPT safeguards commitment.

February 24, 2004: Following meeting with EU-3 in Brussels, Iran notifies IAEA that it will issue orders in March to suspend domestic production of centrifuges.

March 13, 2004: IAEA resolution criticizes Iran for failure to report centrifuge research and fully implement suspension.

April 29, 2004: Iran informs IAEA that it is beginning "hot test" of UF6 production line.

May 7, 2004: IAEA informs Iran that "hot tests" amount to production of feed material for enrichment.

May 18, 2004: Iran informs IAEA that suspension does not include production of UF6.

June 14, 2004: Mohamed El Baradei, Director-General of IAEA, accuses Iran of "less than satisfactory" cooperation during the IAEA investigation.

June 24, 2004: Iran notifies IAEA that it is resuming domestic production and assembly of centrifuges, reversing a voluntary October 2003 pledge to the EU-3 to suspend all uranium enrichment-related activities.

September 18, 2004: IAEA resolution calls on Iran to restore suspension of manufacture of centrifuge components and production of feed material, implicitly threatens referral to UN Security Council.

October 18, 2004: Iran states that it will negotiate with the EU-3 regarding a suspension of its uranium enrichment activities, but that it will never renounce its right to enrich uranium.

October 24, 2004: The EU proposes to provide civilian nuclear technology to Iran in exchange for Iran terminating its uranium enrichment program permanently. Iran rejects this outright

November 15, 2004: EU-3 Iran Paris Agreement in Paris: Iran agrees on comprehensive suspension of enrichment-related activities for the duration of a second round of talks; accord establishes basis for EU-3–Iran negotiations for a long-term agreement on "objective guarantees" that Iran's nuclear program is peaceful.

November 29, 2004: IAEA resolution welcomes Paris Agreement.

March 11, 2005: United States declares support of EU-3 negotiations with Iran.

March 23, 2005: Iran presents new proposal to EU-3.

April 29, 2005: EU-3-Iran Steering Committee meeting in London: Iran threatens to resume conversion if EU-3 does not accept Iran's March proposal as basis for negotiations.

May 10, 2005: EU-3 letter threatens to end talks if Iran resumes conversion.

May 25, 2005: Iran agrees to extend suspension, pending presentation of EU-3 proposal in late July or early August.

August 8, 2005: Iran resumes operations at the Esfahan facility, but does not engage in enrichment of uranium.

August 11, 2005: IAEA resolution calling upon Iran to suspend uranium conversion, implicitly threatening referral to the Security Council.

August 15, 2005: Iran's new president, Mahmoud Ahmadinejad, installs new government.

September 15, 2005: At a United Nations high-level summit, Mahmoud Ahmadinejad declares right to develop a civil nuclear-power programme within the terms of NPT.

November 19, 2005: IAEA releases a report stating that Iran was again blocking nuclear inspectors from the United Nations. Separately, Iran confirms that it had resumed the conversion of new quantities of uranium, despite an IAEA resolution to stop such work.

January 2006: Iran provides the EU-3 with a six-point proposal, offering to suspend uranium enrichment for a period of two years, pending the outcome of continued negotiations. The offer is dismissed by the Europeans.

February 4, 2006: The IAEA votes to report Iran to the United Nations Security Council. After the vote, Iran announced its intention to end voluntary cooperation with the IAEA beyond basic NPT requirements, and to resume enrichment of uranium.

March 2006: The U.S. National Security Strategy states, "Iran has violated its Non-Proliferation Treaty safeguards obligations and refuses to provide objective guarantees that its nuclear programme is solely for peaceful purposes."

April 11, 2006: President Mahmoud Ahmadinejad announces that Iran has enriched uranium. He reiterates that the enrichment was performed solely for civilian purposes.

June 1, 2006: The UN Security Council agrees to a set of proposals designed to reach a compromise with Iran.

July 31, 2006: The UN Security Council gives until August 31, 2006, for Iran to suspend all uranium enrichment and related activities or face the prospect of sanctions.

August 31, 2006: IAEA report announces that Iran has failed to suspend uranium enrichment activities.

September 26, 2006: Russia and Iran sign a deal in Moscow to launch a nuclear reactor at Bushehr in September next year, to be fully operational by November 2007.

October 12, 2006: United States circulates draft of UN resolution calling for sanctions under Chapter VII of UN Charter.

SELECTED UNITED NATIONS SECURITY COUNCIL RESOLUTIONS RELATED TO NORTH KOREA

UN Security Council Resolution 82 (June 25, 1950)

The Security Council,

Recalling the finding of the General Assembly in its Resolution 293 (IV) of 21 October 1949 that the Government of the Republic of Korea is a lawfully established government having effective control and jurisdiction over that part of Korea where the United Nations Temporary Mission on Korea was able to observe and consult and in which the great majority of the people of Korea reside; that this government is based on elections which were a valid expression of the free will of the electorate of that part of Korea and which were observed by the Temporary Commission; and that this is the only such government in Korea,

Mindful of the concern expressed by the General Assembly in its resolutions 195 (III) of 12 December 1948 and 293 (IV) 21 October 1949 about the consequences which might follow unless Member States refrained from acts derogatory to the results sought to be achieved by the United Nations in bringing about the complete independence and unity of Korea; and the concern expressed that the situation described by the United Nations Commission on Korea in its report menaces the safety and well-being of the Republic of Korea and of the people of Korea and might lead to open military conflict there;

Noting with grave concern the armed attack on the Republic of Korea by forces from North Korea,

Determines that this action constitutes a breach of the peace; and

I

Calls for the immediate cessation of hostilities;

Calls upon the authorities in North Korea to withdraw forthwith their armed forces to the 38th parallel;

II

Requests the United Nations Commission on Korea:

(a) To communicate its fully considered recommendations on the situation with the least possible delay;
(b) To observe the withdrawal of North Korean forces to the 38th parallel;
(c) To keep the Security Council informed on the execution of this resolution;

III

Calls upon all Member States to render every assistance to the United Nations in the execution of this resolution and to refrain from giving assistance to the North Korean Authorities.

Adopted by the 473rd meeting by 9 votes to none, with 1 abstention (Yugoslavia).

UN Security Council Resolution 1695 (July 15, 2006)

The Security Council,

Reaffirming its resolutions 825 (1993) of 11 May 1993 and 1540 (2004) of 28 April 2004,

Bearing in mind the importance of maintaining peace and stability on the Korean peninsula and in north-east Asia at large,

Reaffirming that proliferation of nuclear, chemical and biological weapons, as well as their means of delivery, constitutes a threat to international peace and security,

Expressing grave concern at the launch of ballistic missiles by the Democratic People's Republic of Korea (DPRK), given the potential of such systems to be used as a means to deliver nuclear, chemical or biological payloads,

Registering profound concern at the DPRK's breaking of its pledge to maintain its moratorium on missile launching,

Expressing further concern that the DPRK endangered civil aviation and shipping through its failure to provide adequate advance notice,

Expressing its grave concern about DPRK's indication of possible additional launches of ballistic missiles in the near future,

Expressing also its desire for a peaceful and diplomatic solution to the situation and welcoming efforts by Council members as well as other Member States to facilitate a peaceful and comprehensive solution through dialogue,

Recalling that the DPRK launched an object propelled by a missile without prior notification to the countries in the region, which fell into the waters in the vicinity of Japan on 31 August 1998,

Deploring the DPRK's announcement of withdrawal from the Treaty on Non-Proliferation of Nuclear Weapons (the Treaty) and its stated pursuit of nuclear weapons in spite of its Treaty on Non-Proliferation of Nuclear Weapons and International Atomic Energy Agency (IAEA) safeguards obligations,

Stressing the importance of the implementation of the Joint Statement issued on 19 September 2005 by China, DPRK, Japan, Republic of Korea, the Russian Federation and the United States,

Affirming that such launches jeopardize peace, stability and security in the region and beyond, particularly in light of the DPRK's claim that it has developed nuclear weapons,

Acting under its special responsibility for the maintenance of international peace and security,

1. *Condemns* the multiple launches by the DPRK of ballistic missiles on 5 July 2006 local time;
2. *Demands* that the DPRK suspend all activities related to its ballistic missile programme, and in this context re-establish its pre-existing commitments to a moratorium on missile launching;
3. *Requires* all Member States, in accordance with their national legal authorities and legislation and consistent with international law, to exercise vigilance and prevent missile and missile-related items, materials, goods and technology being transferred to DPRK's missile or WMD programmes;
4. *Requires* all Member States, in accordance with their national legal authorities and legislation and consistent with international law, to exercise vigilance and prevent the procurement of missiles or missile related-items, materials, goods and technology from the DPRK, and the transfer of any financial resources in relation to DPRK's missile or WMD programmes;
5. *Underlines*, in particular to the DPRK, the need to show restraint and refrain from any action that might aggravate tension, and to continue to work on the resolution of non-proliferation concerns through political and diplomatic efforts;
6. *Strongly urges* the DPRK to return immediately to the Six-Party Talks without precondition, to work towards the expeditious implementation of 19 September 2005 Joint Statement, in particular to abandon all nuclear weapons and existing nuclear programmes, and to return at an early date to the Treaty on Non-Proliferation of Nuclear Weapons and International Atomic Energy Agency safeguards;
7. *Supports* the Six-Party Talks, calls for their early resumption, and urges all the participants to intensify their efforts on the full implementation of the 19 September 2005 Joint Statement with a view to achieving the verifiable denuclearization of the Korean Peninsula in a peaceful manner and to maintaining peace and stability on the Korean Peninsula and in north-east Asia;
8. *Decides* to remain seized of the matter.

UN Security Council Resolution 1696 (July 31, 2006)

The Security Council,

Recalling the Statement of its President, S/PRST/2006/15, of 29 March 2006,

Reaffirming its commitment to the Treaty on the Non-proliferation of Nuclear Weapons, and recalling the right of States Party, in conformity with

Articles I and II of that Treaty, to develop research, production and use of nuclear energy for peaceful purposes without discrimination,

Noting with serious concern the many reports of the IAEA Director General and resolutions of the IAEA Board of Governors related to Iran's nuclear programme, reported to it by the IAEA Director General, including IAEA Board Resolution GOV/2006/14,

Noting with serious concern that the IAEA Director General's report of 27 February 2006 (GOV/2006/15) lists a number of outstanding issues and concerns on Iran's nuclear programme, including topics which could have a military nuclear dimension, and that the IAEA is unable to conclude that there are no undeclared nuclear materials or activities in Iran,

Noting with serious concern the IAEA Director General's report of 28 April 2006 (GOV/2006/27) and its findings, including that, after more than three years of Agency efforts to seek clarity about all aspects of Iran's nuclear programme, the existing gaps in knowledge continue to be a matter of concern, and that the IAEA is unable to make progress in its efforts to provide assurances about the absence of undeclared nuclear material and activities in Iran,

Noting with serious concern that, as confirmed by the IAEA Director General's report of 8 June 2006 (GOV/2006/38) Iran has not taken the steps required of it by the IAEA Board of Governors, reiterated by the Council in its statement of 29 March and which are essential to build confidence, and in particular Iran's decision to resume enrichment-related activities, including research and development, its recent expansion of and announcements about such activities, and its continued suspension of co-operation with the IAEA under the Additional Protocol,

Emphasizing the importance of political and diplomatic efforts to find a negotiated solution guaranteeing that Iran's nuclear programme is exclusively for peaceful purposes, and noting that such a solution would benefit nuclear non-proliferation elsewhere,

Welcoming the statement by the Foreign Minister of France, Philippe Douste-Blazy, on behalf of the Foreign Ministers of China, France, Germany, the Russian Federation, the United Kingdom, the United States and the High Representative of the European Union, in Paris on 12 July 2006 (S/2006/573),

Concerned by the proliferation risks presented by the Iranian nuclear programme, mindful of its primary responsibility under the Charter of the United Nations for the maintenance of international peace and security, and being determined to prevent an aggravation of the situation,

Acting under Article 40 of Chapter VII of the Charter of the United Nations in order to make mandatory the suspension required by the IAEA,

1. *Calls upon* Iran without further delay to take the steps required by the IAEA Board of Governors in its resolution GOV/2006/14, which are essential to build confidence in the exclusively peaceful purpose of its nuclear programme and to resolve outstanding questions,

2. *Demands*, in this context, that Iran shall suspend all enrichment-related and reprocessing activities, including research and development, to be verified by the IAEA,

3. *Expresses* the conviction that such suspension as well as full, verified Iranian compliance with the requirements set out by the IAEA Board of Governors, would contribute to a diplomatic, negotiated solution that guarantees Iran's nuclear programme is for exclusively peaceful purposes, underlines the willingness of the international community to work positively for such a solution, encourages Iran, in conforming to the above provisions, to re-engage with the international community and with the IAEA, and stresses that such engagement will be beneficial to Iran,

4. *Endorses*, in this regard, the proposals of China, France, Germany, the Russian Federation, the United Kingdom and the United States, with the support of the European Union's High Representative, for a long-term comprehensive arrangement which would allow for the development of relations and cooperation with Iran based on mutual respect and the establishment of international confidence in the exclusively peaceful nature of Iran's nuclear programme (S/2006/521),

5. *Calls upon* all States, in accordance with their national legal authorities and legislation and consistent with international law, to exercise vigilance and prevent the transfer of any items, materials, goods and technology that could contribute to Iran's enrichment-related and re-processing activities and ballistic missile programmes,

6. *Expresses* its determination to reinforce the authority of the IAEA process, strongly supports the role of the IAEA Board of Governors, commends and encourages the Director General of the IAEA and its Secretariat for their ongoing professional and impartial efforts to resolve all remaining outstanding issues in Iran within the framework of the Agency, underlines the necessity of the IAEA continuing its work to clarify all outstanding issues relating to Iran's nuclear programme, and calls upon Iran to act in accordance with the provisions of the Additional Protocol and to implement without delay all transparency measures as the IAEA may request in support of its ongoing investigations,

7. *Requests* by 31 August a report from the Director General of the IAEA primarily on whether Iran has established full and sustained suspension of all activities mentioned in this resolution, as well as on the process of Iranian compliance with all the steps required by the IAEA

Board and with the above provisions of this resolution, to the IAEA Board of Governors and in parallel to the Security Council for its consideration,

8. *Expresses* its intention, in the event that Iran has not by that date complied with this resolution, then to adopt appropriate measures under Article 41 of Chapter VII of the Charter of the United Nations to persuade Iran to comply with this resolution and the requirements of the IAEA, and underlines that further decisions will be required should such additional measures be necessary,

9. *Confirms* that such additional measures will not be necessary in the event that Iran complies with this resolution,

10. *Decides* to remain seized of the matter.

UN Security Council Resolution 1718 (October 14, 2006)

The Security Council,

Recalling its previous relevant resolutions, including resolution 825 (1993), resolution 1540 (2004) and, in particular, resolution 1695 (2006), as well as the statement of its President of 6 October 2006 (S/PRST/2006/41),

Reaffirming that proliferation of nuclear, chemical and biological weapons, as well as their means of delivery, constitutes a threat to international peace and security,

Expressing the gravest concern at the claim by the Democratic People's Republic of Korea (DPRK) that it has conducted a test of a nuclear weapon on 9 October 2006, and at the challenge such a test constitutes to the Treaty on the Non-Proliferation of Nuclear Weapons and to international efforts aimed at strengthening the global regime of non-proliferation of nuclear weapons, and the danger it poses to peace and stability in the region and beyond,

Expressing its firm conviction that the international regime on the non-proliferation of nuclear weapons should be maintained and recalling that the DPRK cannot have the status of a nuclear-weapon state in accordance with the Treaty on the Non-Proliferation of Nuclear Weapons,

Deploring the DPRK's announcement of withdrawal from the Treaty on the Non-Proliferation of Nuclear Weapons and its pursuit of nuclear weapons,

Deploring further that the DPRK has refused to return to the six-party talks without precondition,

Endorsing the Joint Statement issued on 19 September 2005 by China, the DPRK, Japan, the Republic of Korea, the Russian Federation and the United States,

Underlining the importance that the DPRK respond to other security and humanitarian concerns of the international community,

Expressing profound concern that the test claimed by the DPRK has generated increased tension in the region and beyond, and determining therefore that there is a clear threat to international peace and security,

Acting under Chapter VII of the Charter of the United Nations, and taking measures under its Article 41,

1. *Condemns* the nuclear test proclaimed by the DPRK on 9 October 2006 in flagrant disregard of its relevant resolutions, in particular resolution 1695 (2006), as well as of the statement of its President of 6 October 2006 (S/PRST/2006/41), including that such a test would bring universal condemnation of the international community and would represent a clear threat to international peace and security;
2. *Demands* that the DPRK not conduct any further nuclear test or launch of a ballistic missile;
3. *Demands* that the DPRK immediately retract its announcement of withdrawal from the Treaty on the Non-Proliferation of Nuclear Weapons;
4. *Demands* further that the DPRK return to the Treaty on the Non-Proliferation of Nuclear Weapons and International Atomic Energy Agency (IAEA) safeguards, and underlines the need for all States Parties to the Treaty on the Non-Proliferation of Nuclear Weapons to continue to comply with their Treaty obligations;
5. *Decides* that the DPRK shall suspend all activities related to its ballistic missile programme and in this context re-establish its pre-existing commitments to a moratorium on missile launching;
6. *Decides* that the DPRK shall abandon all nuclear weapons and existing nuclear programmes in a complete, verifiable and irreversible manner, shall act strictly in accordance with the obligations applicable to parties under the Treaty on the Non-Proliferation of Nuclear Weapons and the terms and conditions of its International Atomic Energy Agency (IAEA) Safeguards Agreement (IAEA INFCIRC/403) and shall provide the IAEA transparency measures extending beyond these requirements, including such access to individuals, documentation, equipments and facilities as may be required and deemed necessary by the IAEA;
7. *Decides* also that the DPRK shall abandon all other existing weapons of mass destruction and ballistic missile programme in a complete, verifiable and irreversible manner;
8. *Decides* that:
   (a) all Member States shall prevent the direct or indirect supply, sale or transfer to the DPRK, through their territories or by their nationals,

or using their flag vessels or aircraft, and whether or not originating in their territories, of:

(i) any battle tanks, armoured combat vehicles, large calibre artillery systems, combat aircraft, attack helicopters, warships, missiles or missile systems as defined for the purpose of the United Nations Register on Conventional Arms, or related materiel including spare parts, or items as determined by the Security Council or the Committee established by paragraph 12 below (the Committee);

(ii) all items, materials, equipment, goods and technology as set out in the lists in documents S/2006/814 and S/2006/815, unless within 14 days of adoption of this resolution the Committee has amended or completed their provisions also taking into account the list in document S/2006/816, as well as other items, materials, equipment, goods and technology, determined by the Security Council or the Committee, which could contribute to DPRK's nuclear-related, ballistic missile-related or other weapons of mass destruction-related programmes;

(iii) luxury goods;

(b) the DPRK shall cease the export of all items covered in subparagraphs (a) (i) and (a) (ii) above and that all Member States shall prohibit the procurement of such items from the DPRK by their nationals, or using their flagged vessels or aircraft, and whether or not originating in the territory of the DPRK;

(c) all Member States shall prevent any transfers to the DPRK by their nationals or from their territories, or from the DPRK by its nationals or from its territory, of technical training, advice, services or assistance related to the provision, manufacture, maintenance or use of the items in subparagraphs (a) (i) and (a) (ii) above;

(d) all Member States shall, in accordance with their respective legal processes, freeze immediately the funds, other financial assets and economic resources which are on their territories at the date of the adoption of this resolution or at any time thereafter, that are owned or controlled, directly or indirectly, by the persons or entities designated by the Committee or by the Security Council as being engaged in or providing support for, including through other illicit means, DPRK's nuclear-related, other weapons of mass destruction-related and ballistic missile-related programmes, or by persons or entities acting on their behalf or at their direction, and ensure that any funds, financial assets or economic resources are prevented from being made available by their nationals or by any persons or entities within their territories, to or for the benefit of such persons or entities;

(e) all Member States shall take the necessary steps to prevent the entry into or transit through their territories of the persons designated by the Committee or by the Security Council as being responsible for, including through supporting or promoting, DPRK policies in relation to the DPRK's nuclear-related, ballistic missile-related and other weapons of mass destruction-related programmes, together with their family members, provided that nothing in this paragraph shall oblige a state to refuse its own nationals entry into its territory;

(f) in order to ensure compliance with the requirements of this paragraph, and thereby preventing illicit trafficking in nuclear, chemical or biological weapons, their means of delivery and related materials, all Member States are called upon to take, in accordance with their national authorities and legislation, and consistent with international law, cooperative action including through inspection of cargo to and from the DPRK, as necessary;

9. *Decides* that the provisions of paragraph 8 (d) above do not apply to financial or other assets or resources that have been determined by relevant States:

(a) to be necessary for basic expenses, including payment for foodstuffs, rent or mortgage, medicines and medical treatment, taxes, insurance premiums, and public utility charges, or exclusively for payment of reasonable professional fees and reimbursement of incurred expenses associated with the provision of legal services, or fees or service charges, in accordance with national laws, for routine holding or maintenance of frozen funds, other financial assets and economic resources, after notification by the relevant States to the Committee of the intention to authorize, where appropriate, access to such funds, other financial assets and economic resources and in the absence of a negative decision by the Committee within five working days of such notification;

(b) to be necessary for extraordinary expenses, provided that such determination has been notified by the relevant States to the Committee and has been approved by the Committee; or

(c) to be subject of a judicial, administrative or arbitral lien or judgement, in which case the funds, other financial assets and economic resources may be used to satisfy that lien or judgement provided that the lien or judgement was entered prior to the date of the present resolution, is not for the benefit of a person referred to in paragraph 8 (d) above or an individual or entity identified by the Security Council or the Committee, and has been notified by the relevant States to the Committee;

10. *Decides* that the measures imposed by paragraph 8 (e) above shall not apply where the Committee determines on a case-by-case basis that such travel is justified on the grounds of humanitarian need, including religious obligations, or where the Committee concludes that an exemption would otherwise further the objectives of the present resolution;

11. *Calls upon* all Member States to report to the Security Council within thirty days of the adoption of this resolution on the steps they have taken with a view to implementing effectively the provisions of paragraph 8 above;

12. *Decides* to establish, in accordance with rule 28 of its provisional rules of procedure, a Committee of the Security Council consisting of all the members of the Council, to undertake the following tasks:

    (a) to seek from all States, in particular those producing or possessing the items, materials, equipment, goods and technology referred to in paragraph 8 (a) above, information regarding the actions taken by them to implement effectively the measures imposed by paragraph 8 above of this resolution and whatever further information it may consider useful in this regard;

    (b) to examine and take appropriate action on information regarding alleged violations of measures imposed by paragraph 8 of this resolution;

    (c) to consider and decide upon requests for exemptions set out in paragraphs 9 and 10 above;

    (d) to determine additional items, materials, equipment, goods and technology to be specified for the purpose of paragraphs 8 (a) (i) and 8 (a) (ii) above;

    (e) to designate additional individuals and entities subject to the measures imposed by paragraphs 8 (d) and 8 (e) above;

    (f) to promulgate guidelines as may be necessary to facilitate the implementation of the measures imposed by this resolution;

    (g) to report at least every 90 days to the Security Council on its work, with its observations and recommendations, in particular on ways to strengthen the effectiveness of the measures imposed by paragraph 8 above;

13. *Welcomes and encourages further* the efforts by all States concerned to intensify their diplomatic efforts, to refrain from any actions that might aggravate tension and to facilitate the early resumption of the six-party talks, with a view to the expeditious implementation of the Joint Statement issued on 19 September 2005 by China, the DPRK, Japan, the Republic of Korea, the Russian Federation and the United States, to achieve the verifiable denuclearization of the Korean peninsula and to maintain peace and stability on the Korean peninsula and in North-East Asia;

14. *Calls upon* the DPRK to return immediately to the six-party talks without precondition and to work towards the expeditious implementation of the Joint Statement issued on 19 September 2005 by China, the DPRK, Japan, the Republic of Korea, the Russian Federation and the United States;

15. *Affirms* that it shall keep DPRK's actions under continuous review and that it shall be prepared to review the appropriateness of the measures

contained in paragraph 8 above, including the strengthening, modification, suspension or lifting of the measures, as may be needed at that time in light of the DPRK's compliance with the provisions of the resolution;

16. *Underlines* that further decisions will be required, should additional measures be necessary;

17. *Decides* to remain actively seized of the matter.

SELECTED UNITED NATIONS SECURITY COUNCIL RESOLUTIONS RELATED TO IRAN

UN Security Council Resolution 1737 (December 23, 2006)

The Security Council,

Recalling the Statement of its President, S/PRST/2006/15, of 29 March 2006, and its resolution 1696 (2006) of 31 July 2006,

Reaffirming its commitment to the Treaty on the Non-Proliferation of Nuclear Weapons, and recalling the right of States Party, in conformity with Articles I and II of that Treaty, to develop research, production and use of nuclear energy for peaceful purposes without discrimination,

Reiterating its serious concern over the many reports of the IAEA Director General and resolutions of the IAEA Board of Governors related to Iran's nuclear programme, reported to it by the IAEA Director General, including IAEA Board resolution GOV/2006/14,

Reiterating its serious concern that the IAEA Director General's report of 27 February 2006 (GOV/2006/15) lists a number of outstanding issues and concerns on Iran's nuclear programme, including topics which could have a military nuclear dimension, and that the IAEA is unable to conclude that there are no undeclared nuclear materials or activities in Iran,

Reiterating its serious concern over the IAEA Director General's report of 28 April 2006 (GOV/2006/27) and its findings, including that, after more than three years of Agency efforts to seek clarity about all aspects of Iran's nuclear programme, the existing gaps in knowledge continue to be a matter of concern, and that the IAEA is unable to make progress in its efforts to provide assurances about the absence of undeclared nuclear material and activities in Iran,

Noting with serious concern that, as confirmed by the IAEA Director General's reports of 8 June 2006 (GOV/2006/38), 31 August 2006 (GOV/2006/53) and 14 November 2006 (GOV/2006/64), Iran has not established full and sustained suspension of all enrichment-related and reprocessing activities as set out in resolution 1696 (2006), nor resumed its cooperation with the IAEA under the Additional Protocol, nor taken the other steps required of it by the IAEA Board of Governors, nor complied with the provisions of Security Council resolution 1696 (2006) and which are essential to build confidence, and *deploring* Iran's refusal to take these steps,

Emphasizing the importance of political and diplomatic efforts to find a negotiated solution guaranteeing that Iran's nuclear programme is exclusively for peaceful purposes, and *noting* that such a solution would benefit nuclear non-proliferation elsewhere, and *welcoming* the continuing commitment of China, France, Germany, the Russian Federation, the United Kingdom and the United States, with the support of the European Union's High Representative to seek a negotiated solution,

Determined to give effect to its decisions by adopting appropriate measures to persuade Iran to comply with resolution 1696 (2006) and with the requirements of the IAEA, and also to constrain Iran's development of sensitive technologies in support of its nuclear and missile programmes, until such time as the Security Council determines that the objectives of this resolution have been met,

Concerned by the proliferation risks presented by the Iranian nuclear programme and, in this context, by Iran's continuing failure to meet the requirements of the IAEA Board of Governors and to comply with the provisions of Security Council resolution 1696 (2006), *mindful* of its primary responsibility under the Charter of the United Nations for the maintenance of international peace and security,

Acting under Article 41 of Chapter VII of the Charter of the United Nations,

1. *Affirms* that Iran shall without further delay take the steps required by the IAEA Board of Governors in its resolution GOV/2006/14, which are essential to build confidence in the exclusively peaceful purpose of its nuclear programme and to resolve outstanding questions;
2. *Decides*, in this context, that Iran shall without further delay suspend the following proliferation sensitive nuclear activities:
    (a) all enrichment-related and reprocessing activities, including research and development, to be verified by the IAEA; and
    (b) work on all heavy water-related projects, including the construction of a research reactor moderated by heavy water, also to be verified by the IAEA;
3. *Decides* that all States shall take the necessary measures to prevent the supply, sale or transfer directly or indirectly from their territories, or by their nationals or using their flag vessels or aircraft to, or for the use in

or benefit of, Iran, and whether or not originating in their territories, of all items, materials, equipment, goods and technology which could contribute to Iran's enrichment-related, reprocessing or heavy water-related activities, or to the development of nuclear weapon delivery systems, namely:

(a) those set out in sections B.2, B.3, B.4, B.5, B.6 and B.7 of INFCIRC/254/Rev.8/Part 1 in document S/2006/814;

(b) those set out in sections A.1 and B.1 of INFCIRC/254/Rev.8/Part 1 in document S/2006/814, except the supply, sale or transfer of:

   (i) equipment covered by B.1 when such equipment is for light water reactors;

   (ii) low-enriched uranium covered by A.1.2 when it is incorporated in assembled nuclear fuel elements for such reactors;

(c) those set out in document S/2006/815, except the supply, sale or transfer of items covered by 19.A.3 of Category II;

(d) any additional items, materials, equipment, goods and technology, determined as necessary by the Security Council or the Committee established by paragraph 18 below (herein "the Committee"), which could contribute to enrichment-related, or reprocessing, or heavy water-related activities, or to the development of nuclear weapon delivery systems;

4. *Decides* that all States shall take the necessary measures to prevent the supply, sale or transfer directly or indirectly from their territories, or by their nationals or using their flag vessels or aircraft to, or for the use in or benefit of, Iran, and whether or not originating in their territories, of the following items, materials, equipment, goods and technology:

(a) those set out in INFCIRC/254/Rev.7/Part2 of document S/2006/814 if the State determines that they would contribute to enrichment-related, reprocessing or heavy water-related activities;

(b) any other items not listed in documents S/2006/814 or S/2006/815 if the State determines that they would contribute to enrichment-related, reprocessing or heavy water-related activities, or to the development of nuclear weapon delivery systems;

(c) any further items if the State determines that they would contribute to the pursuit of activities related to other topics about which the IAEA has expressed concerns or identified as outstanding;

5. *Decides* that, for the supply, sale or transfer of all items, materials, equipment, goods and technology covered by documents S/2006/814 and S/2006/815 the export of which to Iran is not prohibited by sub-paragraphs 3 (b), 3 (c) or 4 (a) above, States shall ensure that:

(a) the requirements, as appropriate, of the Guidelines as set out in documents S/2006/814 and S/2006/985 have been met; and

(b) they have obtained and are in a position to exercise effectively a right to verify the end-use and end-use location of any supplied item; and

(c) they notify the Committee within ten days of the supply, sale or transfer; and

(d) in the case of items, materials, equipment, goods and technology contained in document S/2006/814, they also notify the IAEA within ten days of the supply, sale or transfer;

6. *Decides* that all States shall also take the necessary measures to prevent the provision to Iran of any technical assistance or training, financial assistance, investment, brokering or other services, and the transfer of financial resources or services, related to the supply, sale, transfer, manufacture or use of the prohibited items, materials, equipment, goods and technology specified in paragraphs 3 and 4 above;

7. *Decides* that Iran shall not export any of the items in documents S/2006/814 and S/2006/815 and that all Member States shall prohibit the procurement of such items from Iran by their nationals, or using their flag vessels or aircraft, and whether or not originating in the territory of Iran;

8. *Decides* that Iran shall provide such access and cooperation as the IAEA requests to be able to verify the suspension outlined in paragraph 2 and to resolve all outstanding issues, as identified in IAEA reports, and *calls upon* Iran to ratify promptly the Additional Protocol;

9. *Decides* that the measures imposed by paragraphs 3, 4 and 6 above shall not apply where the Committee determines in advance and on a case-by-case basis that such supply, sale, transfer or provision of such items or assistance would clearly not contribute to the development of Iran's technologies in support of its proliferation sensitive nuclear activities and of development of nuclear weapon delivery systems, including where such items or assistance are for food, agricultural, medical or other humanitarian purposes, provided that:

(a) contracts for delivery of such items or assistance include appropriate end-user guarantees; and

(b) Iran has committed not to use such items in proliferation sensitive nuclear activities or for development of nuclear weapon delivery systems;

10. *Calls upon* all States to exercise vigilance regarding the entry into or transit through their territories of individuals who are engaged in, directly associated with or providing support for Iran's proliferation sensitive nuclear activities or for the development of nuclear weapon delivery systems, and decides in this regard that all States shall notify the Committee of the entry into or transit through their territories of the persons designated in the Annex to this resolution (herein "the Annex"), as well as of additional persons designated by the Security Council or the Committee as being engaged in, directly associated with or providing support for Iran's proliferation sensitive nuclear activities and for the development of nuclear weapon delivery systems, including through the involvement

in procurement of the prohibited items, goods, equipment, materials and technology specified by and under the measures in paragraphs 3 and 4 above, except where such travel is for activities directly related to the items in subparagraphs 3 (b) (i) and (ii) above;

11. *Underlines* that nothing in the above paragraph requires a State to refuse its own nationals entry into its territory, and that all States shall, in the implementation of the above paragraph, take into account humanitarian considerations as well as the necessity to meet the objectives of this resolution, including where Article XV of the IAEA Statute is engaged;

12. *Decides* that all States shall freeze the funds, other financial assets and economic resources which are on their territories at the date of adoption of this resolution or at any time thereafter, that are owned or controlled by the persons or entities designated in the Annex, as well as those of additional persons or entities designated by the Security Council or by the Committee as being engaged in, directly associated with or providing support for Iran's proliferation sensitive nuclear activities or the development of nuclear weapon delivery systems, or by persons or entities acting on their behalf or at their direction, or by entities owned or controlled by them, including through illicit means, and that the measures in this paragraph shall cease to apply in respect of such persons or entities if, and at such time as, the Security Council or the Committee removes them from the Annex, and *decides further* that all States shall ensure that any funds, financial assets or economic resources are prevented from being made available by their nationals or by any persons or entities within their territories, to or for the benefit of these persons and entities;

13. *Decides* that the measures imposed by paragraph 12 above do not apply to funds, other financial assets or economic resources that have been determined by relevant States:

    (a) to be necessary for basic expenses, including payment for foodstuffs, rent or mortgage, medicines and medical treatment, taxes, insurance premiums, and public utility charges or exclusively for payment of reasonable professional fees and reimbursement of incurred expenses associated with the provision of legal services, or fees or service charges, in accordance with national laws, for routine holding or maintenance of frozen funds, other financial assets and economic resources, after notification by the relevant States to the Committee of the intention to authorize, where appropriate, access to such funds, other financial assets or economic resources and in the absence of a negative decision by the Committee within five working days of such notification;

    (b) to be necessary for extraordinary expenses, provided that such determination has been notified by the relevant States to the Committee and has been approved by the Committee;

(c) to be the subject of a judicial, administrative or arbitral lien or judgement, in which case the funds, other financial assets and economic resources may be used to satisfy that lien or judgement provided that the lien or judgement was entered into prior to the date of the present resolution, is not for the benefit of a person or entity designated pursuant to paragraphs 10 and 12 above, and has been notified by the relevant States to the Committee;

(d) to be necessary for activities directly related to the items specified in subparagraphs 3 (b) (i) and (ii) and have been notified by the relevant States to the Committee;

14. *Decides* that States may permit the addition to the accounts frozen pursuant to the provisions of paragraph 12 above of interests or other earnings due on those accounts or payments due under contracts, agreements or obligations that arose prior to the date on which those accounts became subject to the provisions of this resolution, provided that any such interest, other earnings and payments continue to be subject to these provisions and are frozen;

15. *Decides* that the measures in paragraph 12 above shall not prevent a designated person or entity from making payment due under a contract entered into prior to the listing of such a person or entity, provided that the relevant States have determined that:

(a) the contract is not related to any of the prohibited items, materials, equipment, goods, technologies, assistance, training, financial assistance, investment, brokering or services referred to in paragraphs 3, 4 and 6 above;

(b) the payment is not directly or indirectly received by a person or entity designated pursuant to paragraph 12 above;

and after notification by the relevant States to the Committee of the intention to make or receive such payments or to authorize, where appropriate, the unfreezing of funds, other financial assets or economic resources for this purpose, 10 working days prior to such authorization;

16. *Decides* that technical cooperation provided to Iran by the IAEA or under its auspices shall only be for food, agricultural, medical, safety or other humanitarian purposes, or where it is necessary for projects directly related to the items specified in subparagraphs 3 (b) (i) and (ii) above, but that no such technical cooperation shall be provided that relates to the proliferation sensitive nuclear activities set out in paragraph 2 above;

17. *Calls upon* all States to exercise vigilance and prevent specialized teaching or training of Iranian nationals, within their territories or by their nationals, of disciplines which would contribute to Iran's proliferation sensitive nuclear activities and development of nuclear weapon delivery systems;

18. *Decides* to establish, in accordance with rule 28 of its provisional rules of procedure, a Committee of the Security Council consisting of all the members of the Council, to undertake the following tasks:

(a) to seek from all States, in particular those in the region and those producing the items, materials, equipment, goods and technology referred to in paragraphs 3 and 4 above, information regarding the actions taken by them to implement effectively the measures imposed by paragraphs 3, 4, 5, 6, 7, 8, 10 and 12 of this resolution and whatever further information it may consider useful in this regard;

(b) to seek from the secretariat of the IAEA information regarding the actions taken by the IAEA to implement effectively the measures imposed by paragraph 17 of this resolution and whatever further information it may consider useful in this regard;

(c) to examine and take appropriate action on information regarding alleged violations of measures imposed by paragraphs 3, 4, 5, 6, 7, 8, 10 and 12 of this resolution;

(d) to consider and decide upon requests for exemptions set out in paragraphs 9, 13 and 15 above;

(e) to determine as may be necessary additional items, materials, equipment, goods and technology to be specified for the purpose of paragraph 3 above;

(f) to designate as may be necessary additional individuals and entities subject to the measures imposed by paragraphs 10 and 12 above;

(g) to promulgate guidelines as may be necessary to facilitate the implementation of the measures imposed by this resolution and include in such guidelines a requirement on States to provide information where possible as to why any individuals and/or entities meet the criteria set out in paragraphs 10 and 12 and any relevant identifying information;

(h) to report at least every 90 days to the Security Council on its work and on the implementation of this resolution, with its observations and recommendations, in particular on ways to strengthen the effectiveness of the measures imposed by paragraphs 3, 4, 5, 6, 7, 8, 10 and 12 above;

19. *Decides* that all States shall report to the Committee within 60 days of the adoption of this resolution on the steps they have taken with a view to implementing effectively paragraphs 3, 4, 5, 6, 7, 8, 10, 12 and 17 above;

20. *Expresses* the conviction that the suspension set out in paragraph 2 above as well as full, verified Iranian compliance with the requirements set out by the IAEA Board of Governors, would contribute to a diplomatic, negotiated solution that guarantees Iran's nuclear programme is for

exclusively peaceful purposes, *underlines* the willingness of the international community to work positively for such a solution, *encourages* Iran, in conforming to the above provisions, to re-engage with the international community and with the IAEA, and *stresses* that such engagement will be beneficial to Iran;

21. *Welcomes* the commitment of China, France, Germany, the Russian Federation, the United Kingdom and the United States, with the support of the European Union's High Representative, to a negotiated solution to this issue and encourages Iran to engage with their June 2006 proposals (S/2006/521), which were endorsed by the Security Council in resolution 1696 (2006), for a long-term comprehensive agreement which would allow for the development of relations and cooperation with Iran based on mutual respect and the establishment of international confidence in the exclusively peaceful nature of Iran's nuclear programme;

22. *Reiterates* its determination to reinforce the authority of the IAEA, strongly supports the role of the IAEA Board of Governors, *commends* and *encourages* the Director General of the IAEA and its secretariat for their ongoing professional and impartial efforts to resolve all remaining outstanding issues in Iran within the framework of the IAEA, *underlines* the necessity of the IAEA continuing its work to clarify all outstanding issues relating to Iran's nuclear programme;

23. *Requests* within 60 days a report from the Director General of the IAEA on whether Iran has established full and sustained suspension of all activities mentioned in this resolution, as well as on the process of Iranian compliance with all the steps required by the IAEA Board and with the other provisions of this resolution, to the IAEA Board of Governors and in parallel to the Security Council for its consideration;

24. *Affirms* that it shall review Iran's actions in the light of the report referred to in paragraph 23 above, to be submitted within 60 days, and:

    (a) that it shall suspend the implementation of measures if and for so long as Iran suspends all enrichment-related and reprocessing activities, including research and development, as verified by the IAEA, to allow for negotiations;

    (b) that it shall terminate the measures specified in paragraphs 3, 4, 5, 6, 7, 10 and 12 of this resolution as soon as it determines that Iran has fully complied with its obligations under the relevant resolutions of the Security Council and met the requirements of the IAEA Board of Governors, as confirmed by the IAEA Board;

    (c) that it shall, in the event that the report in paragraph 23 above shows that Iran has not complied with this resolution, adopt further appropriate measures under Article 41 of Chapter VII of the Charter of the United Nations to persuade Iran to comply with this resolution and the requirements of the IAEA, and underlines that further decisions will be required should such additional measures be necessary;

25. *Decides* to remain seized of the matter.

Resolution Annex

A. Entities involved in the nuclear programme

1. Atomic Energy Organisation of Iran
2. Mesbah Energy Company (provider for A40 research reactor—Arak)
3. Kala-Electric (aka Kalaye Electric) (provider for PFEP—Natanz)
4. Pars Trash Company (involved in centrifuge programme, identified in IAEA reports)
5. Farayand Technique (involved in centrifuge programme, identified in IAEA reports)
6. Defence Industries Organisation (overarching MODAFL-controlled entity, some of whose subordinates have been involved in the centrifuge programme making components, and in the missile programme)
7. 7th of Tir (subordinate of DIO, widely recognized as being directly involved in the nuclear programme)

B. Entities involved in the ballistic missile programme

1. Shahid Hemmat Industrial Group (SHIG) (subordinate entity of AIO)
2. Shahid Bagheri Industrial Group (SBIG) (subordinate entity of AIO)
3. Fajr Industrial Group (formerly Instrumentation Factory Plant, subordinate entity of AIO)

C. Persons involved in the nuclear programme

1. Mohammad Qannadi, AEOI Vice President for Research & Development
2. Behman Asgarpour, Operational Manager (Arak)
3. Dawood Agha-Jani, Head of the PFEP (Natanz)
4. Ehsan Monajemi, Construction Project Manager, Natanz
5. Jafar Mohammadi, Technical Adviser to the AEOI (in charge of managing the production of valves for centrifuges)
6. Ali Hajinia Leilabadi, Director General of Mesbah Energy Company
7. Lt Gen Mohammad Mehdi Nejad Nouri, Rector of Malek Ashtar University of Defence Technology (chemistry dept, affiliated to MODALF, has conducted experiments on beryllium)

D. Persons involved in the ballistic missile programme

1. Gen Hosein Salimi, Commander of the Air Force, IRGC (Pasdaran)
2. Ahmad Vahid Dastjerdi, Head of the AIO

3. Reza-Gholi Esmaeli, Head of Trade & International Affairs Dept, AIO

4. Bahmanyar Morteza Bahmanyar, Head of Finance & Budget Dept, AIO

E. Persons involved in both the nuclear and ballistic missile programmes

1. Maj Gen Yahya Rahim Safavi, Commander, IRGC (Pasdaran)

UN Security Council Resolution 1747 (March 24, 2007)

The Security Council,

Recalling the Statement of its President, S/PRST/2006/15, of 29 March 2006, and its resolution 1696 (2006) of 31 July 2006, and its resolution 1737 (2006) of 23 December 2006, and reaffirming their provisions,

Reaffirming its commitment to the Treaty on the Non-Proliferation of Nuclear Weapons, the need for all States party to that Treaty to comply fully with all their obligations, and recalling the right of States parties, in conformity with articles I and II of that Treaty, to develop research, production and use of nuclear energy for peaceful purposes without discrimination,

Recalling its serious concern over the reports of the IAEA Director General as set out in its resolutions 1696 (2006) and 1737 (2006),

Recalling the latest report by the IAEA Director General (GOV/2007/8) of 22 February 2007 and deploring that, as indicated therein, Iran has failed to comply with resolution 1696 (2006) and resolution 1737 (2006),

Emphasizing the importance of political and diplomatic efforts to find a negotiated solution guaranteeing that Iran's nuclear programme is exclusively for peaceful purposes, and noting that such a solution would benefit nuclear non-proliferation elsewhere, and welcoming the continuing commitment of China, France, Germany, the Russian Federation, the United Kingdom and the United States, with the support of the European Union's High Representative, to seek a negotiated solution,

Recalling the resolution of the IAEA Board of Governors (GOV/2006/14), which states that a solution to the Iranian nuclear issue would contribute to global non-proliferation efforts and to realizing the objective of a Middle East free of weapons of mass destruction, including their means of delivery,

Determined to give effect to its decisions by adopting appropriate measures to persuade Iran to comply with resolution 1696 (2006) and resolution 1737 (2006) and with the requirements of the IAEA, and also to constrain Iran's development of sensitive technologies in support of its nuclear and missile programmes, until such time as the Security Council determines that the objectives of these resolutions have been met,

Recalling the requirement on States to join in affording mutual assistance in carrying out the measures decided upon by the Security Council,

Concerned by the proliferation risks presented by the Iranian nuclear programme and, in this context, by Iran's continuing failure to meet the requirements of the IAEA Board of Governors and to comply with the provisions of Security Council resolutions 1696 (2006) and 1737 (2006), mindful of its primary responsibility under the Charter of the United Nations for the maintenance of international peace and security,

Acting under Article 41 of Chapter VII of the Charter of the United Nations,

1. Reaffirms that Iran shall without further delay take the steps required by the IAEA Board of Governors in its resolution GOV/2006/14, which are essential to build confidence in the exclusively peaceful purpose of its nuclear programme and to resolve outstanding questions and, in this context, affirms its decision that Iran shall without further delay take the steps required in paragraph 2 of resolution 1737 (2006);

2. Calls upon all States also to exercise vigilance and restraint regarding the entry into or transit through their territories of individuals who are engaged in, directly associated with or providing support for Iran's proliferation sensitive nuclear activities or for the development of nuclear weapon delivery systems, and decides in this regard that all States shall notify the Committee established pursuant to paragraph 18 of resolution 1737 (2006) (herein "the Committee") of the entry into or transit through their territories of the persons designated in the Annex to resolution 1737 (2006) or Annex I to this resolution, as well as of additional persons designated by the Security Council or the Committee as being engaged in, directly associated with or providing support for Iran's proliferation sensitive nuclear activities or for the development of nuclear weapon delivery systems, including through the involvement in procurement of the prohibited items, goods, equipment, materials and technology specified by and under the measures in paragraphs 3 and 4 of resolution 1737 (2006), except where such travel is for activities directly related to the items in subparagraphs 3 (b) (i) and (ii) of that resolution;

3. Underlines that nothing in the above paragraph requires a State to refuse its own nationals entry into its territory, and that all States shall, in the implementation of the above paragraph, take into account humanitarian considerations, including religious obligations, as well as the necessity to meet the objectives of this resolution and resolution 1737 (2006), including where article XV of the IAEA Statute is engaged;

4. Decides that the measures specified in paragraphs 12, 13, 14 and 15 of resolution 1737 (2006) shall apply also to the persons and entities listed in Annex I to this resolution;

5. Decides that Iran shall not supply, sell or transfer directly or indirectly from its territory or by its nationals or using its flag vessels or aircraft any arms or related materiel, and that all States shall prohibit the procurement of such items from Iran by their nationals, or using their flag vessels or aircraft, and whether or not originating in the territory of Iran;

6. Calls upon all States to exercise vigilance and restraint in the supply, sale or transfer directly or indirectly from their territories or by their nationals or using their flag vessels or aircraft of any battle tanks, armoured combat vehicles, large calibre artillery systems, combat aircraft, attack helicopters, warships, missiles or missile systems as defined for the purpose of the United Nations Register on Conventional Arms to Iran, and in the provision to Iran of any technical assistance or training, financial assistance, investment, brokering or other services, and the transfer of financial resources or services, related to the supply, sale, transfer, manufacture or use of such items in order to prevent a destabilising accumulation of arms;

7. Calls upon all States and international financial institutions not to enter into new commitments for grants, financial assistance, and concessional loans, to the government of the Islamic Republic of Iran, except for humanitarian and developmental purposes;

8. Calls upon all States to report to the Committee within 60 days of the adoption of this resolution on the steps they have taken with a view to implementing effectively paragraphs 2, 4, 5, 6 and 7 above;

9. Expresses the conviction that the suspension set out in paragraph 2 of resolution 1737 (2006), as well as full, verified Iranian compliance with the requirements set out by the IAEA Board of Governors would contribute to a diplomatic, negotiated solution that guarantees Iran's nuclear programme is for exclusively peaceful purposes, underlines the willingness of the international community to work positively for such a solution, encourages Iran, in conforming to the above provisions, to re-engage with the international community and with the IAEA, and stresses that such engagement will be beneficial to Iran;

10. Welcomes the continuous affirmation of the commitment of China, France, Germany, the Russian Federation, the United Kingdom and the United States, with the support of the European Union's High Representative, to a negotiated solution to this issue and encourages Iran to engage with their June 2006 proposals (S/2006/521), attached in Annex II to this resolution, which were endorsed by the Security Council in resolution 1696 (2006), and acknowledges with appreciation that this offer to Iran remains on the table, for a long-term comprehensive agreement

which would allow for the development of relations and cooperation with Iran based on mutual respect and the establishment of international confidence in the exclusively peaceful nature of Iran's nuclear programme;

11. Reiterates its determination to reinforce the authority of the IAEA, strongly supports the role of the IAEA Board of Governors, commends and encourages the Director General of the IAEA and its secretariat for their ongoing professional and impartial efforts to resolve all outstanding issues in Iran within the framework of the IAEA, underlines the necessity of the IAEA, which is internationally recognized as having authority for verifying compliance with safeguards agreements, including the non-diversion of nuclear material for non-peaceful purposes, in accordance with its Statute, to continue its work to clarify all outstanding issues relating to Iran's nuclear programme;

12. Requests within 60 days a further report from the Director General of the IAEA on whether Iran has established full and sustained suspension of all activities mentioned in resolution 1737 (2006), as well as on the process of Iranian compliance with all the steps required by the IAEA Board and with the other provisions of resolution 1737 (2006) and of this resolution, to the IAEA Board of Governors and in parallel to the Security Council for its consideration;

13. Affirms that it shall review Iran's actions in light of the report referred to in paragraph 12 above, to be submitted within 60 days, and:

(a) that it shall suspend the implementation of measures if and for so long as Iran suspends all enrichment-related and reprocessing activities, including research and development, as verified by the IAEA, to allow for negotiations in good faith in order to reach an early and mutually acceptable outcome;

(b) that it shall terminate the measures specified in paragraphs 3, 4, 5, 6, 7 and 12 of resolution 1737 (2006) as well as in paragraphs 2, 4, 5, 6 and 7 above as soon as it determines, following receipt of the report referred to in paragraph 12 above, that Iran has fully complied with its obligations under the relevant resolutions of the Security Council and met the requirements of the IAEA Board of Governors, as confirmed by the IAEA Board;

(c) that it shall, in the event that the report in paragraph 12 above shows that Iran has not complied with resolution 1737 (2006) and this resolution, adopt further appropriate measures under Article 41 of Chapter VII of the Charter of the United Nations to persuade Iran to comply with these resolutions and the requirements of the IAEA, and underlines that further decisions will be required should such additional measures be necessary;

14. Decides to remain seized of the matter.

Resolution Annex I

Entities involved in nuclear or ballistic missile activities

1. Ammunition and Metallurgy Industries Group (AMIG) (aka Ammunition Industries Group) (AMIG controls 7th of Tir, which is designated under resolution 1737 (2006) for its role in Iran's centrifuge programme. AMIG is in turn owned and controlled by the Defence Industries Organisation (DIO), which is designated under resolution 1737 (2006))
2. Esfahan Nuclear Fuel Research and Production Centre (NFRPC) and Esfahan Nuclear Technology Centre (ENTC) (Parts of the Atomic Energy Organisation of Iran's (AEOI) Nuclear Fuel Production and Procurement Company, which is involved in enrichment-related activities. AEOI is designated under resolution 1737 (2006))
3. Kavoshyar Company (Subsidiary company of AEOI, which has sought glass fibres, vacuum chamber furnaces and laboratory equipment for Iran's nuclear programme)
4. Parchin Chemical Industries (Branch of DIO, which produces ammunition, explosives, as well as solid propellants for rockets and missiles)
5. Karaj Nuclear Research Centre (Part of AEOI's research division)
6. Novin Energy Company (aka Pars Novin) (Operates within AEOI and has transferred funds on behalf of AEOI to entities associated with Iran's nuclear programme)
7. Cruise Missile Industry Group (aka Naval Defence Missile Industry Group) (Production and development of cruise missiles. Responsible for naval missiles including cruise missiles)
8. Bank Sepah and Bank Sepah International (Bank Sepah provides support for the Aerospace Industries Organisation (AIO) and subordinates, including Shahid Hemmat Industrial Group (SHIG) and Shahid Bagheri Industrial Group (SBIG), both of which were designated under resolution 1737 (2006)
9. Sanam Industrial Group (subordinate to AIO, which has purchased equipment on AIO's behalf for the missile programme)
10. Ya Mahdi Industries Group (subordinate to AIO, which is involved in international purchases of missile equipment)

Iranian Revolutionary Guard Corps entities

1. Qods Aeronautics Industries (Produces unmanned aerial vehicles (UAVs), parachutes, paragliders, paramotors, etc. Iranian Revolutionary Guard Corps (IRGC) has boasted of using these products as part of its asymmetric warfare doctrine)
2. Pars Aviation Services Company (Maintains various aircraft including MI-171, used by IRGC Air Force)

3. Sho'a' Aviation (Produces micro-lights which IRGC has claimed it is using as part of its asymmetric warfare doctrine)

Persons involved in nuclear or ballistic missile activities

1. Fereidoun Abbasi Davani (Senior Ministry of Defence and Armed Forces Logistics (MODAFL) scientist with links to the Institute of Applied Physics, working closely with Mohsen Fakhrizadeh-Mahabadi, designated below)
2. Mohsen Fakhrizadeh-Mahabadi (Senior MODAFL scientist and former head of the Physics Research Centre (PHRC). The IAEA have asked to interview him about the activities of the PHRC over the period he was head but Iran has refused)
3. Seyed Jaber Safdari (Manager of the Natanz Enrichment Facilities)
4. Amir Rahimi (Head of Esfahan Nuclear Fuel Research and Production Centre, which is part of the AEOI's Nuclear Fuel Production and Procurement Company, which is involved in enrichment-related activities)
5. Mohsen Hojati (Head of Fajr Industrial Group, which is designated under resolution 1737 (2006) for its role in the ballistic missile programme)
6. Mehrdada Akhlaghi Ketabachi (Head of SBIG, which is designated under resolution 1737 (2006) for its role in the ballistic missile programme)
7. Naser Maleki (Head of SHIG, which is designated under resolution 1737 (2006) for its role in Iran's ballistic missile programme. Naser Maleki is also a MODAFL official overseeing work on the Shahab-3 ballistic missile programme. The Shahab-3 is Iran's long-range ballistic missile currently in service)
8. Ahmad Derakhshandeh (Chairman and Managing Director of Bank Sepah, which provides support for the AIO and subordinates, including SHIG and SBIG, both of which were designated under resolution 1737 (2006))

Iranian Revolutionary Guard Corps key persons

1. Brigadier General Morteza Rezaie (Deputy Commander of IRGC)
2. Vice Admiral Ali Akbar Ahmadian (Chief of IRGC Joint Staff.)
3. Brigadier General Mohammad Reza Zahedi (Commander of IRGC Ground Forces)
4. Rear Admiral Morteza Safari (Commander of IRGC Navy)
5. Brigadier General Mohammad Hejazi (Commander of Bassij resistance force)
6. Brigadier General Qasem Soleimani (Commander of Qods force)
7. General Zolqadr (IRGC officer, Deputy Interior Minister for Security Affairs)

Resolution Annex II

Elements of a long-term agreement

Our goal is to develop relations and cooperation with Iran, based on mutual respect and the establishment of international confidence in the exclusively peaceful nature of the nuclear programme of the Islamic Republic of Iran. We propose a fresh start in the negotiation of a comprehensive agreement with Iran. Such an agreement would be deposited with the International Atomic Energy Agency (IAEA) and endorsed in a Security Council resolution.

To create the right conditions for negotiations, we will:

> Reaffirm Iran's right to develop nuclear energy for peaceful purposes in conformity with its obligations under the Treaty on the Non-Proliferation of Nuclear Weapons (hereinafter, NPT), and in this context reaffirm our support for the development by Iran of a civil nuclear energy programme.

> Commit to support actively the building of new light water reactors in Iran through international joint projects, in accordance with the IAEA statute and NPT.

> Agree to suspend discussion of Iran's nuclear programme in the Security Council upon the resumption of negotiations.

Iran will:

> Commit to addressing all of the outstanding concerns of IAEA through full cooperation with IAEA,

> Suspend all enrichment-related and reprocessing activities to be verified by IAEA, as requested by the IAEA Board of Governors and the Security Council, and commit to continue this during these negotiations.

> Resume the implementation of the Additional Protocol.

Areas of future cooperation to be covered in negotiations on a long-term agreement

1. Nuclear

We will take the following steps:

Iran's rights to nuclear energy. Reaffirm Iran's inalienable right to nuclear energy for peaceful purposes without discrimination and in conformity with articles I and II of NPT, and cooperate with Iran in the development by Iran of a civil nuclear power programme. Negotiate and implement a Euratom/Iran nuclear cooperation agreement.

Light water reactors. Actively support the building of new light water power reactors in Iran through international joint projects, in accordance with the IAEA statute and NPT, using state-of-the-art technology, including by authorizing the transfer of necessary goods and the provision of advanced technology to make its power reactors safe against earthquakes. Provide cooperation with the management of spent nuclear fuel and radioactive waste through appropriate arrangements.

Research and development in nuclear energy. Provide a substantive package of research and development cooperation, including possible provision of light water research reactors, notably in the fields of radioisotope production, basic research and nuclear applications in medicine and agriculture.

Fuel guarantees. Give legally binding, multilayered fuel assurances to Iran, based on: Participation as a partner in an international facility in Russia to provide enrichment services for a reliable supply of fuel to Iran's nuclear reactors. Subject to negotiations, such a facility could enrich all uranium hexaflouride (UF6) produced in Iran. Establishment on commercial terms of a buffer stock to hold a reserve of up to five years' supply of nuclear fuel dedicated to Iran, with the participation and under supervision of IAEA. Development with IAEA of a standing multilateral mechanism for reliable access to nuclear fuel, based on ideas to be considered at the next meeting of the Board of Governors.

Review of moratorium

The long-term agreement would, with regard to common efforts to build international confidence, contain a clause for review of the agreement in all its aspects, to follow:

Confirmation by IAEA that all outstanding issues and concerns reported by it, including those activities which could have a military nuclear dimension, have been resolved;

Confirmation that there are no undeclared nuclear activities or materials in Iran and that international confidence in the exclusively peaceful nature of Iran's civil nuclear programme has been restored.

2. Political and economic

Regional security cooperation. Support for a new conference to promote dialogue and cooperation on regional security issues.

International trade and investment. Improving Iran's access to the international economy, markets and capital, through practical support for full integration into international structures, including the World Trade Organization and to create the framework for increased direct investment in Iran and trade with Iran (including a trade and economic cooperation agreement with the European Union). Steps would be taken to improve access to key goods and technology.

Civil aviation. Civil aviation cooperation, including the possible removal of restrictions on United States and European manufacturers in regard to the export of civil aircraft to Iran, thereby widening the prospect of Iran renewing its fleet of civil airliners.

Energy partnership. Establishment of a long-term energy partnership between Iran and the European Union and other willing partners, with concrete and practical applications.

Telecommunications infrastructure. Support for the modernization of Iran's telecommunication infrastructure and advanced Internet provision, including by possible removal of relevant United States and other export restrictions.

High technology cooperation. Cooperation in fields of high technology and other areas to be agreed upon.

Agriculture. Support for agricultural development in Iran, including possible access to United States and European agricultural products, technology and farm equipment.

THE KOREAN ARMISTICE AGREEMENT (JULY 27, 1953)

Agreement between the Commander-in-Chief, United Nations Command, on the one hand, and the Supreme Commander of the Korean People's Army and the Commander of the Chinese People's volunteers, on the other hand, concerning a military armistice in Korea.

Preamble

The undersigned, the Commander-in-Chief, United Nations Command, on the one hand, and the Supreme Commander of the Korean People's Army and the Commander of the Chinese People's Volunteers, on the other hand, in the interest of stopping the Korean conflict, with its great toil of suffering and bloodshed on both sides, and with the objective of establishing an armistice which will insure a complete cessation of hostilities and of all acts of armed force in Korea until a final peaceful settlement is achieved, do individually, collectively, and mutually agree to accept and to be bound and governed by the conditions and terms of armistice set forth in the following articles and paragraphs, which said conditions and terms are intended to be purely military in character and to pertain solely to the belligerents in Korea:

Article I: Military Demarcation Line and Demilitarized Zone

1. A military demarcation line shall be fixed and both sides shall withdraw two (2) kilometers from this line so as to establish a demilitarized zone between the opposing forces. A demilitarized zone shall be established as a buffer zone to prevent the occurrence of incidents which might lead to a resumption of hostilities.

2. The military demarcation line is located as indicated on the attached map.

3. This demilitarized zone is defined by a northern and southern boundary as indicated on the attached map.

4. The military demarcation line shall be plainly marked as directed by the Military Armistice Commission hereinafter established. The Commanders of the opposing sides shall have suitable markers erected along the boundary between the demilitarized zone and their respective areas. The Military Armistice Commission shall supervise the erection of all markers placed along the military demarcation line and along the boundaries of the demilitarized zone.

5. The waters of the Han River Estuary shall be open to civil shipping of both sides wherever one bank is controlled by one side and the other bank is controlled by the other side. The Military Armistice Commission shall prescribe rules for the shipping in that part of the Han River Estuary indicated on the attached map. Civil shipping of each side shall have unrestricted access to the land under the military control of that side.

6. Neither side shall execute any hostile act within, from, or against the demilitarized zone.

7. No person, military or civilian, shall be permitted to cross the military demarcation line unless specifically authorized to do so by the Military Armistice Commission.

8. No, person military of civilian, in the demilitarized zone shall be permitted to enter the territory under the military control of either side unless specifically authorized to do so by the Commander into whose territory entry is sought.

9. No person, military or civilian, shall be permitted to enter the demilitarized zone except persons concerned with the conduct of civil administration and relief and persons specifically authorized to enter by the Military Armistice Commission.

10. Civil administration and relief in that part of the demilitarized zone which is south of the military of the military demarcation line shall be the responsibility of the Commander-in-Chief, United Nations Command; and civil administration and relief in that part of the demilitarized zone which is north of the military demarcation line shall be

the joint responsibility of the Supreme Commander of the Korean People's Army and the Commander of the Chinese People's volunteers. The number of persons, military or civilian, from each side who are permitted to enter the demilitarized zone for the conduct of civil administration and relief shall be as determined by the respective Commanders, but in no case shall the total number authorized by either side exceed one thousand (1,000) persons at any one time. The number of civil police and the arms to be carried by them shall be a prescribed by the Military Armistice Commission. Other personnel shall not carry arms unless specifically authorized to do so by the Military Armistice Commission.

11. Nothing contained in this article shall be construed to prevent the complete freedom of movement to, from, and within the demilitarized zone by the Military Armistice Commission, its assistants, its Joint Observer Teams with their assistants, the Neutral Nations Supervisory Commission hereinafter established, its assistants, its Neutral Nations Inspection teams with their assistants, and of any other persons, materials, and equipment specifically authorized to enter the demilitarized zone by the Military Armistice Commission. Convenience of movement shall be permitted through the territory under the military control of either side over any route necessary to move between points within the demilitarized zone where such points are not connected by roads lying completely within the demilitarized zone.

Article II: Concrete Arrangements for Cease-Fire and Armistice

A. General

12. The Commanders of the opposing sides shall order and enforce a complete cessation of all hostilities in Korea by all armed forces under their control, including all units and personnel of the ground, naval, and air forces, effective twelve (12) hours after this armistice agreement is signed. (See paragraph 63 hereof for effective date and hour of the remaining provisions of this armistice agreement.)

13. In order to insure the stability of the military armistice so as to facilitate the attainment of a peaceful settlement through the holding by both sides of a political conference of a higher level, the Commanders of the opposing sides shall:

    (a) Within seventy-two (72) hours after this armistice agreement becomes effective, withdraw all of their military forces, supplies, and equipment from the demilitarized zone except as otherwise provided herein. Al demolitions, minefields, wire entanglements, and other hazards to the safe movement of personnel of the

Military Armistice Commission or its Joint Observer Teams, known to exist within the demilitarized zone after the withdrawal of military forces therefrom, together with lanes known to be free of all such hazards, shall be reported to the MAC by the Commander of the side whose forces emplaced such hazards. Subsequently, additional safe lanes shall be cleared; and eventually, within forty-five (45) days after the termination of the seventy-two (72) hour period, all such hazards shall be removed from the demilitarized zone as directed by the under the supervision of the MAC. At the termination of the seventy-two (72) hour period, except for unarmed troops authorized forty-five (45) day period to complete salvage operations under MAC and agreed to by the MAC and agreed to by the Commanders of the opposing sides, and personnel authorized under paragraphs 10 and 11 hereof, no personnel of either side shall be permitted to enter the demilitarized zone.

(b) Within ten (10) days after this armistice agreement becomes effective, withdraw all of their military forces, supplies, and equipment from the rear and the coastal islands and waters of Korea of the other side. If such military forces are not withdrawn within the stated time limit, and there is no mutually agreed and valid reason for the delay, the other side shall have the right to take any action which it deems necessary for the maintenance of security and order. The term "coastal islands," as used above, refers to those islands, which, though occupied by one side at the time when this armistice agreement becomes effective, were controlled by the other side on 24 June 1950; provided, however, that all the islands lying to the north and west of the provincial boundary line between HWANGHAE-DO and KYONGGI-DO shall be under the military control of the Supreme Commander of the Korean People's Army and the Commander of the Chinese People's volunteers, except the island groups of PAENGYONG-DO (37 58' N, 124 40' E), TAECHONG-DO (37 50' N, 124 42' E), SOCHONG-DO (37 46' N, 124 46' E), YONPYONG-DO (37 38' N, 125 40' E), and U-DO (37 36'N, 125 58' E), which shall remain under the military control of the Commander-in-Chief, United Nations Command. All the island on the west coast of Korea lying south of the above-mentioned boundary line shall remain under the military control of the Commander in-Chief, United Nations Command. (See Map 3.)

(c) Cease the introduction into Korea of Reinforcing military personnel; provided, however, that the rotation of units and personnel, the arrival in Korea of personnel on a temporary duty basis, and the return to Korea of personnel after short periods of leave or temporary duty outside of Korea shall be permitted within the scope prescribed below: "Rotation" is defined as the replacement of units or personnel by other units or personnel who re commencing a tour of duty in Korea. Rotation personnel shall be introduced into and evacuated from Korea only through the ports of entry enumerated in Paragraph 43 hereof. Rotation shall be conducted on a man-for-man basis; provided, however, that no more than thirty-five thousand (35,000) persons in the military service shall be admitted into Korea by either side in any calendar month under the rotation policy. No military personnel of either side shall be introduced into Korea if the introduction of such personnel will cause the aggregate of the military personnel of that side admitted into Korea since the effective date of this Armistice Agreement to exceed the cumulative total of the military personnel of that side who have departed from Korea since that date. Reports concerning arrivals in and departures from Korea of military personnel shall be made daily to the Military Armistice Commission and the Neutral Nations Supervisory Commission; such reports shall include places of arrival and departure and the number of persons arriving at or departing from each such place. The Neutral Nations Supervisory Commission, through its Neutral Nations Inspection Teams, shall conduct supervision and inspection of the rotation of units and personnel authorized above, at the ports of entry enumerated in Paragraph 43 hereof.

(d) Cease the introduction into Korea of reinforcing combat aircraft, armored vehicles, weapons, and ammunition; provided however, that combat aircraft, armored vehicles, weapons, and ammunition which are destroyed, damaged, worn out, or used up during the period of the armistice may be replaced on the basis piece-for-piece of the same effectiveness and the same type. Such combat aircraft, armored vehicles, weapons, and ammunition shall be introduced into Korea only through the ports of entry enumerated in paragraph 43 hereof. In order to justify the requirements for combat aircraft, armored vehicles, weapons, and ammunition to be introduced into Korea for replacement purposes, reports concerning every incoming shipment of these items shall be made to the MAC and the NNSC; such reports shall include statements regarding the disposition of the items being replaced. Items to be replaced which are removed from Korea shall be removed only through the ports of entry enumerated in paragraph 43 hereof. The NNSC, through its Neutral Nations Inspection Teams, shall conduct supervision and inspection of the replacement of combat aircraft, armored vehicles, weapons, and ammunition authorized above, at the ports of entry enumerated in paragraph 43 hereof.

(e) Insure that personnel of their respective commands who violate any of the provisions of this armistice agreement are adequately punished.

(f) In those cases where places of burial are a matter of record and graves are actually found to exist, permit graves registration personnel of the other side to enter, within a definite time limit after this armistice agreement becomes effective, the territory of Korea under their military control, for the purpose of proceeding to such graves to recover and evacuate the bodies of the deceased military personnel of that side, including deceased prisoners of war. The specific procedures and the time limit for the performance of the above task shall be determined by the Military Armistice Commission. The Commanders of the opposing sides shall furnish to the other side all available information pertaining to the places of burial of the deceased military personnel of the other side.

(g) Afford full protection and all possible assistance and cooperation to the Military Armistice Commission, its Joint Observer Teams, the Neutral Nations Supervisory Commission, and its Neutral Nations Inspection Teams, in the carrying out of their functions and responsibilities hereinafter assigned; and accord to the Neutral Nations Inspection Teams, full convenience of movement between the headquarters of the Neutral Nations supervisory Commission and the ports of entry enumerated in Paragraph 43 hereof over main lines of communication agreed upon by both sides (see Map 4), and between the headquarters of the Neutral Nations Supervisory commission and the places where violations of this Armistice Agreement have been reported to have occurred. In order to prevent unnecessary delays, the use of alternate routes and means of transportation will be permitted whenever the main lines of communication are closed or impassable.

(h) Provide such logistic support, including communications and transportation facilities, as may be required by the military Armistice Commission and the Neutral Nations Supervisory Commission and their Teams.

(i) Each construct, operate, and maintain a suitable airfield in their respective parts of the Demilitarized Zone in the vicinity of the headquarters of the Military Armistice Commission, for such uses as the Commission may determine.

(j) Insure that all members and other personnel of the Neutral Nations Supervisory Commission and of the Neutral Nations Repatriation Commission hereinafter established shall enjoy the freedom and facilities necessary for the proper exercise of their functions, including privileges, treatment, and immunities equivalent to those ordinarily enjoyed by accredited diplomatic personnel under international usage.

14. This Armistice Agreement shall apply to all opposing ground forces under the military control of either side, which ground forces shall respect the Demilitarized Zone and the area of Korea under the military control of the opposing side.

15. This Armistice Agreement shall apply to all opposing naval forces, which naval forces shall respect the water contiguous to the Demilitarized Zone and to the land area of Korea under the military control of the opposing side, and shall not engage in blockade of any kind of Korea.

16. This Armistice Agreement shall apply to all opposing air forces, which air forces shall respect the air space over the Demilitarized Zone and over the area of Korea under the military control of the opposing side, and over the waters contiguous to both.

17. Responsibility for compliance with and enforcement of the terms and provisions of this Armistice Agreement is that of the signatories hereto and their successors in command. The Commanders of the opposing sides shall establish within their respective commands all measures and procedures necessary to insure complete compliance with all of the provisions hereof by all elements of their commands. They shall actively co-operate with one another and with the Military Armistice Commission and the Neutral nations supervisory Commission in requiring observance of both letter and the spirit of all of the provisions of this Armistice Agreement.

18. The costs of the operations of the Military Armistice Commission and of the Neutral Nations supervisory Commission and of their Teams shall be shared equally by the two opposing sides.

B. Military Armistice Commission

1. Composition

19. A Military Armistice Commission is hereby established.

20. The Military Armistice commission shall be composed of ten (10) senior officers, five (5) of whom shall be appointed by the Commander-in-Chief, United Nations Command, and five (5) of whom shall be appointed jointly by the Supreme Commander of the Korean People's Army and the Commander of the Chinese People's Volunteers. Of the ten (10) members, three (3) from each side shall be of general of flag rank. The two (2) remaining members on each side may be major generals, brigadier generals, colonels, or their equivalents.

21. Members of the Military Armistice Commission shall be permitted to use staff assistants as required.

22. The Military Armistice Commission shall be provided with the necessary administrative personnel to establish a Secretariat charged with

assisting the Commission by performing record-keeping, secretarial, interpreting, and such other functions as the Commission may assign to it. Each side shall appoint to the Secretariat a Secretary and an Assistant Secretary and such clerical and specialized personnel as required by the Secretariat. Records shall be kept in English, Korean, and Chinese, all of which shall be equally authentic.

23. (a) The Military Armistice Commission shall be initially provided with and assisted by ten (10) Joint Observer Teams, which number may be reduced by agreement of the senior members of both sides on the Military Armistice Commission.

(b) Each Joint Observer Team shall be composed of not less than four (4) nor more than six (6) officers of field grade, half of whom shall be appointed by the Commander-in-Chief, United Nations Command, and half of whom shall be appointed by the Commander-in-Chief, United Nations Command, and half of whom shall be appointed jointly by the Supreme Commander of the Korean People's Army and the Commander of the Chinese People's Volunteers. Additional personnel such as drivers, clerks, and interpreters shall be furnished by each side as required for the functioning of the Joint Observer Teams.

24. The general mission of the Military Armistice Commission shall be to supervise the implementation of this Armistice Agreement and to settle through negotiations any violations of this Armistice Agreement.

25. The military Armistice Commission shall:

(a) Locate its headquarters in the vicinity of PANMUNJOM (37 57'29" n, 126 40'00" e). The Military Armistice Commission may re-locate its headquarters at another point within the Demilitarized Zone by agreement of the senior members of both sides on the Commission.

(b) Operate as a joint organization without a chairman.

(c) Adopt such rules of procedure as it may, from time to time, deem necessary

(d) Supervise the carrying out of the provisions of this Armistice Agreement pertaining to the Demilitarized Zone and to the Han River Estuary.

(e) Direct the operations of the Joint Observer Teams.

(f) Settle through negotiations any violations of this Armistice Agreement.

(g) Transmit immediately to the Commanders of the opposing sides all reports of investigations of violations of this Armistice Agreement and all other reports and records of proceedings received from the Neutral nations supervisory Commission.

(h) Give general supervision and direction to the activities of the Committee for Repatriation of Prisoners of War and the Committee for Assisting the Return of Displaced Civilians, hereinafter established.

(i) Act as intermediary in transmitting communications between the Commanders of the opposing sides; provided, however, that the foregoing shall not be construed to preclude the Commanders of both sides from communicating with each other by any other means which they may desire to employ.

(j) Provide credentials and distinctive insignia for its staff and its Joint Observer Teams, and a distinctive marking for all vehicles, aircraft, and vessels, used in the performance of its mission.

26. The Mission of the Joint Observer Teams shall be to assist the Military Armistice Commission in supervising the carrying out of the provisions of this Armistice Agreement pertaining to the Demilitarized Zone and to the Han River Estuary.

27. The Military Armistice Commission, or the senior member of either side thereof, is authorized to dispatch Joint Observer Teams to investigate violations of this Armistice Agreement reported to have occurred in the Demilitarized Zone or in the Han River Estuary; provided, however, that not more than one half of the Joint Observer Teams which have not been dispatched by the Military Armistice Commission may be dispatched at any one time by the senior member of either side on the Commission.

28. The Military Armistice Commission, or the senior member of either side thereof, is authorized to request the Neutral Nations Supervisory Commission to conduct special observations and inspections at places outside the Demilitarized Zone where violations of this Armistice Agreement have been reported to have occurred.

29. When the Military Armistice Commission determines that a violation of this Armistice Agreement has occurred, it shall immediately report such violation to the Commanders of the opposing sides.

30. When the Military Armistice Commission determines that a violation of this Armistice Agreement has been corrected to its satisfaction, it shall so report to the Commanders of the opposing sides.

3. General

31. The Military Armistice Commission shall meet daily. Recesses of not to exceed seven (7) days may be agreed upon by the senior members of both sides; provided, that such recesses may be terminated on twenty-four (24) hour notice by the senior member of either side.

32. Copies of the record of the proceedings of all meetings of the Military Armistice Commission shall be forwarded to the Commanders of the opposing sides as soon as possible after each meeting.

33. The Joint Observer teams shall make periodic reports to the Military Armistice Commission as required by the Commission and, in addition,

shall make such special reports as may be deemed necessary by them, or as may be required by the Commission.

34. The Military Armistice Commission shall maintain duplicate files of the reports and records of proceedings required by this Armistice Agreement. The Commission is authorized to maintain duplicate files of such other reports, records, etc., as may be necessary in the conduct of its business. Upon eventual dissolution of the Commission, one set of the above files shall be turned over to each side.

35. The Military Armistice Commission may make recommendations to the Commanders of the opposing sides with respect to amendments or additions to this Armistice Agreement. Such recommended changes should generally be those designed to insure a more effective armistice.

C. Neutral Nations Supervisory Commission

1. Compositions

36. A Neutral Nations Supervisory Commission is hereby established.

37. The Neutral Nations supervisory Commission shall be composed of four (4) senior officers, two (2) of whom shall be appointed by neutral nations nominated by the Commander-in-Chief, United Nations Command, namely, SWEDEN and SWITZERLAND, and two (2) of whom shall be appointed by neutral nations nominated jointly by the Supreme Commander of the Korean People's Army and the Commander of the Chinese People's Volunteers, namely, POLAND and CZECHOSLOVAKIA. The term "neutral nations" as herein used is defined as those nations whose combatant forces have not participated in the hostilities in Korea. Members appointed to the Commission may be from the armed forces of the appointing nations. Each member shall designate an alternate member to attend those meetings which for any reason the principal member is unable to attend. Such alternate members shall be of the same nationality as their principals. The Neutral Nations Supervisory Commission may take action whenever the number of members present from the neutral nations nominated by one side is equal to the number of members present from the neutral nations nominated by the other side.

38. Members of the Neutral Nations Supervisory Commission shall be permitted to use staff assistants furnished by the neutral nations as required. These staff assistants may be appointed as alternate members of the Commission.

39. The neutral nations shall be requested to furnish the Neutral Nations Supervisory Commission with the necessary administrative personnel to establish a Secretariat charged with assisting the Commission by performing necessary record-keeping, secretarial, interpreting, and such other functions as the Commission may assign to it.

40. (a) The Neutral Nations Supervisory Commission shall be initially provided with, and assisted by, twenty (20) Neutral Nations Inspection Teams, which number may be reduced by agreement of the senior members of both sides on the Military Armistice Commission. The Neutral Nations Inspection Teams shall be responsible to, shall report to, and shall be subject to the direction of, the Neutral Nations Supervisory Commission only.

(b) Each Neutral Nations Inspection Team shall be composed of not less than four (4) officers, preferably of field grade, half of whom shall be from the neutral nations nominated by the Commander-in-Chief, United Nations Command, and half of whom shall be from the neutral nations nominated jointly by the Supreme Commander of the Korean People's Army, and the Commander of the Chinese People's Volunteers. Members appointed to the Neutral Nations Inspection Teams may be from the armed forces of the appointed. In order to facilitate the functioning of the Teams, sub-teams composed of not less than two (2) members, one of whom shall be from a neutral nation nominated by the Commander-in-Chief, United Nations Command, and one of whom shall be from a neutral nation nominated jointly by the Supreme Commander of the Korean People's Army and the Commander of the Chinese People's Volunteers, may be formed as circumstances require. Additional personnel such as drivers, clerks, interpreters, and communications personnel, and such equipment as may be required by the Teams to perform their missions, shall be furnished by the Commander of each side, as required, in the Demilitarized Zone and in the territory under his military control. The Neutral Nations Supervisory Commission may provide itself and the Neutral Nations Inspection Teams with such of the above personnel shall be personnel of the same neutral nations of which the Neutral nations supervisory Commission is composed.

2. Functions and Authority

41. The mission of the Neutral Nations Supervisory Commission shall be to carry out the functions of supervision, observation, inspection, and investigation, as stipulated in Sub-paragraphs 13(c) and 13(d) and Paragraph 28 hereof, and to report the results of such supervision, observation, inspection, and investigation to the Military Armistice Commission.

42. The Neutral Nations Supervisory Commission shall:

(a) Locate its headquarters in proximity to the headquarters of the Military Armistice Commission.

(b) Adopt such rules of procedure as it may, from time to time, deem necessary.

(c) Conduct, through its members and its Neutral nations Inspection teams, the supervision and inspection provided for in Sub paragraphs 13(c) and 13(d) of this Armistice Agreement at the ports of entry enumerated in Paragraph 43 hereof, and the special observations and inspections provided for in Paragraph 28 hereof at those places where violations of this Armistice Agreement have been reported to have occurred. The inspection of combat aircraft, armored vehicles, weapons, and ammunition by the Neutral Nations Inspection Teams shall be such as to enable them to properly insure that reinforcing combat aircraft, armored vehicles, weapons, and ammunition are not being introduced into Korea; but this shall not be construed as authorizing inspections or examinations of any secret designs of characteristics of any combat aircraft, armored vehicle, weapon, or ammunition.

(d) Direct and supervise the operations of the Neutral Nations Inspection Teams.

(e) Station five (5) Neutral Nations Inspection Teams at the ports of entry enumerated in Paragraph 43 hereof located in the territory under the military control of the Commander-in-Chief, United Nations Command; and five (5) Neutral Nations Inspection Teams at the ports of entry enumerated in Paragraph 43 hereof located in the territory under the military control of the Supreme Commander of the Korean People's Army and the Commander of the Chinese People's Volunteers; and establish initially ten (10) mobile Neutral Nations Inspection Teams in reserve, stationed in the general vicinity of the headquarters of the Neutral Nations Supervisory Commission, which number may be reduced by agreement of the senior members of both sides on the Military Armistice Commission. Not more than half of the mobile Neutral Nations Inspection Teams shall be dispatched at any one time in accordance with requests of the senior member of either side on the Military Armistice Commission.

(f) Subject to the provisions of the preceding Sub-paragraphs, conduct without delay investigations of reported violations of this Armistice Agreement, including such investigations of reported violations of this Armistice Agreement as may be requested by the Military Armistice Commission or by the senior member of either side on the Commission.

(g) Provide credentials and distinctive insignia for its staff and its Neutral Nations Inspection Teams, and a distinctive marking for all vehicles, aircraft, and vessels used in the performance of this mission.

43. Neutral Nations Inspection Teams shall be stationed at the following ports of entry.

Territory under the military control of the United Nations Command

INCHON . . . .(37 28, 126 38′E)
TAEGU . . . .(35 52′N, 128 36′E)
PUSAN . . . .(35 45′N, 129 02′E)
KANGNUNG . . . .(37 45′N, 128 54′E)
KUNSAN . . . .(35 59′E, 126 43′E)

Territory under the military control of the Korean People's Army and the Chinese People's Volunteers

SINUJU . . . . (40 06′N, 124 24E)
CHONGJIN . . . .(41 46′N, 129 49E)
HUNGNAM . . . .(39 50′N, 127 37′E)
MANPO . . . .(41 46′N, 126 18′E)
SINANJU . . . .(39 36′N, 125 36′E)

These Neutral Nations Inspection Teams shall be accorded full convenience of movement within the areas and over the routes of communication set forth on the attached map (see Map 5).

3. General

44. The Neutral Nations Supervisory Commission shall meet daily. Recesses of not to exceed seven (7) days may be agreed upon by the members of the Neutral Nations Supervisory Commission; provided, that such recesses may be terminated on twenty-four (24) hour notice by any member.

45. Copies of the record of the proceedings of all meetings of the Neutral Nations Supervisory Commission shall be forwarded to the Military Armistice Commission as soon as possible after each meeting. Records shall be kept in English, Korean, and Chinese.

46. The Neutral Nations Inspection Teams shall make periodic reports concerning the results of their supervision observations, inspections, and investigations to the Neutral Nations Supervisory Commission as required by the Commission and, in addition, shall make such special reports as may be deemed necessary by them, or as may be required by the Commission. Reports shall be submitted by a Team as a whole, but may also be submitted by one or more individual members thereof; provided, that the reports submitted by one or more individual members thereof shall be considered as information only.

47. Copies of the reports made by the Neutral Nations Inspection Teams shall be forwarded to the Military Armistice Commission by the Neutral Nations Supervisory Commission without delay and in the language in which received. They shall not be delayed by the process of translation or evaluation. The Neutral Nations Supervisory Commission shall evaluate such reports at the earliest practicable time and shall forward their findings to the Military Armistice Commission as a matter of priority. The Military Armistice Commission shall not take final action with regard to any such report until the evaluation thereof has been received from the Neutral Nations Supervisory Commission. Members of the Neutral Nations Supervisory Commission and of its Teams shall be subject to appearance before the Military Armistice Commission, at the request of the senior member of either side on the Military Armistice Commission, for clarification of any report submitted.

48. The Neutral Nations Supervisory Commission shall maintain duplicate files of the reports and records of proceedings required by this Armistice Agreement. The Commission is authorized to maintain duplicate files of such other reports, records, etc., as may be necessary in the conduct of its business. Upon eventual dissolution of the Commission, one set of the above files shall be turned over to each side.

49. The Neutral Nations Supervisory Commission may make recommendations to the Military Armistice Commission with respect to amendments or additions to this Armistice Agreement. Such recommended changes should generally be those designed to insure a more effective armistice.

50. The Neutral Nations Supervisory Commission, or any member thereof, shall be authorized to communicated with any member of the Military Armistice Commission.

Article III: Arrangement Relating to Prisoners of War

51. The release and repatriation of all prisoners of war held in the custody of each side at the time this armistice agreement becomes effective shall be effected in conformity with the following provisions agreed upon by both sides prior to the signing of this armistice agreement.

    (a) Within sixty (60) days after this agreement becomes effective each side shall, without offering any hindrance, directly repatriate and hand over in groups all those prisoners of war in its custody who insist on repatriation to the side to which they belonged at the time of capture. Repatriation shall be accomplished in accordance with the related provisions of this Article. In order to expedite the repatriation process of such personnel, each side shall, prior to the signing of the Armistice Agreement, exchange the total numbers, by nationalities, or personnel to be directly repatriated. Each group of prisoners of war delivered to the other side shall be accompanied by rosters, prepared by nationality, to include name, rank (if any) and internment or military serial number.

(b) Each side shall release all those remaining prisoners of war, who are not directly repatriated, from its military control and from its custody and hand them over to the Neutral Nations Repatriation Commission for disposition in accordance with the provisions in the Annex hereto, "Terms of Reference for Neutral Nations Repatriation Commission."

(c) So that there may be no misunderstanding owing to the equal use of three languages, the act of delivery of a prisoner of war by one side to other side shall, for the purposes of the Armistice Agreement, be called "repatriation" in English, ( ) "Song Hwan" in Korean and ( ) "Ch'ien Fan" in Chinese, notwithstanding the nationality or place of residence of such prisoner of war.

52. Each side insures that it will not employ in acts of war in the Korean conflict any prisoner of war released and repatriated incident to the coming into effect of this armistice agreement.

53. All the sick and injured prisoners of war who insist upon repatriation shall be repatriated with priority. Insofar as possible, there shall be captured medical personnel repatriated concurrently with the sick and injured prisoners of war, so as to provide medical care and attendance enroute.

54. The repatriation of all of the prisoners of war required by Sub-paragraph 51 (a) hereof shall be completed within a time limit of sixty (60) days after this Armistice Agreement becomes effective. Within this time limit each side undertakes to complete repatriation of the above-mentioned prisoners of war in its custody at the earliest practicable time.

55. PANMUNJOM is designated as the place where prisoners of war will be delivered and received by both sides. Additional place(s) of delivery and reception of prisoners of war in the Demilitarized Zone may be designated, if necessary, by the Committee for Repatriation of Prisoners of War.

56. (a) A committee for Repatriation of Prisoners of War is hereby established. It shall be composed of six (6) officers of field grade, three (3) of whom shall be appointed by the Commander-in-Chief, United Nations Command, and three (3) of whom shall be appointed jointly by the Supreme Commander of the Korean People's Army and the Commander of the Chinese People's Volunteers. This Committee shall, under the general supervision and direction of the Military Armistice Commission, be responsible for co-ordinating the specific plans of both sides for the repatriation of prisoners of

war and for supervision of the execution by both sides of all of the provisions of this Armistice Agreement relating to the repatriation of prisoners of war. It shall be the duty of this Committee to co-ordinate the timing of the arrival of prisoners of war at the place(s) of delivery and reception of prisoners of war from the prisoner of war camps of both sides; to make, when necessary, such special arrangements as may be required with regard to the transportation and welfare of sick and injured prisoners of war; to co-ordinate the work of the joint Red Cross teams, established in Paragraph 57 hereof, in assisting in the repatriation of prisoners of war; to supervise the implementation of the arrangements for the actual repatriation of prisoners of war stipulated in Paragraphs 53 and 54 hereof; to select, when necessary, additional place(s) of delivery and reception of prisoners of war; and to carry out such other related functions as are required for the repatriation of prisoners of war.

(b) When unable to reach agreement on any matter relating to its responsibilities, the committee for Repatriation of Prisoners of War shall immediately refer such matter to the Military Armistice Commission for decision. The Committee for Repatriation of Prisoners of War shall maintain its headquarters in proximity to the headquarters of the Military Armistice Commission.

(c) The Committee for Repatriation of Prisoners of War shall be dissolved by the Military Armistice Committee upon completion of the program of repatriation of prisoners of war.

57. (a) Immediately after this Armistice Agreement becomes effective, joint Red Cross teams composed of representatives of the national Red Cross Societies of countries contributing forces to the United Nations Command on the one hand, and representatives of the Red Cross Society of the Democratic People's Republic of Korea and representatives of the Red Cross Society of the People's Republic of China on the other hand, shall be established. The joint Red Cross teams shall assist in the execution by both sides of those provisions of this Armistice Agreement relating to the repatriation of all the prisoners of war specified in Sub-paragraph 51 (a) hereof, who insist upon repatriation, by the performance of such humanitarian services as are necessary and desirable for the welfare of the prisoners of war. To accomplish this task, the joint Red Cross teams shall provide assistance in the delivering and receiving of prisoners of war by both sides at the place(s) of delivery and reception of prisoners of war, and shall visit the prisoner-of-war camps of both sides to comfort the prisoners of war.

(b) The joint Red Cross teams shall be organized as set forth below:
   1. One team shall be composed of twenty (20) members, namely, ten (10) representatives from the national Red Cross Societies

of each side, to assist in the delivering and receiving of prisoners of war by both sides at the place(s) of delivery and reception of prisoners of war. The chairmanship of this team shall alternate daily between representative from the Red Cross Societies of the two sides. The work and services of this team shall be coordinated by the Committee for Repatriation of Prisoners of War.

2. One team shall be composed of sixty (60) members, namely, thirty (30) representatives from the national Red Cross Societies of each side, to visit the prisoner-of-war camps under the administration of the Korean People's Army and the Chinese People's Volunteers. This team may provide services to prisoners of war while en route from the prisoner of war camps to the place(s) of delivery and reception of prisoners of war. A representative of a Red Cross Society of the Democratic People's Republic of Korea or of the Red Cross Society of the People's Republic of China shall serve as chairman of this team.

3. One team shall be composed of sixty (60) members, namely, thirty (30) representatives from the national Red Cross Societies of each side, to visit the prisoner of war camps under the administration of the United Nations Command. This team may provide services to prisoners of war while en route from the prisoner of war camps to the place(s) of delivery and reception of prisoners of war. A representative of a Red Cross Society of a nation contributing to forces to the United Nations Command shall serve as chairman of this team.

4. In order to facilitate the functioning of each joint Red Cross team, sub-teams composed of not less than two (2) members from this team, with an equal number of representatives from each side, may be formed as circumstances require.

5. Additional personnel such as drivers, clerks, and interpreters, and such equipment as may be required by the joint Red Cross teams to perform their missions, shall be furnished by the Commander of each side to the team operating in the territory under his military control.

6. Whenever jointly agreed upon by the representatives of both sides on any joint Red Cross team, the size of such team may be increased or decreased, subject to confirmation by the committee for Repatriation of Prisoners of War.

(c) The Commander of each side shall co-operate fully with the joint Red Cross teams in the performance of their functions, and undertakes to insure the security of the personnel of the Joint Red Cross team in the area under his military control. The Commander of each side shall provide such logistic, administrative, and communications facilities as may be required by the team operating in the territory under his military control.

(d) The joint Red Cross teams shall be dissolved upon completion of the program of repatriation of all of the prisoners of war specified in Sub-paragraph 51 (a) hereof, who insist upon repatriation.

58. (a) The Commander of each side shall furnish to the Commander of the other side as soon as practicable, but not later than ten (10) days after this Armistice Agreement becomes effective, the following information concerning prisoners of war:

1. Complete data pertaining to the prisoners of war who escaped since the effective date of the data last exchanged.

2. Insofar as practicable, information regarding name, nationality, rank, and other identification data, date and cause of death, and place of burial, of those prisoners of war who died while in his custody.

(b) If any prisoners of war escape or die after the effective date of the supplementary information specified above, the detaining side shall furnish to the other side, through the Committee for Repatriation of Prisoners of War, the data pertaining thereto in accordance with the provisions of Sub-paragraph 58 (a) hereof. Such data shall be furnished at ten-day intervals until the completion of the program of delivery and reception of prisoners of war.

(c) Any escaped prisoner of war who returns to the custody of the detaining side after the completion of the program of delivery and reception of prisoners of war shall be delivered to the Military Armistice Commission for disposition.

59. (a) All civilians who, at the time this Armistice Agreement becomes effective, are in territory under the military control of the Commander-in-Chief, United Nations Command, and who, on 24 June 1950, resided north of the Military Demarcation Line established in this Armistice Agreement shall, if they desire to return home, be permitted and assisted by the Commander-in-Chief, United Nations Command, to return to the area north of the Military Demarcation Line; and all civilians who, at the time this Armistice Agreement becomes effective, are in territory under the military control of the Supreme Commander of the Korean People's Army and the Commander of the Chinese People's Volunteers, and who on 24 June 1950, resided south of the Military Demarcation Line established in this Armistice Agreement shall, if they desire to return home, be permitted and assisted by

the Supreme Commander of the Korean People's Army and the Commander of the Chinese People's Volunteers to return to the area south of the Military Demarcation Line. The Commander of each side shall be responsible for publicizing widely throughout the territory under his military control the contents of the provisions of this Sub-paragraph, and for calling upon the appropriate civil authorities to give necessary guidance and assistance to all such civilians who desire to return home.

(b) All civilians of foreign nationality who, at the time this Armistice Agreement becomes effective, are in territory under the military control of the Supreme Commander of the Korean People's Army and the Commander of the Chinese People's Volunteers shall if they desire to proceed to territory under the military control of the Commander-in-Chief, United Nations command, be permitted and assisted to do so; all civilians of foreign nationality who, at the time this Armistice Agreement becomes effective, are in territory under the military control of the Commander-in-Chief, United Nations Command, shall, if they desire to proceed to territory under the military Control of the Supreme Commander of the Korean People's Army and the Commander of the Chinese People's Volunteers, be permitted and assisted to do so. The Commander of each side shall be responsible for publicizing widely throughout the territory under his military control of contents of the provisions of this sub-paragraph, and for calling upon the appropriate civil authorizes to give necessary guidance and assistance to all such civilians of foreign nationality who desire to proceed to territory under the military control of the Commander of the other side.

(c) Measures to assist in the return of civilians provided for in Sub-paragraph 59 (a) hereof and the movement of civilians provided for in Sub-paragraph 59 (b) hereof shall be commenced by both sides as soon as possible after this Armistice Agreement becomes effective.

(d) 1. A Committee for Assisting the Return of Displaced Civilians is hereby established. It shall be composed of four (4) officers of field grade, two (2) of whom shall be appointed jointly by the Commander-in-Chief, United Nations Command, and two (2) of whom shall be appointed jointly by the Supreme Commander of the Korean People's Army and the Commander of the Chinese People's Volunteers. This committee shall, under the general supervision and direction of the Military Armistice Commission, be responsible for coordinating the specific plans of both sides for assistance to the return of the above-mentioned civilians. It shall be the duty of this Committee to make necessary arrangements, including those of transportation, for expediting and coordinating the movement of the above-mentioned civilians; to select the crossing point(s) through which the above-mentioned civilians will cross the Military Demarcation Line; to arrange for security at the crossing point(s), and to carry out such other functions as are required to accomplish the return of the above-mentioned civilians.

2. When unable to reach agreement on any matter relating to its responsibilities, the Committee for Assisting the return of Displaced Civilians shall immediately refer such matter to the Military Armistice Commission for decision. The Committee for assisting the Return of Displaced Civilians shall maintain its headquarters in proximity to the headquarters of the Military Armistice Commission.

3. The Committee for Assisting the Return of Displaced Civilians shall be dissolved by the Military Armistice Commission upon fulfillment of its mission.

Article IV: Recommendations to the Governments Concerned on Both Sides

60. In order to insure the peaceful settlement of the Korean question, the military Commanders of both sides hereby recommend to the governments of the countries concerned on both sides that, within three (3) months after the Armistice Agreement is signed and becomes effective, a political conference of a higher level of both sides be held by representatives appointed respectively to settle through negotiation the questions of the withdrawal of all foreign forces from Korea, the peaceful settlement of the Korean question, etc.

Article V: Miscellaneous

61. Amendments and additions to this Armistice Agreement must be mutually agreed to by the Commanders of the opposing sides.
62. The Articles and Paragraphs of this Armistice Agreement shall remain in effect until expressly superseded either by mutually acceptable amendments and additions or by provision in an appropriate agreement for a peaceful settlement at a political level between both sides.
63. All of the provisions of this Armistice Agreement, other than Paragraph 12, shall become effective at 2200 hours on 27 July 1953.

Done at Panmunjom, Korea at
10:00 hours on the 27th day of
July 1953, in English, Korean
and Chinese, all texts being
equally authentic.

NAM IL
_____

General, Korea People's Army
Senior Delegate,
Delegation of the Korean People's
Army and the Chinese People's
Volunteers

WILLIAM K. HARRISON, JR.
_____

Lieutenant General, United States Army
Senior Delegate,
United Nations Command Delegation

MUTUAL DEFENSE TREATY BETWEEN THE REPUBLIC OF KOREA AND THE UNITED STATES OF AMERICA (SIGNED AT WASHINGTON: OCTOBER 1, 1953; ENTERED INTO FORCE: NOVEMBER 17, 1954)

The Parties to this Treaty,

Reaffirming their desire to live in peace with all governments, and desiring to strengthen the fabric of peace in the Pacific area,

Desiring to declare publicly and formally their common determination to defend themselves against external armed attack so that no potential aggressor could be under the illusion that either of them stands alone in the Pacific area,

Desiring further to strengthen their efforts for collective defense for the preservation of peace and security pending the development of a more comprehensive and effective system of regional security in the Pacific area,

Have agreed as follows:

Article 1

The Parties undertake to settle any international disputes in which they may be involved by peaceful means in such a manner that international peace and security and justice are not endangered and to refrain in their international relations from the threat or use of force in any manner inconsistent with the purposes of the United Nations, or obligations assumed by any Party towards the United Nations.

Article 2

The Parties will consult together whenever, in the opinion of either of them, the political independence or security of either of the Parties is threatened by external armed attack. Separately and jointly, by self-help and mutual aid, the Parties will maintain and develop appropriate means to deter armed attack and will take suitable measures in consultation and agreement to implement this Treaty and to further its purposes.

Article 3

Each Party recognizes that an armed attack in the Pacific area on either of the Parties in territories now under their respective administrative control, or hereafter recognized by one of the Parties as lawfully brought under the administrative control of the other, would be dangerous to its own peace and safety and declares that it would act to meet the common danger in accordance with its constitutional processes.

Article 4

The Republic of Korea grants, and the United States of America accepts, the right to dispose United States land, air and sea forces in and about the territory of the Republic of Korea as determined by mutual agreement.

Article 5

This Treaty shall be ratified by the United States of America and the Republic of Korea in accordance with their respective constitutional processes and will come into force when instruments of ratification thereof have been exchanged by them at Washington.

Article 6

This Treaty shall remain in force indefinitely. Either party may terminate it one year after notice has been given to the other Party.

IN WITNESS WHEREOF the undersigned plenipotentiaries have signed this Treaty.

Done in duplicate at Washington, in the Korean and English languages, this first day of October, 1953.

> For the Republic of Korea: For the United States of America:
> (signed) Y.T. Pyun   (signed) John Foster Dulles

AGREED FRAMEWORK BETWEEN THE DEMOCRATIC PEOPLE'S REPUBLIC OF KOREA AND THE UNITED STATES OF AMERICA (GENEVA, OCTOBER 21, 1994)

Delegations of the governments of the Democratic People's Republic of Korea (DPRK) and the United States of America (U.S.) held talks in Geneva from September 23 to October 21, 1994, to negotiate an overall resolution of the nuclear issue on the Korean Peninsula.

Both sides reaffirmed the importance of attaining the objectives contained in the August 12, 1994 agreed statement between the DPRK and the U.S. and upholding the principles of the June 11, 1993 joint statement of the DPRK and the U.S. to achieve peace and security on a nuclear-free Korean Peninsula. The DPRK and the U.S. decided to take the following actions for the resolution of the nuclear issue:

I. Both sides will cooperate to replace the DPRK's graphite-moderated reactors and related facilities with light-water reactor (LWR) power plants.

   1) In accordance with the October 20, 1994 letter of assurance from the U.S. President, the U.S. will undertake to make arrangements for the provision to the DPRK of a LWR project with a total generating capacity of approximately 2,000 MW (e) by a target date of 2003.
      – The U.S. will organize under its leadership an international consortium to finance and supply the LWR project to be provided to the DPRK. The U.S., representing the international consortium, will serve as the principal point of contact with the DPRK for the LWR project.
      – The U.S., representing the consortium, will make best efforts to secure the conclusion of a supply contract with the DPRK within six months of the date of this document for the provision of the LWR project. Contract talks will begin as soon as possible after the date of this document.
      – As necessary, the DPRK and the U.S. will conclude a bilateral agreement, for cooperation in the field of peaceful uses of nuclear energy.
   2) In accordance with the October 20, 1994 letter of assurance from the U.S. President, the U.S., representing the consortium, will make arrangements to offset the energy forgone due to the freeze of the DPRK's graphite-moderated reactors and related facilities, pending completion of the first LWR unit.
      – Alternative energy will be provided in the form of heavy oil for heating and electricity production.
      – Deliveries of heavy oil will begin within three months of the date of this document and will reach a rate of 500,000 tons annually, in accordance with an agreed schedule of deliveries.
   3) Upon receipt of U.S. assurances for the provision of LWRs and for arrangements for interim energy alternatives, the DPRK will freeze its graphite-moderated reactors and related facilities and will eventually dismantle these reactors and related facilities.
      – The freeze on the DPRK's graphite-moderated reactors and related facilities will be fully implemented within one month of the date

of this document. During this one-month period, and throughout the freeze, the International Atomic Energy Agency (IAEA) will be allowed to monitor this freeze, and the DPRK will provide full cooperation to the IAEA for this purpose.

- Dismantlement of the DPRK's graphite-moderated reactors and related facilities will be completed when the LWR project is completed.
- The DPRK and the U.S. will cooperate in finding a method to store safely the spent fuel from the 5 MW (e) experimental reactor during the construction of the LWR project, and to dispose of the fuel in a safe manner that does not involve reprocessing in the DPRK.

4) As soon as possible after the date of this document. DPRK and U.S. experts will hold two sets of experts talks.

- At one set of talks, experts will discuss issues related to alternative energy and the replacement of the graphite-moderated reactor program with the LWR project.
- At the other set of talks, experts will discuss specific arrangements for spent fuel storage and ultimate disposition.

II. The two sides will move toward full normalization of political and economic relations.

1) Within three months of the date of this document, both sides will reduce barriers to trade and investment, including restrictions on telecommunications services and financial transactions.

2) Each side will open a liaison office in the other's capital following resolution of consular and other technical issues through expert-level discussions.

3) As progress is made on issues of concern to each side, the DPRK and the U.S. will upgrade bilateral relations to the ambassadorial level.

III. Both sides will work together for peace and security on a nuclear-free Korean Peninsula.

1) The U.S. will provide formal assurances to the DPRK against the threat or use of nuclear weapons by the U.S.

2) The DPRK will consistently take steps to implement the North-South Joint Declaration on the Denuclearization of the Korean Peninsula.

3) The DPRK will engage in north-south dialogue, as this agreed framework will help create an atmosphere that promotes such dialogue.

IV. Both sides will work together to strengthen the international nuclear non-proliferation regime.

1) The DPRK will remain a party to the Treaty on the Non-Proliferation of Nuclear Weapons (NPT) and will allow implementation of its safeguards agreement under the treaty.

2) Upon conclusion of the supply contract for the provision of the LWR project, ad hoc and routine inspections will resume under the DPRK's

safeguards agreement with the IAEA with respect to the facilities not subject to the freeze. Pending conclusion of the supply contract, inspections required by the IAEA for the continuity of safeguards will continue at the facilities not subject to the freeze.

3) When a significant portion of the LWR project is completed, but before delivery of key nuclear components, the DPRK will come into full compliance with its safeguards agreement with the IAEA (INFCIRC/403), including taking all steps that may be deemed necessary by the IAEA, following consultations with the agency with regard to verifying the accuracy and completeness of the DPRK's initial report on all nuclear material in the DPRK.

Kang Sok Ju	Robert L. Gallucci
Head of the Delegation of the Democratic People's Republic of Korea, First Vice-Minister of Foreign Affairs of the Democratic People's Republic of Korea	Head of the Delegation of the United States of America, Ambassador at Large of the United States of America

CHAIRMAN'S STATEMENT AFTER THE SECOND ROUND OF SIX-PARTY TALKS (FEBRUARY 28, 2004)

1. The Second Round of Six-Party Talks was held in Beijing among the People's Republic of China, the Democratic People's Republic of Korea, Japan, the Republic of Korea, the Russian Federation, and the United States of America from 25th to 28th of February, 2004.

2. The heads of delegations were Mr. Wang Yi, Vice Minister, Ministry of Foreign Affairs of the PRC; Mr. Kim Kye-gwan, Vice Minister, Ministry of Foreign Affairs of DPRK; Ambassador Mitoji Yabunaka, Director-General for the Asian and Oceanian Affairs, Ministry of Foreign Affairs of Japan; Ambassador Lee Soo-Hyuck, Deputy Minister, Ministry of Foreign Affairs and Trade of the ROK; Ambassador Alexander Losiukov, Vice Minister, Ministry of Foreign Affairs of Russia; Mr. James Kelly, Assistant Secretary of State for East Asian and Pacific Affairs, United States Department of State.

3. The Parties agreed that the second round of the Six-Party Talks had launched the discussion on substantive issues, which was beneficial and positive, and that the attitudes of all parties were serious in the discussion. Through the talks, while differences remained, the Parties enhanced their understanding of each other's positions.

4. The Parties expressed their commitment to a nuclear–weapon-free Korean Peninsula, and to resolving the nuclear issue peacefully through

dialogue in a spirit of mutual respect and consultations on an equal basis, so as to maintain peace and stability on the Korean Peninsula and the region at large.

5. The Parties expressed their willingness to coexist peacefully. They agreed to take coordinated steps to address the nuclear issue and address the related concerns.

6. The Parties agreed to continue the process of the talks and agreed in principle to hold the third round of the Six-Party Talks in Beijing no later than the end of the second quarter of 2004. They agreed to set up a working group in preparation for the plenary. The terms of reference of the working group will be established through diplomatic channels.

7. The delegations of the DPRK, Japan, the ROK, Russia and the USA have expressed their appreciation to the Chinese side for the efforts aimed at the successful staging of the two rounds of the Six-Party Talks.

CHAIRMAN'S STATEMENT AFTER THE THIRD ROUND OF SIX-PARTY TALKS (JUNE 26, 2004)

1. The third round of the six-party talks were held in Beijing among the People's Republic of China (PRC), the Democratic People's Republic of Korea (DPRK), Japan, the Republic of Korea (ROK), the Russian Federation (Russia) and the United States of America (USA) from June 23 to 26, 2004.

2. The heads of delegation were Mr. Wan Yi, vice-foreign minister of China; Mr. Kim Kye-gwan, vice-foreign minister of DPRK; Ambassador Mitoji Yabunaka, director-general for Asian and Oceanian Affairs of Ministry of Foreign Affairs of Japan; Ambassador Lee Soo-Hyuck, deputy minister of Foreign Affairs and Trade of ROK; Ambassador Alexander Alekseyev, special envoy of the Ministry of Foreign Affairs of Russia; Mr. James A. Kelly, assistant secretary of State for East Asian and Pacific Affairs, United States Department of State.

3. In preparation of the third round of the six-party talks, two sessions of the Working Group were held in Beijing from May 12 to 15 and from June 21 to 22, 2004. The parties approved the Concept Paper on the Working Group in the plenary.

4. During the third round of the talks, the parties had constructive, pragmatic and substantive discussions. Based on the consensus reached at the second round of the talks, as reflected in its Chairman's Statement, they reaffirmed their commitments to the goal of denuclearization of the Korean Peninsula and stressed the need to take first steps toward that goal as soon as possible.

5. The parties stressed the need for a step-by-step process of "words for words" and "action for action" in search for a peaceful solution to the nuclear issue.

6. In this context, proposals, suggestions and recommendations were put forward by all parties. The parties welcomed the submission of those proposals, suggestions and recommendations, and noted some common elements, which would provide a useful basis for future work, while differences among the parties remained. The parties believed that further discussions were needed to expand their common ground and reduce existing differences.

7. The parties agreed in principle to hold the fourth round of the six-party talks in Beijing by the end of Sept. 2004, at a date to be decided through diplomatic channels with due consideration to the proceedings of the working group. The parties authorized the working group to convene at the earliest possible date to define the scope, duration and verification as well as corresponding measures for first steps for denuclearization, and as appropriate, make recommendations to the fourth round of the talks.

8. The delegations of the DPRK, Japan, the ROK, Russia and the USA expressed their appreciation to the Chinese side for its efforts for the success of the third round of the six-party talks.

U.S. TREASURY DEPARTMENT PRESS RELEASE CITING BANCO DELTA ASIA FOR MONEY LAUNDERING, OTHER CRIMES (SEPTEMBER 15, 2005)

Treasury Designates Banco Delta Asia as Primary Money Laundering Concern under USA Patriot Act

The U.S. Department of the Treasury today designated Banco Delta Asia SARL as a "primary money laundering concern" under Section 311 of the USA PATRIOT Act because it represents an unacceptable risk of money laundering and other financial crimes.

"Banco Delta Asia has been a willing pawn for the North Korean government to engage in corrupt financial activities through Macau, a region that needs significant improvement in its money laundering controls," said Stuart Levey, the Treasury's Under Secretary for Terrorism and Financial Intelligence (TFI). "By invoking our USA PATRIOT Act authorities, we are working to protect U.S. financial institutions while warning the global community of the illicit financial threat posed by Banco Delta Asia."

In conjunction with this finding, Treasury's Financial Crimes Enforcement Network (FinCEN) issued a proposed rule that, if adopted as final, will prohibit U.S. financial institutions from directly or indirectly establishing, maintaining, administering or managing any correspondent account in the United States for or on behalf of Banco Delta Asia.

Banco Delta Asia SARL

Banco Delta Asia is located and licensed in the Macau Special Administrative Region, China. The bank operates eight branches in Macau, including a branch at a casino, and is served by a representative office in Japan. In addition, Banco Delta Asia maintains correspondent accounts in Europe, Asia, Australia, Canada, and the United States.

Deficiencies at Banco Delta Asia noted in the finding include, but are not limited to, the following:

- Banco Delta Asia has provided financial services for over 20 years to Democratic People's Republic of Korea (DPRK) government agencies and front companies. It continues to develop relationships with these account holders, which comprise a significant amount of Banco Delta Asia's business. Evidence exists that some of these agencies and front companies are engaged in illicit activities.
- Banco Delta Asia has tailored its services to the needs and demands of the DPRK with little oversight or control. The bank also handles the bulk of the DPRK's precious metal sales, and helps North Korean agents conduct surreptitious, multi-million dollar cash deposits and withdrawals.
- Banco Delta Asia's special relationship with the DPRK has specifically facilitated the criminal activities of North Korean government agencies and front companies. For example, sources show that senior officials in Banco Delta Asia are working with DPRK officials to accept large deposits of cash, including counterfeit U.S. currency, and agreeing to place that currency into circulation.
- One well-known North Korean front company that has been a client of Banco Delta Asia for over a decade has conducted numerous illegal activities, including distributing counterfeit currency and smuggling counterfeit tobacco products. In addition, the front company has also long been suspected of being involved in international drug trafficking. Moreover, Banco Delta Asia facilitated several multi-million dollar wire transfers connected with alleged criminal activity on behalf of another North Korean front company.
- In addition to facilitating illicit activities of the DPRK, investigations reveal that Banco Delta Asia has serviced a multi-million dollar account on behalf of a known international drug trafficker.

Background on Section 311

Title III of the USA PATRIOT Act amends the anti-money laundering provisions of the Bank Secrecy Act (BSA) to promote the prevention, detection and prosecution of international money laundering and the financing of terrorism. Section 311 authorizes the Secretary of the Treasury – in consultation with the Departments of Justice and State and appropriate Federal financial regulators – to find that reasonable grounds exist for concluding that a foreign jurisdiction, institution, class of transactions or type of account is of "primary money laundering concern" and to require U.S. financial institutions to take certain "special measures" against those jurisdictions, institutions, accounts or transactions.

These special measures range from enhanced recordkeeping or reporting obligations to a requirement to terminate correspondent banking relationships with the designated entity. The measures are meant to provide Treasury with a range of options to bring additional pressure on institutions that pose specific money laundering threats.

The Treasury Department has previously identified the following financial institutions as being of "primary money laundering concern," pursuant to Section 311:

- Multibanka and VEF Bank of Latvia in April 2005;
- First Merchant Bank of the "Turkish Republic of Northern Cyprus" ("TRNC") and Infobank of Belarus in August 2004;
- Commercial Bank of Syria and its subsidiary Syrian Lebanese Commercial Bank in May 2004; and
- Myanmar Mayflower Bank and Asia Wealth Bank in November 2003.

The Bush Administration has also taken action, pursuant to Section 311, against the foreign jurisdictions of Burma, Nauru and the Ukraine. The finding of the Ukraine as being of "primary money laundering concern" was lifted after Ukrainian authorities took subsequent and aggressive steps to address the concerns and risks identified in the 311 action.

FIRST JOINT STATEMENT OF THE FOURTH ROUND OF THE SIX-PARTY TALKS, BEIJING (SEPTEMBER 19, 2005)

The Fourth Round of the Six-Party Talks was held in Beijing, China among the People's Republic of China, the Democratic People's Republic of Korea, Japan, the Republic of Korea, the Russian Federation, and the United States of America from July 26th to August 7th, and from September 13th to 19th, 2005.

Mr. Wu Dawei, Vice Minister of Foreign Affairs of the PRC, Mr. Kim Gye Gwan, Vice Minister of Foreign Affairs of the DPRK; Mr. Kenichiro Sasae, Director-General for Asian and Oceanian Affairs, Ministry of Foreign Affairs of Japan; Mr. Song Min-soon, Deputy Minister of Foreign Affairs and Trade of the ROK; Mr. Alexandr Alekseyev, Deputy Minister of Foreign Affairs of the Russian Federation; and Mr. Christopher Hill, Assistant Secretary of State for East Asian and Pacific Affairs of the United States attended the talks as heads of their respective delegations.

Vice Foreign Minister Wu Dawei chaired the talks.

For the cause of peace and stability on the Korean Peninsula and in Northeast Asia at large, the Six Parties held, in the spirit of mutual respect and equality, serious and practical talks concerning the denuclearization of the Korean Peninsula on the basis of the common understanding of the previous three rounds of talks, and agreed, in this context, to the following:

1. The Six Parties unanimously reaffirmed that the goal of the Six-Party Talks is the verifiable denuclearization of the Korean Peninsula in a peaceful manner.

   The DPRK committed to abandoning all nuclear weapons and existing nuclear programs and returning, at an early date, to the Treaty on the Non-Proliferation of Nuclear Weapons and to IAEA safeguards.
   The United States affirmed that it has no nuclear weapons on the Korean Peninsula and has no intention to attack or invade the DPRK with nuclear or conventional weapons.
   The ROK reaffirmed its commitment not to receive or deploy nuclear weapons in accordance with the 1992 Joint Declaration of the Denuclearization of the Korean Peninsula, while affirming that there exist no nuclear weapons within its territory.
   The 1992 Joint Declaration of the Denuclearization of the Korean Peninsula should be observed and implemented.
   The DPRK stated that it has the right to peaceful uses of nuclear energy. The other parties expressed their respect and agreed to discuss, at an appropriate time, the subject of the provision of light water reactor to the DPRK.
2. The Six Parties undertook, in their relations, to abide by the purposes and principles of the Charter of the United Nations and recognized norms of international relations.

   The DPRK and the United States undertook to respect each other's sovereignty, exist peacefully together, and take steps to normalize their relations subject to their respective bilateral policies.
   The DPRK and Japan undertook to take steps to normalize their relations in accordance with the Pyongyang Declaration, on the basis of the settlement of unfortunate past and the outstanding issues of concern.
3. The Six Parties undertook to promote economic cooperation in the fields of energy, trade and investment, bilaterally and/or multilaterally.

China, Japan, ROK, Russia and the US stated their willingness to provide energy assistance to the DPRK.

The ROK reaffirmed its proposal of July 12th 2005 concerning the provision of 2 million kilowatts of electric power to the DPRK.

4. The Six Parties committed to joint efforts for lasting peace and stability in Northeast Asia.

    The directly related parties will negotiate a permanent peace regime on the Korean Peninsula at an appropriate separate forum.

    The Six Parties agreed to explore ways and means for promoting security cooperation in Northeast Asia.

5. The Six Parties agreed to take coordinated steps to implement the afore-mentioned consensus in a phased manner in line with the principle of "commitment for commitment, action for action."

6. The Six Parties agreed to hold the Fifth Round of the Six-Party Talks in Beijing in early November 2005 at a date to be determined through consultations.

ANNOUNCEMENT MADE BY THE NORTH KOREAN CENTRAL NEWS AGENCY FOLLOWING THE OCTOBER 9, 2006, NUCLEAR TEST

The field of scientific research in the DPRK successfully conducted an underground nuclear test under secure conditions on October 9, 2006, at a stirring time when all the people of the country are making a great leap forward in the building of a great, prosperous, powerful socialist nation.

It has been confirmed that there was no such danger as radioactive emission in the course of the nuclear test as it was carried out under scientific consideration and careful calculation.

The nuclear test was conducted with indigenous wisdom and technology 100 percent. It marks a historic event as it greatly encouraged and pleased the KPA [Korean People's Army] and people that have wished to have powerful self-reliant defense capability.

It will contribute to defending the peace and stability on the Korean Peninsula and in the area around it.

CHAIRMAN'S STATEMENT AFTER FIRST SESSION OF THE FIFTH ROUND OF SIX-PARTY TALKS (NOVEMBER 9–11, 2005)

The First Session of the Fifth Round of the Six-Party Talks was held in Beijing from November 9th to 11th, 2005. The Parties conducted serious, pragmatic and constructive discussions and put forward proposals on how to implement the Joint Statement of the Fourth Round of the Six-Party Talks.

The Parties reaffirmed that they would fully implement the Joint Statement in line with the principle of "commitment for commitment, action for action," so as to realize the verifiable denuclearization of the Korean Peninsula at an early date and contribute to lasting peace and stability of the Korean Peninsula and Northeast Asia.

The Parties emphasized that they are willing to comprehensively implement the Joint Statement through confidence building, carry out all commitments in different areas, commence and conclude the process in a timely and coordinated manner and achieve balanced interests and win-win result through cooperation.

The Parties agreed to formulate concrete plans, measures and steps to fulfill the Joint Statement in accordance with the afore-mentioned spirit.

The Parties agreed to hold the Second Session of the Fifth Round of Six-Party Talks at the earliest possible date.

CHAIRMAN'S STATEMENT AFTER SECOND SESSION OF THE FIFTH ROUND OF THE SIX-PARTY TALKS (DECEMBER 22, 2006)

The Second Session of the Fifth Round of the Six-Party Talks was held in Beijing from December 18 to 22, 2006.

The Parties reviewed changes and developments in the situation of the Six-Party Talks and reaffirmed their common goal and will to achieve the peaceful denuclearization of the Korean Peninsula through dialogue. They reiterated that they would earnestly carry out their commitments in the Joint Statement of 19 September 2005,and agreed to take coordinated steps to implement the Joint Statement as soon as possible in a phased manner in line with the principle of "action for action."

The Parties held useful discussions on measures to implement the Joint Statement and on actions to be taken by the Parties in the starting phase and put forward some initial ideas. The Parties, through intensive bilateral consultations, had candid and in-depth exchange of views to address their concerns.

The Parties agreed to recess to report to capitals and to reconvene at the earliest opportunity.

JOINT STATEMENT AFTER THE THIRD SESSION OF THE FIFTH ROUND OF SIX-PARTY TALKS (FEBRUARY 13, 2007)

The Third Session of the Fifth Round of the Six-Party Talks was held in Beijing among the People's Republic of China, the Democratic People's

Republic of Korea, Japan, the Republic of Korea, the Russian Federation and the United States of America from 8 to 13 February 2007.

Mr. Wu Dawei, Vice Minister of Foreign Affairs of the PRC; Mr. Kim Kye Gwan, Vice Minister of Foreign Affairs of the DPRK; Mr. Kenichiro Sasae, Director-General for Asian and Oceanian affairs, Ministry of Foreign Affairs of Japan; Mr. Chun Yung-woo, Special Representative for Korean Peninsula Peace and Security Affairs of the ROK, Ministry of Foreign Affairs and Trade; Mr. Alexander Losyukov, Deputy of Minister of Foreign Affairs of the Russian Federation; and Mr. Christopher Hill, Assistant Secretary of East Asian and Pacific Affairs of the Department of State of the United States attended the talks as heads of their respective delegations.

Vice Minister Wu Dawei chaired the talks.

I. The parties held serious and productive discussions on the actions each party will take in the initial phase for the implementation of the joint statement of September 19 of 2005. The parties reaffirmed their common goal and will to achieve early denuclearization of the Korean Peninsula in a peaceful manner and reiterated that they would earnestly fulfill their commitments in the Joint Statement. The parties agreed to take coordinated steps to implement the Joint Statement in a phased manner in line with the principle of "action for action."

II. The parties agreed to take the following actions in parallel in the initial phase:

1. The DPRK will shut down and seal for the purpose of the eventual abandonment the Yongbyon nuclear facility, including the reprocessing facility and invite back IAEA personnel to conduct all necessary monitoring and verification as agreed between the IAEA and the DPRK.

2. The DPRK will discuss with other parties a list of all its nuclear programs as described in the joint statement, including plutonium extracted from used fuel rods, that would be abandoned pursuant to the Joint Statement.

3. The DPRK and the U.S. will start bilateral talks aimed at resolving bilateral issues and moving toward full diplomatic relations. The U.S. will begin the process of removing the designation of the DPRK as a state sponsor of terrorism, and advance the process of terminating the application of the Trading with the Enemy Act with respect with the DPRK.

4. The DPRK and Japan will start bilateral talks aimed at taking steps to normalize their relations in accordance to the Pyongyang Declaration, on the basis of the settlement of unfortunate past and the outstanding issues of concern.

5. Recalling Section 1 and 3 of the Joint Statement of 19 September 2005, the Parties agreed to cooperate in economic, energy and humanitarian

assistance to the DPRK. In this regard, the Parties agreed to the provision of emergency energy assistance to the DPRK in the initial phase. The initial shipment would be the equivalent of 50,000 tons of heavy fuel oil, which will start in the next 60 days.

The Parties agreed that the above mentioned will be implemented in the next 60 days and that they will take coordinated steps toward this goal.

III. The Parties agreed on the establishment of the following Working Groups in order to carry out the initial actions and for the purpose of full implementation of the joint statement:

1. Denuclearization of the Korean Peninsula
2. Normalization of DPRK-U.S. relations
3. Normalization of DPRK-Japan relations
4. Economy and energy cooperation
5. Northeast Asia Peace and Security Mechanism

The Working Groups will discuss and formulate specific plans for the implementation of the Joint Statement in their respective areas. The Working Groups shall report to the Six-Party Heads of Delegation Meeting on the progress of their work. In principle, progress in one Working Group shall not affect the progress in other Working Groups. Plans made by the five Working Groups will be implemented as a whole in a coordinated manner. The Parties agreed that all working groups will meet within the next 30 days.

IV. During the period of the Initial Actions phase and in the next phase—which includes provision by the DPRK of a complete declaration of all nuclear programs and disablement of all existing nuclear facilities including graphite-moderated reactors and repossessing plants—economic, energy and humanitarian assistance up to the equivalent of 1 million tons of heavy fuel oil, including the initial shipment equivalent to 50,000 tons of heavy fuel oil, will be provided to the DPRK.

The detailed modalities of the said assistance will be determined through consultation and appropriate assessment in the working group on Economic and Energy Cooperation.

V. Once the initial actions are implemented, the Six Parties will promptly hold a ministerial meeting to confirm implementation of the Joint Statement and explore ways and means for promoting security cooperation in Northeast Asia.

VI. The Parties reaffirmed that they will take positive steps to increase mutual trust, and will make joint efforts for lasting peace and stability in Northeast Asia. The directly related Parties will negotiate a permanent peace regime on the Korean Peninsula at an appropriate separate forum.

VII. The Parties agreed to hold the Sixth Round of the Six-Party Talks on 19 March 2007 to hear reports by the Working Groups and discuss action for the next phase.

U.S. TREASURY STATEMENT ON BANCO DELTA ASIA (MARCH 14, 2007)

Treasury Finalizes Rule against Banco Delta Asia (BDA Cut off from U.S. Financial System)

The U.S. Department of the Treasury today finalized its rule against Banco Delta Asia SARL (BDA) under Section 311 of the USA PATRIOT Act. When the final rule takes effect in 30 days, U.S. financial institutions will be prohibited from opening or maintaining correspondent accounts for or on behalf of BDA. This action bars BDA from accessing the U.S. financial system, either directly or indirectly.

"Our investigation of BDA confirmed the bank's willingness to turn a blind eye to illicit activity, notably by its North Korean-related clients," said Stuart Levey, Treasury's Under Secretary for Terrorism and Financial Intelligence (TFI). "In fact, in exchange for a fee, the bank provided its North Korean clients access to the banking system with little oversight or control."

The Treasury's Financial Crimes Enforcement Network (FinCEN) in September 2005 found BDA to be of "primary money laundering concern" under Section 311 and issued its proposed rule, citing the bank's systemic failures to safeguard against money laundering and other financial crimes.

The U.S. Treasury has since been engaged in an ongoing investigation of BDA with the cooperation of Macanese authorities. The information derived from that investigation and the failure of the bank to address adequately the full scope of concerns described in the proposed rule has laid the groundwork for today's action.

Over the past 18 months, the Macanese authorities have taken substantial steps to strengthen Macau's anti-money laundering and counter-terrorist financing regime, notably by passing a new law to strengthen these controls and standing up the jurisdiction's first-ever Financial Intelligence Unit (FIU). Today's regulatory action is targeted at BDA as an institution, not Macau as a jurisdiction.

"We are pleased that Macau has made important progress in strengthening its anti-money laundering controls and safeguarding the Macanese financial system. However, Banco Delta Asia's grossly inadequate due diligence and systematic facilitation of deceptive financial practices have run too deep for the bank to be allowed access to the U.S. financial system," said Levey.

The Treasury would review and, if appropriate, rescind the rule if the concerns laid out in it are adequately addressed, including if BDA were to be brought under the long-term control of responsible management and ownership.

Abuses at the bank included the facilitation of financial transactions related to illicit activities, including North Korea's trade in counterfeit U.S. currency, counterfeit cigarettes, and narcotics. In addition, several front companies may have laundered hundreds of millions of dollars in cash through the bank. The final rule highlights the bank's grossly inadequate due diligence, which facilitated deceptive financial practices by these clients including:

- Suppressing the identity and location of originators of transactions and arranging for funds transfers via third parties;
- Repeated bank transfers of large, round-figure sums both to and from accounts held at other banks that have no apparent licit purpose; and
- The routine use of cash couriers to move large amounts of currency, usually U.S. dollars, in the absence of any credible explanation of the origin or purpose for the cash transactions.

Background on Section 311

Title III of the USA PATRIOT Act amended the anti-money laundering provisions of the Bank Secrecy Act (BSA) to promote the prevention, detection and prosecution of international money laundering and the financing of terrorism. Section 311 authorizes the Secretary of the Treasury—in consultation with the Departments of Justice and State and appropriate Federal financial regulators—to find that reasonable grounds exist for concluding that a foreign jurisdiction, institution, class of transactions or type of account is of "primary money laundering concern" and to require U.S. financial institutions to take certain "special measures" against those jurisdictions, institutions, accounts or transactions.

These special measures range from enhanced recordkeeping or reporting obligations to a requirement to terminate correspondent banking relationships with the designated entity. The measures are meant to provide Treasury with a range of options to bring additional pressure on institutions that pose specific money laundering threats.

The Treasury Department has previously issued final rules against the following financial institutions under Section 311, prohibiting U.S. financial institutions from opening or maintaining correspondent accounts for or on their behalf:

- VEF Banka (Latvia)
- Commercial Bank of Syria (Syria) and Syrian Lebanese Commercial Bank (Lebanon)
- Myanmar Mayflower Bank (Burma)
- Asia Wealth Bank (Burma)

THE TREATY ON THE NON-PROLIFERATION OF NUCLEAR WEAPONS (COMMONLY REFERRED TO AS THE NUCLEAR NON-PROLIFERATION TREATY OR THE NPT AND ORIGINALLY SIGNED ON JULY 1, 1968)

The States concluding this Treaty, hereinafter referred to as the "Parties to the Treaty,"

Considering the devastation that would be visited upon all mankind by a nuclear war and the consequent need to make every effort to avert the danger of such a war and to take measures to safeguard the security of peoples,

Believing that the proliferation of nuclear weapons would seriously enhance the danger of nuclear war,

In conformity with resolutions of the United Nations General Assembly calling for the conclusion of an agreement on the prevention of wider dissemination of nuclear weapons,

Undertaking to cooperate in facilitating the application of International Atomic Energy Agency safeguards on peaceful nuclear activities,

Expressing their support for research, development and other efforts to further the application, within the framework of the International Atomic Energy Agency safeguards system, of the principle of safeguarding effectively the flow of source and special fissionable materials by use of instruments and other techniques at certain strategic points,

Affirming the principle that the benefits of peaceful applications of nuclear technology, including any technological by-products which may be derived by nuclear-weapon States from the development of nuclear explosive devices, should be available for peaceful purposes to all Parties of the Treaty, whether nuclear-weapon or non-nuclear weapon States,

Convinced that, in furtherance of this principle, all Parties to the Treaty are entitled to participate in the fullest possible exchange of scientific information for, and to contribute alone or in cooperation with other States to, the further development of the applications of atomic energy for peaceful purposes,

Declaring their intention to achieve at the earliest possible date the cessation of the nuclear arms race and to undertake effective measures in the direction of nuclear disarmament,

Urging the cooperation of all States in the attainment of this objective,

Recalling the determination expressed by the Parties to the 1963 Treaty banning nuclear weapon tests in the atmosphere, in outer space and under water in its Preamble to seek to achieve the discontinuance of all test explosions of nuclear weapons for all time and to continue negotiations to this end,

Desiring to further the easing of international tension and the strengthening of trust between States in order to facilitate the cessation of the manufacture of nuclear weapons, the liquidation of all their existing stockpiles, and the elimination from national arsenals of nuclear weapons and the means of their delivery pursuant to a Treaty on general and complete disarmament under strict and effective international control,

Recalling that, in accordance with the Charter of the United Nations, States must refrain in their international relations from the threat or use of force against the territorial integrity or political independence of any State, or in any other manner inconsistent with the Purposes of the United Nations, and that the establishment and maintenance of international peace and security are to be promoted with the least diversion for armaments of the worlds human and economic resources,

Have agreed as follows:

Article I

Each nuclear-weapon State Party to the Treaty undertakes not to transfer to any recipient whatsoever nuclear weapons or other nuclear explosive devices or control over such weapons or explosive devices directly, or indirectly; and not in any way to assist, encourage, or induce any non-nuclear weapon State to manufacture or otherwise acquire nuclear weapons or other nuclear explosive devices, or control over such weapons or explosive devices.

Article II

Each non-nuclear-weapon State Party to the Treaty undertakes not to receive the transfer from any transferor whatsoever of nuclear weapons or other nuclear explosive devices or of control over such weapons or explosive devices directly, or indirectly; not to manufacture or otherwise acquire nuclear weapons or other nuclear explosive devices; and not to seek or receive any assistance in the manufacture of nuclear weapons or other nuclear explosive devices.

Article III

1. Each non-nuclear-weapon State Party to the Treaty undertakes to accept safeguards, as set forth in an agreement to be negotiated and concluded with the International Atomic Energy Agency in accordance with the

Statute of the International Atomic Energy Agency and the Agency's safeguards system, for the exclusive purpose of verification of the fulfillment of its obligations assumed under this Treaty with a view to preventing diversion of nuclear energy from peaceful uses to nuclear weapons or other nuclear explosive devices. Procedures for the safeguards required by this article shall be followed with respect to source or special fissionable material whether it is being produced, processed or used in any principal nuclear facility or is outside any such facility. The safeguards required by this article shall be applied to all source or special fissionable material in all peaceful nuclear activities within the territory of such State, under its jurisdiction, or carried out under its control anywhere.

2. Each State Party to the Treaty undertakes not to provide: (a) source or special fissionable material, or (b) equipment or material especially designed or prepared for the processing, use or production of special fissionable material, to any non-nuclear-weapon State for peaceful purposes, unless the source or special fissionable material shall be subject to the safeguards required by this article.

3. The safeguards required by this article shall be implemented in a manner designed to comply with article IV of this Treaty, and to avoid hampering the economic or technological development of the Parties or international cooperation in the field of peaceful nuclear activities, including the international exchange of nuclear material and equipment for the processing, use or production of nuclear material for peaceful purposes in accordance with the provisions of this article and the principle of safeguarding set forth in the Preamble of the Treaty.

4. Non-nuclear-weapon States Party to the Treaty shall conclude agreements with the International Atomic Energy Agency to meet the requirements of this article either individually or together with other States in accordance with the Statute of the International Atomic Energy Agency. Negotiation of such agreements shall commence within 180 days from the original entry into force of this Treaty. For States depositing their instruments of ratification or accession after the 180-day period, negotiation of such agreements shall commence not later than the date of such deposit. Such agreements shall enter into force not later than eighteen months after the date of initiation of negotiations.

Article IV

1. Nothing in this Treaty shall be interpreted as affecting the inalienable right of all the Parties to the Treaty to develop research, production and use of nuclear energy for peaceful purposes without discrimination and in conformity with articles I and II of this Treaty.

2. All the Parties to the Treaty undertake to facilitate, and have the right to participate in, the fullest possible exchange of equipment, materials and scientific and technological information for the peaceful uses of nuclear energy. Parties to the Treaty in a position to do so shall also cooperate in contributing alone or together with other States or international organizations to the further development of the applications of nuclear energy for peaceful purposes, especially in the territories of non-nuclear-weapon States Party to the Treaty, with due consideration for the needs of the developing areas of the world.

Article V

Each party to the Treaty undertakes to take appropriate measures to ensure that, in accordance with this Treaty, under appropriate international observation and through appropriate international procedures, potential benefits from any peaceful applications of nuclear explosions will be made available to non-nuclear-weapon States Party to the Treaty on a nondiscriminatory basis and that the charge to such Parties for the explosive devices used will be as low as possible and exclude any charge for research and development. Non-nuclear-weapon States Party to the Treaty shall be able to obtain such benefits, pursuant to a special international agreement or agreements, through an appropriate international body with adequate representation of non-nuclear-weapon States. Negotiations on this subject shall commence as soon as possible after the Treaty enters into force. Non-nuclear-weapon States Party to the Treaty so desiring may also obtain such benefits pursuant to bilateral agreements.

Article VI

Each of the Parties to the Treaty undertakes to pursue negotiations in good faith on effective measures relating to cessation of the nuclear arms race at an early date and to nuclear disarmament, and on a Treaty on general and complete disarmament under strict and effective international control.

Article VII

Nothing in this Treaty affects the right of any group of States to conclude regional treaties in order to assure the total absence of nuclear weapons in their respective territories.

Article VIII

1. Any Party to the Treaty may propose amendments to this Treaty. The text of any proposed amendment shall be submitted to the Depositary

Governments which shall circulate it to all Parties to the Treaty. Thereupon, if requested to do so by one-third or more of the Parties to the Treaty, the Depositary Governments shall convene a conference, to which they shall invite all the Parties to the Treaty, to consider such an amendment.

2. Any amendment to this Treaty must be approved by a majority of the votes of all the Parties to the Treaty, including the votes of all nuclear-weapon States Party to the Treaty and all other Parties which, on the date the amendment is circulated, are members of the Board of Governors of the International Atomic Energy Agency. The amendment shall enter into force for each Party that deposits its instrument of ratification of the amendment upon the deposit of such instruments of ratification by a majority of all the Parties, including the instruments of ratification of all nuclear-weapon States Party to the Treaty and all other Parties which, on the date the amendment is circulated, are members of the Board of Governors of the International Atomic Energy Agency. Thereafter, it shall enter into force for any other Party upon the deposit of its instrument of ratification of the amendment.

3. Five years after the entry into force of this Treaty, a conference of Parties to the Treaty shall be held in Geneva, Switzerland, in order to review the operation of this Treaty with a view to assuring that the purposes of the Preamble and the provisions of the Treaty are being realized. At intervals of five years thereafter, a majority of the Parties to the Treaty may obtain, by submitting a proposal to this effect to the Depositary Governments, the convening of further conferences with the same objective of reviewing the operation of the Treaty.

Article IX

1. This Treaty shall be open to all States for signature. Any State which does not sign the Treaty before its entry into force in accordance with paragraph 3 of this article may accede to it at any time.

2. This Treaty shall be subject to ratification by signatory States. Instruments of ratification and instruments of accession shall be deposited with the Governments of the United States of America, the United Kingdom of Great Britain and Northern Ireland and the Union of Soviet Socialist Republics, which are hereby designated the Depositary Governments.

3. This Treaty shall enter into force after its ratification by the States, the Governments of which are designated Depositaries of the Treaty, and forty other States signatory to this Treaty and the deposit of their instruments of ratification. For the purposes of this Treaty, a nuclear-weapon State is one which has manufactured and exploded a nuclear weapon or other nuclear explosive device prior to January 1, 1967.

4. For States whose instruments of ratification or accession are deposited subsequent to the entry into force of this Treaty, it shall enter into force on the date of the deposit of their instruments of ratification or accession.
5. The Depositary Governments shall promptly inform all signatory and acceding States of the date of each signature, the date of deposit of each instrument of ratification or of accession, the date of the entry into force of this Treaty, and the date of receipt of any requests for convening a conference or other notices.
6. This Treaty shall be registered by the Depositary Governments pursuant to article 102 of the Charter of the United Nations.

Article X

1. Each Party shall in exercising its national sovereignty have the right to withdraw from the Treaty if it decides that extraordinary events, related to the subject matter of this Treaty, have jeopardized the supreme interests of its country. It shall give notice of such withdrawal to all other Parties to the Treaty and to the United Nations Security Council three months in advance. Such notice shall include a statement of the extraordinary events it regards as having jeopardized its supreme interests.
2. Twenty-five years after the entry into force of the Treaty, a conference shall be convened to decide whether the Treaty shall continue in force indefinitely, or shall be extended for an additional fixed period or periods. This decision shall be taken by a majority of the Parties to the Treaty.

Article XI

This Treaty, the English, Russian, French, Spanish and Chinese texts of which are equally authentic, shall be deposited in the archives of the Depositary Governments. Duly certified copies of this Treaty shall be transmitted by the Depositary Governments to the Governments of the signatory and acceding States.

IN WITNESS WHEREOF the undersigned, duly authorized, have signed this Treaty.

DONE in triplicate, at the cities of Washington, London and Moscow, this first day of July one thousand nine hundred sixty-eight.

Index

About the Contributors

ALEXEI G. ARBATOV has, since 1976, worked at the Russian Academy of Sciences' Institute for World Economy and International Relations (IMEMO). He serves as the Head of the Institute's Center for International Security, comprising departments on nuclear nonproliferation, strategic studies, regional conflicts, and terrorism. From 1994 until 2003, Dr. Arbatov was the Deputy Chairman of the Russian Parliament Defence Committee. He is a consultant to the Russian Foreign and Defence Ministries and has participated in numerous official delegations and working groups in support of major arms control negotiations. Dr. Arbatov is also a Scholar-in-Residence of Moscow Carnegie Center, a member of the Governing Board of the Stockholm International Peace Research Institute, and a member of the international advisory board of both the Centre for the Democratic Control of Armed Forces in Geneva and the Center for Nonproliferation Studies at the Monterey Institute of International Studies. Dr. Arbatov graduated from the Moscow State Institute of International Relations in 1973. In 1982, he received a postdoctorate degree, completing his dissertation on American-Russian strategic relations. In 2003, Dr. Arbatov became a Corresponding Member of the Academy of Sciences. He is the author of a number of books and numerous articles on issues of global security, strategic stability, disarmament, Russian military reform, and various current domestic and foreign political issues.

SHAHRAM CHUBIN is Director of Studies at the Geneva Centre for Security Policy (GCSP). At the Centre, Dr. Chubin plans, coordinates, and contributes to research which is mainly focused on enhancing training programs; teaches; runs a course on arms control for diplomats and military officers from the Middle East; and organizes conferences on topical subjects. Dr. Chubin was born in Iran, educated in Britain and the United States, and is a Swiss national. Before joining the GCSP, he taught at the Graduate Institute for International Studies in Geneva from 1981–1996. He has been Director of Regional Security Studies at the IISS and a fellow of the Woodrow Wilson Center in Washington, DC, Dr. Chubin has published widely in such journals as *Survival*, *Foreign Affairs*, *Foreign Policy*, *International Security*, and *Daedalus*. Among his many recent publications are *Iran's Nuclear Ambitions* (Washington, DC: Carnegie Endowment for International Peace, 2006) and *Whither Iran? Reform, Domestic Policy and National Security* (IISS Adelphi Paper 342, 2002).

PATRICK M. CRONIN is Director of Studies at the International Institute for Strategic Studies (IISS) in London. He serves concurrently as Editor of the Institute's monograph series, the *Adelphi Papers*, and he has directed a global Armed Conflict Database. Prior to joining the IISS, Dr. Cronin was Director of Research and Senior Vice President at the Center for Strategic and International Studies in Washington, DC, In 2001, Dr. Cronin was appointed by President George W. Bush and confirmed by the Senate to the third-ranking post at the U.S. Agency for International Development. While serving as Assistant Administrator for Policy and Program Coordination, Dr. Cronin led the interagency task force that designed a new development agency, the Millennium Challenge Corporation. Prior to holding government office, Dr. Cronin served as Director of Research at the U.S. Institute of Peace and then Director of Studies at the National Defense University's Institute for National Strategic Studies, where he was simultaneously a Senior Research Professor and Deputy Director of the Institute. Dr. Cronin has also been a senior analyst at the Center for Naval Analyses, a U.S. Naval Reserve intelligence officer, and an analyst with the Congressional Research Service and SRI International. Dr. Cronin was the founding Executive Editor of *Joint Force Quarterly* and Associate Editor of *Strategic Review*. He has been an adjunct professor at Georgetown University's Security Studies Program, The Johns Hopkins University's Paul H. Nitze School of Advanced International Studies, and the University of Virginia's Woodrow Wilson Department of Government. His major publications include *The United States and Coercive Diplomacy*, *The U.S.-Japan Alliance: Past Present and Future*; *2015: Power and Progress*, and *From Globalism to Regionalism: New Perspectives on American Foreign and Defense Policies*. He read international relations at St. Antony's

College, University of Oxford, where he received both his M.Phil. and D.Phil. degrees.

LIRU CUI was appointed President of the China Institute of Contemporary International Relations (CICIR) in 2005; he is simultaneously Research Professor at CICIR, which is the primary institution for comprehensive international studies in the People's Republic of China (PRC). Dr. Cui graduated from Fudan University in 1976 and then joined CICIR as a research fellow. Before working as a counselor at the PRC Mission to the United Nations Headquarters in New York from 1992 to 1994, he was the Deputy Director of the Division for North American Studies and then the Director of the Division for International Exchanges at CICIR. Dr. Cui subsequently served as the Director of the Division of American Studies of CICIR and the Director General of the State Information Center's Institute of World Information.

MARK FITZPATRICK is Senior Fellow for Non-Proliferation at the International Institute for Strategic Studies in London. Before joining the Institute, Mr. Fitzpatrick had a distinguished twenty-six-year career in the U.S. Department of State, where for the last ten years he focused on nonproliferation issues. In his last posting, he served as Deputy Assistant Secretary for Non-Proliferation, responsible for policies to address the proliferation problems posed by Iran, North Korea, Libya, Iraq, South Asia, and other regions of concern. Among his duties, he also oversaw implementation of the Proliferation Security Initiative, advanced conventional arms and technology controls, proliferation sanctions, and export control cooperation programs. Mr. Fitzpatrick had previously served for four years at the U.S. Mission to International Organizations in Vienna, including as *Chargé d'Affaires* and as Counselor for Nuclear Policy, in charge of liaison with the International Atomic Energy Agency. In previous State Department postings, he headed the South Asia Regional Affairs Office, responsible for nonproliferation and security policies regarding India and Pakistan; served as special assistant to Deputy Secretary Strobe Talbott; headed the Political-Military Branch of the U.S. Embassy in Tokyo; served as North Korea desk officer; and held postings in South Korea and New Zealand.

SUNG-JOO HAN is Professor Emeritus of International Relations at Korea University and President of the Seoul Forum for International Affairs. Previously, he served as South Korea's Minister of Foreign Affairs from 1993 to 1994. Dr. Han also held a variety of other senior positions, including the United Nations Secretary-General's Special Representative for Cyprus from 1996 to 1997, a member of the UN Inquiry Commission on the 1994 Rwanda Genocide in 1999, Chairman of the East Asia Vision Group from 2000 to 2001, and Ambassador of the Republic of Korea to the United

States in 2003–2005. Professor Han is a graduate of Seoul National University (1962) and received a Ph.D. in political science from the University of California, Berkeley, in 1970. Previously he taught at the City University of New York from 1970 to 1978, and was a visiting professor at Columbia University from 1986 to 1987, and Stanford University in 1992 and 1995. Dr. Han was also a distinguished fellow at the Rockefeller Brothers Fund from 1986 to 1987. His English publications include *Korean Diplomacy in an Era of Globalization* (1995); *Korea in a Changing World* (1995); and *Changing Values in Asia* (1999). He has many publications in Korean, including *Nam gwa Puk, kurigo Sekye*, "The Two Koreas and the World" (2000).

NARUSHIGE MICHISHITA is a Senior Research Fellow at the National Institute for Defense Studies in Tokyo. Dr. Michishita earned his Ph.D. in international relations at the Johns Hopkins University's Paul H. Nitze School of Advanced International Studies (SAIS) in Washington, DC A specialist in strategic and Korean studies, Dr. Michishita's recent publications include "Calculated Adventurism: North Korea's Military-Diplomatic Campaigns," in *The Korean Journal of Defense Analysis* (Fall 2004); "North Korea's 'Second Nuclear Diplomacy': Rising Risks and Expectations," and "Korean Peninsula in the Renewed Process for Change," in The National Institute for Defense Studies, ed., *East Asian Strategic Review 2004* (Tokyo, Japan Times, 2004); "Changing Faces of Japanese Defense Policy: Past and Future," *Global Economic Review* (2002); and "Alliances After Peace in Korea," *Survival* (Autumn 1999).

MITCHELL B. REISS is currently Vice Provost for International Affairs at the College of William & Mary in Williamsburg, Virginia. From 2003 to 2005 Dr. Reiss served as Director of the Office of Policy Planning at the U.S. Department of State, where he served under Secretary of State Colin L. Powell. He also served concurrently as the President's Special Envoy for the Northern Ireland Peace Process with the rank of Ambassador, a post he held until February 2007. From 1999 to 2003, Dr. Reiss was Dean of International Affairs and Director of the Wendy and Emery Reves Center for International Studies at William & Mary; he also held appointments at the Marshall-Wythe School of Law and in the Department of Government. Prior to coming to William & Mary, he was chief negotiator with the North Koreans at the Korean Peninsula Energy Development Organization (KEDO), a multinational organization designed to deliver energy to North Korea as part of the 1994 Agreed Framework. Dr Reiss has also been a Guest Scholar at the Woodrow Wilson International Center for Scholars in Washington, DC. He practiced corporate and banking law for three years at Covington & Burling, and was Special Assistant to the National Security Advisor as a White House Fellow in 1988–1989. He served as a consultant to the Office of the Legal Advisor at the State Department, the General Counsel's Office at the U.S. Arms Control and Disarmament Agency, and the Los Alamos and Livermore National Laboratories. Dr. Reiss has a law degree from Columbia Law School, a D.Phil. from Oxford University, a master's degree from the Fletcher School of Law & Diplomacy, and a bachelor's degree from Williams College. He has published widely, including two books on international security.